NIGERIA

NIGERIA

The Politics of Adjustment & Democracy

JULIUS O. IHONVBERE

Transaction Publishers
New Brunswick (U.S.A.) and London (U.K.)

Library of Congress Catalog Number: 92-36996
ISBN: 1-56000-093-7
Printed in the United States of America

Library of Congress Cataloging-in-Publication Data
Ihonvbere, Julius Omozuanvbo.
Nigeria : the politics of adjustment and democracy / Julius O. Ihonvbere.
p. cm.
Includes bibliographical references and index.
ISBN 1-56000-093-7
1. Nigeria—Economic conditions—1970- 2. Nigeria—Politics and government—1984- 3. Structural adjustment (Economic policy)—Nigeria. 4. Democracy—Nigeria. 5. Academic freedom—Nigeria. I. Title.
HC1055.I378 1993
338.9669—dc20

92-36996
CIP

To Grace, Oje, Ikhide, and Efe
with love

Contents

Acknowledgments

Several organizations and individuals contributed to the writing of this book in one way or the other. I would like to thank in particular Professor Andrew Evwaraye, former deputy vice-chancellor, University of Port Harcourt, Nigeria for having the courage to support and befriend the cause of truth, justice, and fair play. Dr. Eme Ekekwe for his invaluable and unparalleled encouragement and support, and for "attracting" me to the University of Port Harcourt from the University of Ife in 1986. Segun Osoba, Toye Olorode, Idowu Awopetu, Segun Adewoye, Dipo Fasina, Biodun Jeyifo, Femi Falana, and G. G. Darah are owed thanks for their fraternal encouragement and total political support since 1975; as are Bade Onimode, Ola Oni, Festus Iyayi, Atahiru Jega, Bene Madunagu, Princewill Alozie, Osita Eze, I. D. Ayu, Tunde Fatunde, Bala Usman, Okwudiba Nnoli, Maurice Iwu, Humphrey Asobie, Ugochukwu Uba, Ralph Onwuka, Dauda Abubakar, Femi Taiwo, Ayo Dunmoye, Andrew Okolie, and Lucky Akaruese, whose ideas, debates and political struggles have over the years shaped my ideas, strengthened my commitments, and clarified my arguments. I would like to express my appreciation to Pita Agbese, for sharing his ideas and materials and to my students at the universities of Ife, Port Harcourt, Toronto, and Texas at Austin, whose unending questions encouraged me to write this book. In particular to the Students Union Government at the University of Port Harcourt, 1986–90, and the National Association of Nigerian Students Executive, 1987–90, I owe tremendous debt for their belief in me, their support, their sacrifices and their courage in standing against tyranny in the so-called ivory tower. I would also like to thank Enst Ekobay, Ayodele Momodu, Bobo Brown, and Ken Anegwoje for their support with materials and information even while I was out of the country. Chris Adepoju, Femi Vaughn, Pade Badru, George Caffentzis, Silvia Federici, Michael Hanchard, Doyin and Yinka Odunsi, Tony Mba, Samuel Atteh and Ed Ferguson are owed thanks for being part of my academic family in the United States. Words cannot express my appreciation to Suzanne Colwell of the Department of Government, The University of Texas at Austin, whose technical touch turned the manuscript into a presentable finished work. Finally, I thank members of the Committee for the Defence of Human Rights (CDHR) and the National Association of Democratic Lawyers (NADL) in Nigeria for providing a forum for concrete struggles in a difficult era.

Introduction

The Nigerian social formation is in a very deep crisis. Military rule has not only suffocated civil society, but has also entrenched a culture of repression, corruption, privatization of public office, official irresponsibility, arrogance, and nonaccountability to the public. The Babangida era witnessed the massive incorporation of popular forces, the accentuation of existing political and social antagonisms and differences, the further disarticulation of the economy, and the near total asphyxiation of popular organizations. The only group that has managed to escape being crushed or incorporated or domesticated by the regime is the National Association of Nigerian Students (NANS). In today's Nigeria, what was once a very creative society has become one in which people live in fear; the youths are voting with their feet and seeking greener pastures all over the world, even in apartheid South Africa, and the rural and urban areas are in total decay and confusion. Crime, corruption, waste, the use of public facilities and positions to advance personal interests, prostitution, and alienation from the state, its agents and agencies, have never been higher in the political history of Nigeria.

The Nigerian situation is so bad that people are generally saying that the inglorious days of colonialism were much better than the present, that suffering and fear were not as widespread and real during the civil war of the late 1960s, and that it is now impossible to survive or make progress in the country without (1) belonging to a particular religion; (2) having connections with top military officers, their spouses, or traditional rulers; (3) coming from particular sections of the country; and (4) getting involved directly in one form of corruption or another. Involvement in drug pushing and murder are no longer seen as crimes. Whatever limited legitimacy the state and its institutions enjoyed in the past have been eroded as a precipitate of the retrenchment of hundreds of thousands of workers; the commercialization or elimination of social services; the repression of popular forces; the detention and imprisonment of journalists, critical scholars, hundreds of students, and social critics; the rehabilitation of discredited military officers and politicians who looted the treasury in the past or who had been probed and found guilty by tribunals; widespread unemployment, even of graduates; the erosion of academic freedom and university autonomy; the arrogance of the military and all those in uniform; official indifference to the conditions of disillusionment, dehumanization, and poverty; and official toleration of religious extremism, the frequent religious riots, and constant army-civilian clashes. To be sure, the list can go on without end.

The conditions above have raised several questions with implications for theory and analysis. Yet, the answers cannot be found from looking at Ibrahim Babangida as a soldier, president, or individual, even if his reign has meant near total disaster for the country. In the words of Segun Osoba, one of Nigeria's most respected historians, Babangida "is one leader that has inflicted the greatest suffering on the Nigerian people." The answers cannot be found by merely looking at the structural adjustment program and the officials of state, even if more than any other policy, adjustment has caused pains and hardships of untold proportions in Nigeria. As well, the answers cannot be found by looking at the *manifestations* of structural contradictions in the system. Rather, the answers to the Nigerian predicament can be found in the country's historical experience and the reproduction of the implications and consequences of that experience since political independence through the alignment and realignment of class forces. The crystallization of class forces, the efforts by the state and bourgeoisie to build hegemony, the struggles to expand and consolidate the accumulative bases of the local bourgeois classes, the rationalization of the unequal relations between foreign capital and the local bourgeoisie, and the overall struggles to consolidate the marginal location and role of the social formation in the international division of labor constitute some of the major aspects of the development of state, society, and economy in postcolonial Nigeria.

Recent developments in the global political economy, in particular, the disintegration of the Soviet Union as a superpower and as a nation, have tended to encourage a negative revisionist intellectual approach among scholars. This is rather unfortunate because the disintegration of the Soviet empire in no way means the end of ideology or, to be more specific, the end of socialism. As well, the disintegration of the Stalinist bureaucracy in the former Soviet Union does not mean the end of exploitation, repression, foreign domination, vulnerability to foreign manipulation, and the marginalization of Africa in a highly unequal and ruthlessly exploitative global order. The end of the cold war in no way implies increased resource flows to Africa, an improvement in the status of blacks the world over, the elimination of stereotypes and discrimination against people of color, and an end to the near total irrelevance of a rich continent like Africa in the global system. To be sure, African leaders and several political figures in the West have been gloating over the demise of the Soviet Union and interpreting the implications in a very narrow way. The real point is that what happened in Eastern Europe demonstrates the failure of the *practice* of socialism in a global economy dominated by capitalist interests, the encumbrances imposed on growth and development by a heavy bureaucracy, the need to build democracy into the process of socialism right at the onset, the costs of bearing the burdens of ideological reconstruction in the world (support for liberation movements, socialist regimes and fighting imperialism in international organizations), the constraints of heavy deployment of capital for military purposes, the difficulties of building socialism without fundamentally restructuring relations of production and significantly expanding and strengthening the economic base of the social formation, and the implications of political opportunism, ideological posturing, and social infantilism.

The Eastern European experience should of course dictate an urgent need, at the levels of theory, praxis, and intellectual work, to reexamine old ideological positions and prescriptions and reformulate alliances and tactics of struggle for change. While it marks an epoch in the development of human society, it does not represent the end of inequality, neocolonialism, dependence, poverty, underdevelopment, and discrimination against weaker actors in the international division of labor. For African countries, the Eastern European experience only provides evidence of what is possible and what is to be avoided in the process of change. It will be a mistake to assume that as a precipitate of the Eastern European experience, all African states will become viable, productive, and prosperous capitalist societies overnight. In fact, many African states will never experience any improvement in their economic, social, and political development to the extent that crass individualism, exploitation, and inequalities continue to dominate social and political relations. If anything, the emerging global security and political order shows very clearly what the future holds for African states. The responses to developments in Yugoslavia, Kuwait, the Soviet Republics, Poland, Israel, and so on, compared to responses to developments in Liberia, Sudan, Somalia, Mozambique, and Ethiopia show very clearly that Africa cannot expect any sympathy from the developed capitalist world. With the disintegration of the Soviet Union, the world economy is now open for undisturbed domination and exploitation by western capitalist interests.

The developments mentioned above only dictate a need to look inward, support the emergence of popular organizations, promote democracy and the strengthening of civil society, and initiate policies to meet the basic human needs of the vast majority. Africa has no future in an unequal, exploitative, and ruthlessly insensitive capitalist world economy. This is largely because it is so weak, marginal, vulnerable, and disarticulated that it cannot compete with the developed centers of world capitalism. The bogus ideology of "democratization under structural adjustment" as advocated by the International Monetary Fund (IMF), the World Bank, and Western donors has no future in Africa as there is no direct and immediate relationship between democracy and development. Yet, the inability to promote *democracy* as against the genuine *democratization* of society, as well as the inability to keep foreign-designed and supervised structural adjustment programs on course will serve as sufficient excuses by the West to divert resources and investments to other parts of the world, away from Africa. The American economy itself is in great trouble. Millions are out of work. The technology is unable to compete with Japanese technology. There are over 33 million Americans without health insurance. Thousands of people are living on the streets. Crime, gang violence, and drug problems have become major political issues. By A.D. 2000, about half the number of American children will be without health insurance. At the end of 1991 and early 1992, the U.S. president had to travel to Japan and parts of Asia to seek concessions for American business interests. Urban riots and looting have become the fastest way for the deprived to acquire the basic necessities of life, as was seen recently in 1992 with the riots in Los Angeles and other major cities. Thus, there is a need to reexamine the mistaken notion in Africa that the American economic model, in spite of the benefits it reaped from the slave trade and the worldwide extraction and repatriation of capital by its multinationals, is, in every respect, the best system in the world.

Africa cannot reinvent the slave trade. It cannot colonize other countries for boundless exploitation. It lacks the multinationals capable of repatriating profits. It lacks modern technology, skills, and resources. Yet, in the midst of the crisis, there is hope. One thing we cannot accuse

African leaders of is that they promoted mobilization, growth, and development. Ironically, in their policies of subservience, repression, human rights abuses, nepotism, waste, corruption, and mismanagement, we can find the options for the future. Africa needs to map out its own program of mobilization, recovery, growth, development, and transformation. It is not sufficient for African leaders and their organizations to make and adopt declarations that are not taken seriously or implemented. African leaders have rightly noted in the 1990 *African Charter for Popular Participation in Development* that "there must be an opening up of political process to accommodate freedom of opinions, tolerate differences, accept consensus on issues as well as ensure the effective participation of the people and their organizations and associations" and that independent people's organizations that are "genuinely grass-root, voluntary, democratically administered and self-reliant and that are rooted in the tradition and culture of the society so as to ensure community empowerment and self-development" are established at various levels. However, it is time, given the increasing disinterest in Africa and its marginalization in the global system, to move beyond declarations to actions. Of course, the majority of the corrupt and repressive leaders, many of whom are on their way out of power, cannot be relied upon to support the calls and struggles for change and the drastic reconstitution and recomposition of political, economic, and social relations.

The Nigerian situation, as presently constituted, does not hold out much hope for the people and the political economy. After seven years of gross mismanagement and inability to carry out serious and far-reaching structural reforms, the Babangida regime has admitted its failure. Yet, this has not meant a commitment to a drastic restructuring of socioeconomic and political relations. On the contrary it has meant the further harassment of scholars, students, and journalists and the total surrender of the economy to the IMF. Hence, in early 1992, the currency was further devalued by 100 percent and import duties were removed from virtually all imports through Decree No. 13 of March 1992. Ironically, the conditions of neglect, waste, mismanagement, repression, and the gross violation of popular rights have encouraged the emergence of several popular organizations in the last five or more years. In fact, students, workers, market women, youths, progressive intellectuals, professionals, and the unemployed are forging new alliances beyond ethnic, regional, and religious differences. These interest groups are resisting the politics of manipulation, antagonism, and anxiety. The language of political discourse has expanded beyond the traditional ideological phrases to include at a concrete level, issues of participation, empowerment, mobilization, human rights, the environment, gender, democracy, democratization, and social justice. It is at this emerging level of struggle and interaction, which transcends narrow political and ideological interests, that the future of Nigeria can be conceptualized. Beyond the military, beyond the ongoing prodemocracy movements, beyond the programmed transition to bourgeois democracy, beyond the hired praise singers and intellectual rationalizers in the Presidential Advisory Council and in other arms of government, beyond foreign praise singers who advise the regime on its usually wrong courses of action, and beyond the IMF and World Bank-inspired structural adjustment program, is a whole new agenda of mobilization, accountability, empowerment, self-reliance, and democratization that draws from current failures and achievements of other societies. The struggle ahead has no room for so-called objectivity and neutrality at any levels. The struggle ahead has no room for political posturing and opportunism. But out of current experiences, whether Nigerians (and Africans) like it or not, internal and external developments and pressures will force commitment to change and progress on all.

1

The State and Underdevelopment in Nigeria

> The rising tide of statism, the proliferation of bureaucratic apparatuses and a parasitical class feeding on the limited surplus in the face of protracted stagnation has brought the state to the point of collapse. It has squeezed the economy to the point where there is hardly any margin for the further extraction of surplus. . . . Certain adjustments are being made in a desperate attempt to contain the crisis and save the state. . . . Unfortunately these measures are replete with contradictions and address the symptoms and not the causes of the problems.[1]

> The point, simply, is that, explanations of political instability in Nigeria that focus on the various primordialisms of tribe, region and more recently state and religion are partial and superficial.[2]

A critical study of the crisis and contradictions of Nigeria's political economy since achieving political independence in October 1960 will reveal that the social formation is yet to recover from its historical experiences and from the constraints of the neocolonial inheritance. To be sure, so much has been achieved since political independence. Postcolonial alignment and realignment of political and social forces have facilitated the generation, even establishment, of new social relations, new contradictions, new coalitions, and new institutions as well as new dimensions of conflicts and contradictions. Yet, in spite of these seemingly novel developments, which have impacted on the character of state and class, the fundamental character of the Nigerian social formation as a dependent, foreign dominated, underdeveloped, crisis-ridden, and marginalized actor in the international division of labor remains constant.

The argument in this chapter is that the depth and dimensions of internal crisis as well as the reproduction of Nigeria's peripheralization in the global capitalist system is largely the precipitate of the structure of the state and the nature of its custodians. We recognize that the state's agents and agencies have, since political independence, initiated and attempted to implement an array of policies and programs aimed at redefining the patterns and structures of power and accumulation in the country.[3] It is our contention, however, that the structural weaknesses of the bourgeoisie as well as the nonhegemony and instability of the state have, among other factors, contributed to the overall inability to restructure the economy in the direction of the Newly Industrializing Countries (NICs) or toward an appreciable degree of self-reliance. Nigeria, especially in the 1970s, might have become a Newly Influential Country (NIC), thanks to its oil wealth. This influence has not translated into power, and the Physical Quality of Life Index (PQLI) continues to show that Nigeria has not achieved much since *political* independence in 1960. It is in this context of social/class factionalization and fractionalization, instability, mass poverty, class conflicts and antagonisms, foreign domination and exploitation, and increasing vulnerability in a very hostile global system, that we must contextualize the inability of the state and bourgeoisie to promote *development* in Nigeria,[4] in spite of huge material and human resources.

We begin by examining the inheritance of structural distortions and vulnerability to imperialist penetration and exploitation. We then discuss postcolonial economic policies, the civil war, and the oil boom showing the implications of export concentration and deepening crisis. In the third part, we discuss the post-oil boom crash, mounting foreign debt, corruption, and mismanagement that made the adoption of IMF and World Bank-dictated adjustment programs inevitable by the early 1980s.

The Colonial Experience and the Roots of Nigeria's Economic Crisis

As we have noted above, any serious discussion of Nigeria's economic and, indeed, other problems must begin with the country's historical experiences. This implies a careful understanding of the nature of precolonial society, the contact with the forces of imperialism, the impacts of that contact, and the implications of the contact for postcolonial politics, production, and exchange relations. Today, there is almost total agreement on the fact that colonialism stultified, terminated, and distorted all social, political, and economic dynamics of precolonial society. The whole basis and character of communal and property relations, political traditions, culture, and beliefs were completely affected in ways that have been largely dysfunctional to the postcolonial society. The natural processes of state and class formation, and possibilities of improvement on indigenous technology and industrial patterns were either destroyed, deformed, or recomposed to serve alien interests and support the imposed political, economic, and administrative structures in the service of colonial penetration, subjugation, domination, and exploitation. By 1851, contact had been established between the precapitalist formations in the area today called Nigeria and the forces of imperialism, mainly British interests. By 1900, the Royal Niger Company (RNC), representing the economic and political interests of the British state and dominant classes, had established some degree of hegemony over the area now known as Southern Nigeria. By 1902, this influence had extended up to the northern parts of the territory.

The point that is of interest to us is not the description of the precolonial society or the patterns of colonial conquest. This has been done elsewhere.[5] Rather, we are interested in the ways in which this historic contact contributed to the underdevelopment and distortion of the economic, political, and social relations, in particular, how it deformed the state structure and the dominant classes, marginalized them in the internal production and exchange processes, and peripheralized the social formation in the international division of labor. Thus, through a process of manipulation, lies, tricks, threats, violence, and several other extralegal mechanisms, British capitalist interests succeeded in taking over the territory that is today Nigeria as well as imposing its interests on all social and political interests and structures. It is from this stage that the history of Nigeria can be said to be the history of its domination, exploitation, underdevelopment, and marginalization in an unequal and highly exploitative international division of labor.

To put it mildly, Nigeria's colonial experience was a disastrous one. This is not to say that there was a colony that could be said to have benefitted from the brutal experience in the African continent or elsewhere. It is little use drawing a balance sheet of colonialism. Colonialism was never designed to develop its victims. It never pretended to represent the interests of the colonized. The church, as well as metropolitan political and economic interests, considered the colonized peoples as savages and the colonies as mere markets and sources of raw materials. It is no wonder, therefore, that decades of colonialism left Nigeria a severely backward, underdeveloped, distorted, disarticulated, dependent, and poverty-stricken formation. The country lacked any capacity for a relatively independent participation in international economic relations. Science and technology were backward and the level of literacy was very low. The colonial state, which had relied on extreme violence and ruthlessness, had bequeathed a culture of political intolerance, repression, and abuses to the colony. Infrastructural development was virtually nil as transportation, communications, and administrative institutions and structures were not only scanty but severely underdeveloped in comparison with what existed in Britain at that time. The economy was under the full control of foreign capital, which dominated every sector of society from prospecting, through distribution, to consumption.

One major area where the colonial impact was most severe was in the development of local bourgeois classes. Colonialism had not come to Nigeria to create competitors for itself. Having very little regard for the "savages," its goal was the creation of an adjunct and dependent dominant elite that was to contribute to its surplus extraction in the colonized society. As well, this elite was to be the agent for the reproduction of its interests in the territory following political freedom, which the British knew would eventually come anyway. This explains the reluctance to invest in Nigeria and the very shabby administrative, industrial, and infrastructural programs that were pursued by the colonial state. At political independence in 1960, the local bourgeois classes had been severely retarded and incorporated into the service of foreign capital in a largely dependent manner.[6]

Though one can argue, that the Nigerian bourgeoisie has moved a long way since achieving political independence, this is only at the surface level. Its ranks have expanded. Some of its members have become extremely wealthy. It has succeeded in using the state to facilitate the process of accumulation. It has restructured internal political structures to suit its own political and economic interests. It has also strengthened, in several ways, its unequal relations with foreign capital. In spite of these advances, the bourgeoisie remains essentially what it was at the time it was given political independence—an underdeveloped, dependent, corrupt, unproductive, undisciplined, unpatriotic, wasteful, and highly factionalized elite in charge of a dependent economy and an unstable state.[7] Its relationship to production remains very weak and, in fact, tenuous.

The most predominant route to wealth is corruption, politics, drug pushing, sinecure political apopointments, currency trafficking, import-export activities, real estate, and fronting for powerful transnational interests.[8]

Through the process of monetization, metropolitan capital ensured that the economy was structured to depend on the global capitalist market through the production and exportation of a narrow range of raw materials to feed industries in the metropole. New tastes, ideologies, language, religion, administrative structures, worldview, and social relations had been imposed and reified in the society while indigenous culture, products, and traditions were discriminated against and treated with disdain. Through the effective manipulation of ethnic, religious, and regional differences, the colonial state, its agents and agencies, had succeeded in accentuating the level of antagonisms, contradictions, and suspicions within and between various ethnic groups in the country. The contemporary distrust within and between ethnic groups in Nigeria, which has culminated in several riots and a major civil war, is a direct precipitate of the politicization of ethnic differences under colonialism and the inequalities introduced among the various ethnic groups and regions.

The colonial state had no responsibility to any Nigerian. Its main interests were the exploitation of the colonized, the guarantee of control of the colonized economy to foreign capital, and serving the interests of metropolitan industrialists in the extraction and transfer of surpluses. As Eme Ekekwe has rightly noted,

> The state's role "was to supervise the initial and necessary penetration of pre-capitalist formations, to organize the conditions of exploitation of labour and land." This entailed, in effect, restructuring the pre-capitalist economy, making it more conducive to the production and marketing of commodities required by the trading companies. It required a series of policies and programmes by the colonial state, over a period of time, to effect such changes in the pre-capitalist structural pattern. The policies and programmes of the colonial state defined new needs and obligations which forced the cultivators to go into commodity production.[9]

To do this effectively, the colonial state had to distance itself from the objective needs of the people, dispense with any morality on the mechanisms of exploitation, underdevelop and marginalize indigenous elites, divide the colonized along primordial lines, and promote the social formation's structural incorporation into global capitalism as a periphery:

> Colonialism blocked the further evolution of national solidarity, because it destroyed the particular Asian and African states which were principal agents for achieving the liquidation of fragmented loyalties. . . . What came to be called tribalism at the beginning of the new epoch of political independence . . . was itself a product of the way people were brought together under colonialism so as to be exploited.[10]

Bade Onimode expatiates further on the mechanisms of colonial domination and exploitation of Nigeria by arguing that, overall, colonialism had very negative designs for Nigeria like other colonized societies while going for minimum investment for maximum gain:

> The mechanisms of colonialism in Nigeria centred around the colonial state and economy. They included military conquest and political coercion through British monopoly of the colonial state apparatus, the manipulation of this political power for unequal trade, capital import, cultural penetration through christianity and colonial education as well as the dissemination of the British "illusion of the colonial epoch."[11]

Onimode goes on to reiterate the point that colonialism in Nigeria not only dedicated itself to the creation of a docile population but also to ensuring the permanent structural dependence and underdevelopment of the territory through economic and cultural policies. Hence, while the colonial adventure provided employment for a portion of the British labor force, "political and cultural domination, like the imposition of English language, dress, education, religion and law, were not goals in themselves but means of integrating Nigeria into Britain to facilitate exploitation."[12]

The consequence of this combined assault was that the social formation, in particular the agricultural sector that provided employment for over 98 percent of the population in the colonial period, "lost any internal stimulus for development. Indeed, the naked exposure of the country's agriculture to the vagaries of the imperialist market may well be one of the most permanent damages of British colonialism to Nigerian development. It has ensured the stagnation, or even degradation, of Nigerian agriculture to this day."[13] Of course, more than cultural penetration and political repression was the collusion between the colonial state and foreign capital to ensure first, the *domination* of the colonial economy; second, the effective structural *marginalization* of the emerging indigenous bourgeois elements; and third, the ruthless *exploitation* of the economy and the massive transfer of surpluses to the metropole:

> The loss of local control over the new production process marked the beginning of the loss of self-reliance by the Nigerian economy. This loss was exacerbated and

> reinforced by the external orientation of the colonial economy. In sharp contrast to their pre-colonial production of goods and services for their own use, Nigerian participants in the colonial economy produced excessively for the world market.[14]

This process of eliminating the possibilities for, as well as the existing structures of, self-reliance and autocentric development was a deliberate colonial policy. It was part of the grand strategy of ensuring the underdevelopment of Nigeria and its incorporation into the exploitative orbit of British interests. As Onimode has rightly noted:

> The fundamental reason for the abysmal backwardness of the colonial industrial sector in Nigeria and elsewhere, was deliberate imperialist economic policy. This policy had two salient components. First, as a matter of calculated economic policy, the imperialists banned and suppressed industries in the colonies. Their motive was the maintenance of monopoly over the raw materials, technology, and the markets for manufacturers in these imperial estates. This industrial prohibition was an integral part of the policy of exclusion of "Nigerians from engaging in processing, packing, sorting and grading of the produce for export." . . . Second, the colonialist policy of expanding the import of manufactures and encouraging export of raw materials had the dual effect of eliminating both the market for domestic manufactures, and the domestic supply of raw materials to Nigerian industries. Both factors operated to the satisfaction of British ambitions in Nigeria.[15]

In sum, therefore, colonialism laid the foundations for Nigeria's current crisis, dependence, instability, poverty, underdevelopment, and marginalization in the international division of labor. By terminating the dynamic and natural processes of state and class formation and by imposing alien interests, structures, institutions, and cultures, the colonial experience ensured the contemporary reproduction of crisis and conflicts. As we have noted, colonialism laid this background by bequeathing a weak, unstable, and nonhegemonic *state*; an unproductive, dependent, and weak *bourgeois class*; foreign domination of all sectors of the economy; science and technology backwardness; imposition of an inefficient and ineffective bureaucracy that was alienated from the people; structuring of the economy to depend on the production and exportation of a narrow range of cash crops to metropolitan markets; accentuation of rural-urban inequities; concentration of power, resources, facilities, and opportunities in the urban centers; the politicization of regional, religious, and ethnic differences; dependence on foreign aid, information, technology, tastes, ideologies, and worldview; and the partial transformation of precapitalist modes and relations of power, production, and exchange.

The fact that the Nigerian economy moved from a precapitalist stage to a monopoly stage with excessive state intervention, evidenced in the very prominent and interventionist role of the colonial state in the economy, equally laid the foundation for the contemporary nature and role of the state in Nigeria. As well, the colonial state collaborated effectively with foreign capital to enjoy monopoly over the purchase of raw materials, contracts, and the control of the growth of local investors. This meant that the colonial bourgeoisie depended on the colonial state heavily for capital accumulation. This equally laid the basis for the reliance of the postcolonial indigenous bourgeoisie on the state for accumulation, a factor largely responsible for its instability and tenuous hegemony today. Finally, the fact that the Nigerian bourgeois class today relies on politics and access to political power rather than on production and investments to accumulate is also a product of the colonial experience. Since they were structurally divorced from production, the only option available to the indigenous bourgeoisie after political independence was politics and political power. After all, the Nigerian economy was under the total domination of foreign capital at political independence in 1960. This weakness and poverty deprived the local elites of opportunities to pursue independent and viable economic policies. They had no options but to rely on the manipulation of politics and the control of public power to facilitate a form of primitive accumulation. This situation increased the premium on politics and political power. Hence, the competition for state power became a life or death battle. The political culture of "winner takes all" was enthroned since the resources available to the state was limited. Given the primacy of the state in the accumulation process, political intolerance, manipulation, and violence became mechanisms for winning control over the state, its institutions, and resources. As well, lacking a material base, the indigenous elites resorted to the manipulation of primordial loyalties—religion, ethnicity, and region. These developments contributed to eroding the tenuous hegemony of the state and promoting nonbourgeois challenges to it. This, of course, has been one of the fundamental obstacles to growth and development in Nigeria.

From our discussion thus far it is clear that there was no way in which the Nigerian economy and society could have escaped the sort of crisis that followed political independence. Because the crises are deep-rooted in the structural distortions of the colonial era, even the oil boom of the

1970s had no substantial impact on the deepening contradictions of the country. The political economy was not just underdeveloped, but it was also structurally incorporated into a hostile, exploitative, and unequal international system. Its weaknesses made it extremely vulnerable to the vagaries of the world capitalist system. This system, into which the economy is integrated, has not been restructured in any way in favor of poor, dependent, and vulnerable economies like Nigeria. This means that at best what the postcolonial dominant classes have done is to attempt to integrate themselves and the Nigerian economy within this unequal exchange relations, which, given the structure of internal and external power balances, has continued to operate against the development of the Nigerian economy.

Dimensions of the Crisis of Development

Since political independence, the Nigerian state and its custodians have tried to come to terms with the structural contradictions, coalitions, and crisis of the social formation. Other than political engineering and direct state intervention in the economy, *development planning* has been the basic weapon for redressing the deepening crisis of state and society. From the first national plan of 1948 to the current rolling plan, the goals, at least on paper, have included: the strengthening of the state by the promotion of industrialization, rural development, the revitalization of food and agricultural production, the mobilization of the masses for national development, the construction of infrastructures and the provision of basic needs for the majority, and the promotion of economic growth and development in all sectors.

These goals were clearly spelled out as constituting the "ideological" framework of the Second National Development Plan, 1970–74, which was introduced after the civil war. It has since then been incorporated into the nation's constitution and regarded as the goals of public policy. The so-called five principles are:

1. a united, strong, and self-reliant nation;
2. a great and dynamic economy;
3. a just and egalitarian society;
4. a land of bright and full opportunities; and
5. a free and democratic society.

One does not require a degree in economics to know that the Nigerian economy and society, in spite of vitriolic and suffocating propaganda by the state and its agents, has not succeeded since the 1970s in meeting any of these objectives. In fact, with the current national crisis, the country seems to have moved farther away from the "principles."[16] The reasons for this are of course embedded in (a) the character of planning; (b) the content and context of planning, in particular, the ideology of plan initiation and implementation; (c) the role of the state in the planning processes; (d) the use to which planning has been put by the dominant classes since political independence; (e) the role of imperialist forces, in particular, foreign capital in the planning processes; (f) the discovery of oil, which accentuated corruption, waste, mismanagement, and the diversion of investment and interest away from rural and agricultural development toward massive importation of goods, food, and services; and (g) misplaced priorities and vulnerability to manipulation and pressures by international capital and finance institutions.

Since political independence, planning has tended to widen the gap between the rich and the poor, promote alienation and tensions, increase the marginalization of the majority from the planning processes, and weaken the state and its institutions in relation to primordial institutions. The elitist nature of the planning processes has also contributed to the unequal distribution of power, opportunities, and resources in the country:

> The collective impact of elitist conception of planning with bureaucrats and bourgeois economists alone and the grossly unequal distribution of the gains of development have been the inability of Nigeria to mobilize a mass base for planning. . . . In spite of . . . propaganda about planning from the grassroots, the truth is that the masses of Nigerian peasants, workers, market women, artisans, youths and patriotic professional people have not been participating actively in our national planning at any level.[17]

In the context described above, planning becomes a ritual. It has little bearing on the objective needs of the people beyond the paper on which it is written. It will be wrong to claim that the majority of Nigerians have any confidence in or know anything about the planning process and the planners or that they believe that, at the end of each plan period, their lives will be improved in any substantial way. The Nigerian experience has been one in which planning has become an avenue to divert attention from pressing national matters by creating the impression that something is being done about the numerous problems often listed in the plan document. It has also become a mechanism for penetrating the rural areas in the name of promoting agriculture and rural development and encapsulating the peasantry in order to facilitate the process of surplus extraction. More importantly, planning in Nigeria has become a way of using public funds to subsidize private accumulation by providing the social overhead from which private corporations benefit. This is often rationalized through unequal and exploitative joint venture agreements. Unfortunately for the Nigerian state, its past mismanagement of resources, waste, and corruption caught up with it in the mid-1980s. As a result of declining foreign exchange, closure of credit lines, capital flight, and general economic crisis, it was forced to withdraw from a socially based planning methodology and adopt an IMF and World Bank-inspired monetarist strategy of recovery. With this development, all the moral, humane, social, and culturally specific aspects of planning and resource deployment adopted since political independence gave way to crass individualism, privatization, and the triumph of market forces.

Finally, planning has bred corruption in Nigeria.[18] Contract mania has become the order of the day. Within months of the announcement of any new national plan or budget, millions of naira (N) simply disappear through inflated contracts and direct stealing of public funds by bureaucrats, military officers, politicians and their friends in the business world. Because there is a collusion between the politician or bureaucrat and the contractor or businessperson, accountability is thrown to the winds as bribes are exchanged. Plan indiscipline takes over, disbursements fall behind allocations, projects are redefined and restructured, and the people suffer.

As we have mentioned, these conditions are promoted by the weak nature of the state and its institutions, the unproductive nature of the indigenous bourgeois class, the domination of the economy by foreign capital, and the marginalization of the economy in world capitalism. Planning programs are easily subverted by the inability of the state to control its agents and agencies as well as the general lack of control over the economy. True, a mechanical view of the state as weak and generally unable to control developments in society might not always be helpful if we are to understand the specific character of postcolonial alignment and realignment of class forces. Yet, unless we wish to engage in some intellectual dishonesty, by seeing what is not there or making projections from unrealistic conceptualization of existing realities, it is essential that we understand the state the way it is.

The Nigerian state has simply been unable to manage the economy and plan its way out of dependence and underdevelopment. It has remained the fastest avenue to wealth and power in a country manipulated by the rich and powerful to enrich only themselves. It has failed to inspire creativity, innovation, productivity, hope, justice, and patriotism among the Nigerian people. If anything, Nigerians see the state as a wicked, ruthless, exploitative, and distant structure, a force "owned" by the rich and employed to exploit and dehumanize the poor majority. As Claude Ake notes, "The Nigerian state is constituted in a way that it reflects a narrow range of interests, mainly that of the Nigerian bourgeoisie and metropolitan capital. The apparatuses of the state express the power and interests of labour in a limited way; that of the peasants and subsistence farmers, not at all."[19] In spite of the collection of huge oil rents, several development plans, massive state intervention in the economy, partnership with foreign capital, and the establishment of countless boards and panels to deal with the problems of agriculture, among others, the lot of the Nigerian people has hardly changed for the better. The most glaring evidences of its weaknesses and failures include: the recent adoption of the structural adjustment program,[20] the World Bank reclassification of Nigeria as a "low income country" as against its former "middle income" status, and the fact that the country is now eligible "to receive loans on concessionary terms, reserved for the world's poorest countries."[21] The beginning of the 1990s saw the quality of life of nonbourgeois forces at the very lowest point ever. At the beginning of 1992, Nigeria was classified in the International Index of Human Suffering as the thirteenth poorest country in the world.

There is sufficient ground to argue that Nigerians are worse off today than they were at the time they received political independence.[22] The International Labour Office was clear on this point in its 1981 report; and that period would seem like a golden era in comparison to today's reality:

> Since the overall rate of economic growth has apparently been fast in the past two decades, there should be by now signs of substantial improvements in the living conditions of the majority of the Nigerian people. These are not evident. Indeed . . . large numbers are worse off in numerous respects, especially in the rural areas but also in the big new slums of the cities.[23]

Eleven years later, specifically in April 1992, Dapo Olorunyomi described the Nigerian reality thus:

> The economy has, truly, been galloping from one crisis to another, inflicting damages on the social standard and welfare of the average citizen. Prices are daily shooting up, especially of basic necessities. Rents have quadrupled in urban areas shooting through the roofs and heading for the skies. Transportation is a sore topic. Public transporters on intra and inter state routes are gleefully fleecing commuters; wages have turned ash in the mouths of workers. Doctors are busy still canvassing steep rises in medical bills. And airlines have tripled the fares for foreign trips.[24]

In April 1992, the president of the Federal Republic, General Ibrahim Babangida, after six years of a poorly managed structural adjustment program, admitted that the economy had "defied all logic," and that he had not found the answers to the crisis of underdevelopment and dependence.[25]

The Politics and Contradictions of Accumulation and Development in Nigeria

The crisis of growth and development in Nigeria can be properly conceptualized within the overall dynamics of class contradictions and struggles that have historically militated against stability, national autonomy, self-reliance, and investment in productive activities.[26] It cannot be argued that the fundamental problems of the economy is the lack of resources. It also cannot be contended that it is the lack of qualified person power that has militated against the ability to promote even capitalist development. On the contrary, the deepening crisis of growth and development since achieving political independence can be found in the constraints of the neocolonial inheritance, in particular, the weakness of the local bourgeoisie and the instability and nonhegemony of the state. It is the combination of these factors that has militated against the ability to manage scarce resources, mobilize the huge population for development, control the impact of foreign capital, and strengthen the productive base of the economy. Let us look, for instance, at what happened even in an era when the country collected huge rents from the production and exportation of crude oil after the civil war in 1970. This would support our position that the problem with the Nigerian economy is structural—the underdevelopment of the state and its custodians—rather than material.

The story of oil and development in Nigeria is one of waste, mismanagement, corruption, the neglect of structural development, and a doom instead of a boom. Today there is unanimous agreement that the country mismanaged its huge oil rents, which had, in the 1970s, made it financially independent in the international system.[27] The history of oil production in Nigeria need not detain us here. The point is that as production moved from 2.1 million barrels per day in 1970 to its peak of 2.4 million barrels per day in 1979, revenues also increased from N1,403.3 million in 1973 to N10 billion in 1979. At the same time, food imports increased from N88 million in 1971 to N1.86 billion in 1981. The national budget climbed from millions to billions, Nigeria pursued a flamboyant and extravagant foreign policy, the state expanded its role in the economy, invested in infrastructures and education while it tried to use oil wealth in the expansion of the power and accumulative bases of the bourgeoisie.[28] The custodians of the state replaced economic reality and planning with dreams about becoming another Japan or, at the very least, the "Brazil of Africa."

It is difficult to put together a catalogue of the ways in which oil wealth accentuated and consolidated the underdevelopment Nigeria. Suffice it to note that the current problems of the country are in very many ways not unconnected with the massive inflow of oil rents, the low absorptive capacity of the economy, large-scale and unprecedented corruption and waste, as well as the enthronement of a mediocre and extravagant culture among the bourgeois classes. With oil wealth, the Nigerian state and bourgeois classes almost went crazy. Millionaires and billionaires were made overnight, not through investment in production, but largely through connections to the state and other unproductive ventures. The mismanagement of billions of oil money reflects clearly the ways in which the bourgeoisie has become an obstacle to development.[29]

The country declared itself the "giant of Africa" and a "distant frontline state" in the struggle against apartheid. It took on the struggle of blacks in diaspora. It neglected agriculture and the rural areas. It paid the salaries of civil servants in Grenada. It invested heavily in prestige projects and cultural jamborees like the 1977 International Festival of Arts and Culture (FESTAC).[30] A minister for finance, Major General J. J. Oluleye, once declared in the 1970s that the country's problem was not money but how to spend money. The elites, in the traditional culture of decadence resorted to accumulation, not through production, but by constructing direct and indirect linkages to the public treasury and looting it dry. With the loot, it organized wild all-night parties as prostitution, drug pushing, and foreign currency speculation became lucrative businesses. The country's monthly import bill by 1981 stood at N2 billion. The government consistently spent more than it was making and by the end of the 1970s, it was forced to raise its first jumbo loan from a consortium of international banks. As Ukpabi Asika, onetime civilian administrator of the East Central State under the Gowon administration, rightly noted on recent reflection, "Oil misled us . . . oil created false impression that all was well and that money was no longer a problem. . . . The temptations were extraordinary. Nigeria, like many countries, misled by oil wealth, was not strong enough to resist the temptation."[31] Asika was right because the Nigerian economy, in spite of the boom in the 1970s, is still structurally weak, vulnerable, dependent, underdeveloped, and full of serious contradictions and negative coalitions. The managing director of the state-owned Nigerian National Petroleum Corporation (NNPC) had cause to warn the country several times on the way in which oil wealth was being used to deepen the country's dependence and backwardness. On one occasion, Lawrence Amu noted that "oil revenue is spent on the importation of various consumer goods, capital goods, rice, and other agricultural produce which could be cultivated in Nigeria. Thus we earned our oil revenue only to use it to keep foreign industries going."[32]

The 1970s witnessed a massive import boom as import bills rose from N1,737 million in 1974 to N5,140 million in 1976 and by the end of 1979 had reached N1 billion. Contracts were awarded for virtually everything from the supply of firewood to prisons to the supply of water to military barracks. The government undertook the importation of food, stock fish, custom-made wines and cars, frozen meat and chicken, and whatever foreign multinational corporations and international crooks were willing to supply to the country, irrespective of quality or implications for local industry and investments. Every small bureaucrat had an official car. Loans were granted to students, bureaucrats, and soldiers to pay school fees, buy cars, and build houses. To put it simply, Nigerian leaders roamed the world seeking opportunities to spend money. Rather than promote genuine industrialization, the government concentrated on the establishment of assembly plants. Rather than create a conducive environment for the development of science and technology, the state concentrated on the establishment of bogus universities of science and technology where the faculties of law and business were often larger than the science and engineering faculties. The construction of expressways without feeder roads, international-size swimming pools, stadia, and airports was seen as indicators of growth and development. All sorts of international businessmen, tricksters, crooks, and criminals rushed to Nigeria to take advantage of the boom with the active connivance of members of the Nigerian bourgeoisie.

The result of this extravagance, mismanagement, and misplaced priorities had begun to register by the mid-1970s. General Olusegun Obasanjo, then Nigeria's head of state, noted in his 1976–77 budget speech that "while government revenue for the 1975–76 fiscal year was N3.9 billion, recurrent and capital expenditures totalled N4.7 billion." This left a deficit of N0.8 billion. In his next budget speech, 1977–78, the general had cause to note that the situation had not improved in any way as the economy became characterized by "rapidly accelerating price inflation, economically crippling congestion of ports, widespread shortages of essential commodities, a deficit in Federal Government finances and deterioration in balance of payments position." This deteriorating economic situation scared the state but not the bourgeois classes. While the government introduced some so-called belt-tightening measures, which had virtually no effect on the deepening crisis, the bureaucrats, contractors, top military officers, and other fractions of the bourgeois classes continued to loot the treasury and engage in largely unproductive activities.

The Nigerian economy rapidly gained an international reputation of being one of the most open economies in the world, an economy where quick returns could be made with minimal investments. The export concentration led to the direct neglect of agriculture and of course the rural areas and rural people. Thus, while crude oil accounted for 2.7 percent of Nigeria's exports in 1960 and nonoil exports accounted for 97.3 percent, by 1975 oil was accounting for 97.6 percent and nonoil exports 2.4 percent. By 1985, the situation had not changed much as oil accounted for 95.8 percent of total exports, while nonoil exports accounted for only 4.2 percent. In 1990, oil accounted for 97 percent and nonoil exports accounted for only 3.0 percent. As the United Bank for Africa (UBA) noted recently,

> A critical examination of the non-oil export sub-sector shows that the sector is still structurally defective even with a liberalized exchange rate regime. For example, crude oil still dominates the export sector.[33]

Specifically on the decline of the nonoil sector of the economy, the UBA noted that

> before the discovery of oil in commercial quantity, export of basic commodities, semi-processed products and minerals used to be the main source of foreign exchange earnings for the country. With the arrival of oil as a source of foreign exchange earnings, other items declined in importance. Long before the introduction of SAP which brought about exchange rate liberalization, commodities such as groundnut, cotton and palm oil had virtually disappeared from the export list. Apparently, production could not even meet local demand so much that substantial quantities of these products had to be imported when foreign exchange was substantially available. . . . With the introduction of SAP (exchange rate liberalization) in 1986 the structure has not changed substantially. . . . On aggregate, export volume of non-oil items have increased only marginally.[34]

By the time the civilian administration of Alhaji Shehu Shagari came to power, following a military hand over of power in October 1979, the Nigerian economy was in ruins. It had been bled dry, the treasury was empty, contractors were being owed, public projects were abandoned uncompleted, food scarcity and inflation were common features of the economy, the majority of Nigerians were living below the poverty line, and the dangerous road to the debtors club was wide open for Nigeria. The Shagari administration, to put it mildly, was a major disaster in the country's political history.[35] The politicians in all the parties without exception (it was merely a matter of degree reflecting access to public resources) reveled in decadence, political intolerance, waste, corruption, irresponsibility, thuggery, political manipulation, ethnic and religious politics, and collusion with foreign interests to divert public funds to foreign bank accounts. The regime violated all known rules of political competition and moral uprightness. It paid little attention to food and cash crop production, and when it did, it was only on television. Its Green Revolution Programme was simply an avenue to divert public funds into private pockets and foreign bank accounts. Its Ethical Revolution had very little meaning beyond radio jingles and television announcements. With its generally misguided economic and political policies, constant manipulation of the media and judiciary, and the wanton use of the secret police to harass nonbourgeois forces, the state lost its credibility, and the slide toward total economic decline became inevitable.

It is interesting to note that the civilian administration ran down the economy in spite of the fact that it collected more revenue from oil exports than any other regime before it. As F. R. A. Marinho has noted:

> At the height of Nigeria's petroleum boom, during the Civilian Administration from 1979–1983, Nigeria earned more foreign exchange from petroleum exports (over N43.6 billion in those four years) than it ever did in all the preceding 21 years of production (1958–1979) during which it earned just over N42.0 billion. Nigeria could have earned much more during those four years but for the large scale leakages through "bunkering" and other yet to be discovered sharp practices. . . . Nigeria totalled up . . . more domestic and foreign debts in the four years of the same Civilian Administration than the cumulative debt ever owed before it. The total indebtedness during those four years of the Civilian Administration amounted to N24 billion compared to a total of N5 billion for the period 1970–79. In other words, the administration spent more than 200% more money than this country had ever spent from the time of its independence.[36]

Thus, the crisis that was to engulf post-civil rule regimes—closure of credit lines, high foreign debt profile, capital flight, declining foreign assistance, weak productive base, inability to pay workers and meet contractual obligations, inflation, and a perverse culture of waste, corruption, and bureaucratic decay—was effectively consolidated under the Shehu Shagari administration. The gross mismanagement of the economy and the accentuation of political violence and tensions by the politicians easily encouraged the return of the generals on New Year's Eve, 31 December 1983. The popular Nigerian news daily, *The Guardian*, reflecting on the mood of the nation in its 1983 Christmas Eve editorial noted in a very somber mood that "(t)his year, all is quiet and sober. Economic hardship increasing almost daily in ugly dimensions, has taken all calculations to shreds, leaving pockets empty, markets deserted. . . . This is the legacy of the economic crisis and the Nigerian twins: government mismanagement and corruption."[37] This mood is quite unusual in Nigeria; even during the civil war between 1967 and 1970 the nation was not so somber.

The oil glut that occurred in 1981 did not send the right signals to the civilians. While revenues from oil exports declined precipitously as a result of falling international prices and oil exports, the Nigerian government and its custodians continued to squander away scarce resources. In fact, the Shagari government expanded its cabinet by appointing two ministers for each ministry after the 1983 "landslide" election victory:

> Since 1981 when the oil glut became a world wide phenomenon, oil revenue which had constituted about 73% of total revenue collected by the Federal Government at the peak of the oil boom began to decline. For example, from a peak of N13,632 million in 1980, the value of exports of oil declined to N10,535.5 million in 1981 and N8,583.8 million in 1982. This resulted in the slow down of economic activities because the various governments that had controlled the economy were facing declining revenue. . . . The effects of the oil glut was worsened by the economic mismanagement by governments of the Federation, giving rise to increased budgetary deficits and acute shortages of foreign exchange reserves.[38]

In spite of these obvious warnings, the Nigerian state did virtually nothing beyond lip service to organize the haphazard stabilization measures that were still at the early stages of formulation before the civilians were unceremoniously dismissed from Nigeria's political scene.[39] The economy has yet to recover from the profligacy, indiscipline, and mismanagement of the civilians. To most Nigerians, the period from 1979 to 1983 was a nightmare:

> Even if the scale of corruption was no greater than before, it was more visible. In part this was because it was more brazen. . . . What the people got was not performance but arrogance, displays of wealth that were stupidly insensitive to the economic realities of recession, scarcity and suffering. Naira was sprayed around at social functions and donated to political causes by ministers and legislators in amounts that exceeded and often dwarfed their legitimate annual incomes. Draped in gold and magnificent dress, they assumed the bearing of aristocracy, and became considerably more distant from the people. . . . The disastrous decline in Nigeria's oil income meant that every naira stolen or wasted sank the country further into debt and depression.[40]

The military regime that ousted the civilians hardly fared better. Generals Muhammadu Buhari and Tunde Idiagbon inherited a bleeding economy and a society plagued by alienation, frustration, cynicism, and massive opposition to the state. Poverty, hunger, unemployment, inefficiency, prostitution, crime, and violence had become common features of Nigerian society. As they correctly put it in their coup broadcast statement, the hospitals had become mere consulting clinics. Schools had been largely deserted. Industries were either closed or operating at below a third of their normal capacities. The country had become a beggar and debtor nation, and the nation had become a dumping ground for all sorts of goods and services with obviously dubious quality.

The regime relied foremost on political repression and the suffocation of democratic spaces to maintain its hegemony over the polity. It banned popular organizations, threw scores of social critics, intellectuals, students, and trade unionists into jail, and prohibited any discussion of the country's political future. Its second strategy of reform and recovery was countertrade, the bartering of Nigeria's oil for vehicle spare parts, goods, food, and services with Poland, Italy, Brazil, and other Western sources. The regime's third strategy was to continue negotiations for a short-term facility loan with the IMF. In its 1984 budget, it outlined a recovery program aimed at restoring investor confidence in the economy, cutting waste, and stimulating production. The basic components of the policy included:

1. a rapid repayment of external loans in order to reestablish the country's credit worthiness;
2. a high rate of repayment of internal debts to placate local investors and contractors;
3. an increase in the rate and volume of internal revenue raised through taxes, levies, tolls, and fees;
4. overall reduction in public expenditure, particularly on social services like education and health;
5. a freeze on wages and salaries and a reduction in the total amount paid as wages through the drastic reduction of allowances;
6. large-scale reduction of the labor force in the public services and parastatals to reduce the wage bill and promote efficiency and proper resource management;
7. closer monitoring and taxing of the economic activities of petty traders, artisans, and other self-employed professionals as a way of raising revenue;
8. expanded incentives to foreign investors and the review of the indigenization regulations promulgated in the 1970s;
9. encouragement of large-scale private investment in agriculture through a review of the land use decree and the indigenization program;
10. the privatization and commercialization of public parastatals, even those making profit, as a way of generating revenue and rolling back the role of the state in the economy;
11. review of all ongoing projects with funding for only "core projects" especially in the areas of basic raw material production;
12. priority investment in power and telecommunications;
13. more effective coordination of the budgeting processes, particularly at the level of monitoring; and
14. strict foreign exchange control in order to build up the foreign reserves and encourage the inflow of foreign investors.[41]

Unfortunately these measures failed to revive the economy, improve foreign reserves, restore investor confidence, or open up closed credit lines. As popular opposition to the policies grew, the regime relied more and more on repression, threats, and massive human rights abuses. It also refused to reach agreement with the IMF on devaluation of the naira the removal of subsidies from petroleum, and the blanket liberalization of trade. The regime, right wing as it was, felt that such policies would make life more difficult for the poor, open up the economy to all sorts of foreign goods to the detriment of local producers, and lead to uncontrollable inflation.[42]

In a bloodless palace coup d'etat in August 1985, the regime was overthrown over "irreconcilable differences" by General Ibrahim Babangida. In a recent book, Ibrahim Ayagi, former chairman of Continental Merchant Bank (CMB) of Nigeria and now chairman of the Kano Foundation, argued that the regime was overthrown by the IMF for failing to reach an accord with it on its structural adjustment package.[43] There is certainly some measure of truth to this claim as one of the first policies of the Babangida regime on coming to power was reaching agreement with the IMF on all the contentious issues that had separated the Buhari regime and the IMF. In its coup broadcast statement, the Babangida regime blamed the ousted regime of mismanagement, authoritarianism, disrespect for elders and traditional rulers, human rights abuses, and general inability to meet the basic needs of the people. One fact has become clear by now; all regimes and administrations since political independence have advanced virtually the same complaints and excuses in their efforts to explain the deepening crisis of the economy and win legitimacy.[44] Beyond these, however, is the fact that the Nigerian state and its custodians have not recovered from the constraints imposed on their development in the colonial era. Consequently, the management of oil rents generated deeper contradictions and conflicts in the country further pushing the society to the periphery of the global system. As the rest of this volume would show, the Babangida regime has not done any better than previous governments.

Conclusion

Explanations of the Nigerian crisis that focus on corruption and the idiosyncracies of the Nigerian bourgeoisie do not address the critical factors responsible for the country's backwardness. True, corruption has contributed to economic confusion, the failure of development plans, the massive transfer of resources abroad, the debt problem, and the preference for unproductive activities in the process of accumulation.

Yet, corruption is only one aspect of the country's predicament. It is a mere manifestation of more fundamental contradictions and conflicts that continue to militate against the ability to create a viable and productive economic base in spite of ideologies, regimes, plan methodology, resource availability, and personalities. What we have tried to establish in this chapter, therefore, is that to understand the background to the country's economic crisis, it is essential to have a holistic understanding of the country's historical experience and the implications of that experience.

The inability to construct a viable and productive economic base, build state hegemony, promote the comodification of production forces, and expand democratic spaces is directly connected to the underdevelopment and dependence of Nigeria. To be sure, the state has tried to promote and subsidize the emergence of a disciplined and productive bourgeois class. As well, some members of the bourgeoisie have moved into productive sectors—agriculture, local manufacturing, and science and technology development. But this tiny *productive* fraction of the bourgeoisie is not in direct control of the state. The state is still under the control of politicians, drug pushers, military officers, currency traffickers, technocrats, and traditional rulers. Their accumulative *bases* are in lucrative but unproductive relations with foreign capital. As Trevor Parfitt and Stephen Riley have correctly noted, the "process of capital accumulation is not contingent on productive activities, but on control of the state and its revenues, which are subject to large scale misappropriation of one sort or another;"[45] and the "oil boom in the 1970s was to make the state an even richer prize."[46]

The Nigerian bourgeoisie, no matter what concessions foreign intellectuals concerned with purely theoretical analysis might wish to make to it, is still very fractionalized, factionalized, unproductive, dependent, undisciplined, and subservient to foreign capital. A look at the behaviour of the political elite in the transition to democracy under the supervision of the military junta shows clearly that it has learnt very little, and changed very little in its political goals and methods. The masses of the people are still seen as objects for political manipulation rather than forces of participation. The state is still used for resolving personal conflicts and for private accumulation. Politics is still seen as a business, an investment in which legal and extralegal mechanisms are employed to win access to the state and its resources. It still lacks hegemony and a relatively common sense of purpose. Its relationship to *production* is still very tenuous and marginal; in fact, it has an open distaste for long-term *investment.* It lacks a worldview and remains incapable of mobilizing the populace along its own determined ideological lines. The basis of its power and survival remains the accentuation and manipulation of particularistic differences. The bourgeoisie is still very impatient with the norms and expectations of a democratic political culture. These conditions and tendencies have combined with structural deformations and distortions to deepen the country's economic crisis.

By the time the Babangida regime came to power, it had very few alternatives left: credit lines were closed, inflation was out of control, food shortages were rampant, drug abuse, prostitution, and crime had become commonly talked about issues, and the economy had virtually grounded to a halt. Given the constraints of decline in oil revenues, increasing protectionism in the international economy, and the insistence by creditors and suppliers that the regime reach agreement with the IMF and the World Bank on a stabilization and structural adjustment package, the regime had no bargaining power against more powerful external interests. This was the more so since it was politically divorced from the Nigerian people and their organizations, and was completely unprepared to make any concessions to civil society. It embraced the structural adjustment package with both hands and grafted it on a sea of alienation, instability, poverty, inefficiency, corruption, institutional decay, urban dislocation, migration to the urban centers, agricultural stagnation, rising crime and unemployment, and deindustrialization.[47]

The adjustment program has achieved very little in concrete terms as unemployment has risen, the country's foreign debt has more than doubled reaching $37 billion at the end of 1991, and foreign investors have yet to take a renewed interest in the economy (see chapter 4).[48] It is difficult to say, therefore, that the neocolonial inheritance has been checked, restructured, and reconstituted since becoming politically independent. Chief John Odigie-Oyegun, the newly elected Third Republic civilian governor of Edo State, assessed the state of the Nigerian economy at the end of 1991 this way:

> It is an economy that is in recession, it is an economy in which the productive capacity, installed capacity, is today being utilized at about—if we are lucky—at about 30 per cent, 29-30 per cent of installed capacity. It is an economy where the value of the currency due to inflation has depreciated rather rapidly in a way that is now becoming counter-productive. Counter-productive in the sense that all we have to sell is oil. So

> the devaluation of the naira has not as much resulted in a great explosion of export which is the only way in which it could really have benefited from it. It makes importation much more expensive so that tended to curtail our outlay. But again, that has not succeeded as it ought to have succeeded.
>
> It is an economy in which there is a lack of new investments and that is critical because if you are recessing the only way you can get out again is for new investments to be created, new jobs to be created and the best indicator is that you watch the construction industry. . . . So, we are basically in recession. The world economy itself globally is to some extent in recession. But the Nigerian economy did not have to do as badly as it has done because when you come to think of it, we have virtually all the resources.[49]

Thus, at the beginning of the 1990s, the Nigerian economy is in very deep trouble. Such deep contradictions and constraints are bound to have far-reaching implications for the future. Such a future will ultimately be shaped not only by available resources and room to maneuver in the global economy but by the character of the state's agents and agencies: the ability to mobilize the people, carefully deploy scarce resources, promote accumulation and investments, exploit developments in the global economy, and encourage the populace to make sacrifices and be creative and productive. As presently constituted, there is no reason to expect much from the present and incoming governments. This is largely because the Nigerian state lacks the required capabilities that are prerequisites for stability, efficiency, planning, and autonomy. These include capabilities to "*penetrate* society, *regulate* social relationships, *extract* resources, and *appropriate* or use resources in determined ways."[50] As Okey Ndibe has noted,

> Prices for crude oil, which accounts for 95 percent of Nigeria's exports, have been falling steadily. The oil boom of the 1970s, which lasted until 1982, left Nigeria with more money than its leaders knew how to invest wisely. The country embarked on a spending binge for such luxury items as champagne and expensive cars, as well as international airports and a brand new federal capitol. The coming civilian regime will inherit a bloated external debt . . ., rising unemployment, widening impatience with official corruption, a decaying educational system and infrastructures that are in shambles. The future is bleak for the so-called "new breed" politicians, many of whom have embraced a political style short on meaningful issues and ideas but long on exploiting raw ethnic and religious nerves.[51]

In spite of its commitment to returning the country to bourgeois democracy, its repressive and manipulative tactics seem to have dislocated civil society and its economic policies have impoverished the masses so badly that the basis for sustaining a democratic culture is, in reality, inexistent in Nigeria today (see chapters 5 and 6). The decade of the 1990s will be tough and rough for economies like Nigeria in the context of declining foreign investment, the redirection of aid and investment to Eastern Europe, and the deepening contradictions of state and society arising from the weaknesses of the state and the local bourgeoisie.[52] The increasing alliances between popular organizations, the breakdown of old ideological orthodoxies, and the increasing demands for justice, accountability, democracy, redistribution, and empowerment hold out the alternative path out from underdevelopment and crisis in the next decade.

Notes

1. Claude Ake, "The Present Crisis in Africa: Economic Crisis or a Crisis of the State?" in Julius O. Ihonvbere, ed., *The Political Economy of Crisis and Underdevelopment in Africa: Selected Works of Claude Ake* (Lagos, Nigeria: JAD Publishers, 1989), 48.
2. Aaron T. Gana, *The Limits of Political Engineering: A Critique of the Transition Programme* (Jos, Nigeria: 12th Convocation Lecture, University of Jos, 2 February 1990), 14.
3. See Festus Iyayi, "The Primitive Accumulation of Capital in a Neo-Colony," *Review of African Political Economy* 35 (May 1986).
4. Here, we conceive of development as a dynamic process of structural change and capital accumulation that empowers a people and society to generate the required resources, structures and institutions for survival and reproduction. In this process of change, the cost and gains of progress are distributed among all in society. The emerging institutions support the strengthening of popular power and the environment is conducive for the self-realization and creativity of the citizen.
5. See Toyin Falola, ed., *Britain and Nigeria: Exploitation or Development?* (London: Zed Press, 1986).
6. See works by Toyin Falola, Bade Onimode, Ade Ajayi, Omafume Onogie, Segun Osoba, Bala Usman, and Obaro Ikime.
7. See Edwin Madunagu, *Problems of Socialism: The Nigerian Challenge* (London: Zed Press, 1982); Okwudiba Nnoli, ed., *Path to Nigerian Development* (Dakar, Senegal: CODESRIA, 1981); and Paul M. Lubeck, ed., *The African Bourgeoisie: Capitalist Development in Nigeria, Kenya and the Ivory Coast* (Boulder, CO: Lynne Rienner, 1986).
8. See the works of Eddie Madunagu, Bade Onimode, Inya Eteng, Segun Osoba, Otonti Nduka, Bala Usman, Okwudiba Nnoli, Festus Iyayi, and Adeoye Akinsanya.
9. Eme Ekekwe, *Class and State in Nigeria* (London: Longman, 1986), 31.
10. Walter Rodney, *How Europe Underdeveloped Africa* (Washington, DC: Howard University Press, 1974), 205.
11. Bade Onimode, "Imperialism and Nigerian Development," in Okwudiba Nnoli, ed., *Path to Nigerian Development* (Dakar, Senegal: CODESRIA, 1981), 81.
12. Ibid.
13. Ibid., 82–83.

14. Okwudiba Nnoli, "A Short History of Nigerian Underdevelopment," in his collection *Path to Nigerian Development*, 105.
15. Bade Onimode, *Imperialism and Underdevelopment in Nigeria* (London: Macmillan, 1983), 77.
16. See Julius O. Ihonvbere and Toyin Falola, "The Illusion of Economic Development," in Toyin Falola, ed., *Britain and Nigeria: Exploitation or Development?"*
17. Bade Onimode, "A Critique of Planning Concepts and Methodology in Nigeria," *Review of Black Political Economy* 7, no. 3 (Spring 1977), 301.
18. See Okwudiba Nnoli, ed., *Path to Nigerian Development.*
19. Claude Ake, "The Nigerian State: The Antinomies of a Periphery Formation," in his collection *Political Economy of Nigeria* (London: Longman, 1985): 31.
20. See Adeotun Phillips, *Economic Impact of Nigeria's Structural Adjustment Programme* (Ibadan, Nigeria: NISER, 1990); and Federal Government of Nigeria, *Structural Adjustment Programme for Nigeria July 1986–June 1988* (Lagos, Nigeria: Government Printer, 1986).
21. *The Europa World Yearbook 1990 Volume II* (London: Europa Publishers Limited, 1990), 1938.
22. See Mokwugo Okoye, "A Time for Sadness," *The African Guardian* (24 September 1990); Ademola Oguntayo, "The Hard Times," *African Concord* (3 September 1990); Ben Olawunmi et al., "Winners and Losers," *African Concord* (3 September 1990); Abdul Oroh, "Budget 89: Promises of More Pains—Dwindling Oil Fortunes, Naira Value, Paint a Gloomier Year," *The African Guardian* (12 December 1988); and Demola Abimboye, "And the SAP Song is Sad," *African Concord* (3 September 1990).
23. International Labour Office, *First Things First: Meeting the Basic Needs of the People of Nigeria* (Addis Ababa, Ethiopia: JASPA, 1981), v.
24. Dapo Olorunyomi, "Defeated by Nigeria?" *African Concord* (13 April 1992), 25. See also "All the President's Men: 'Tourists' in Government," *TELL* (27 January 1992).
25. Dapo Olorunyomi, "Defeated by Nigeria?" *African Concord* (13 April 1992).
26. See Julius O. Ihonvbere and Timothy M. Shaw, *Towards a Political Economy of Nigeria: Petroleum and Politics at the (Semi-) Periphery* (Aldershot, England: Avebury/Gower, 1988).
27. See Julius O. Ihonvbere and Toyin Falola eds., *Oil and the Nigerian Economy* (Lagos, Nigeria: Longman, 1992).
28. See ibid. and Julius O. Ihonvbere, *The Oil Industry in Nigeria: An Annotated Bibliography* (Montreal: Centre for Developing-Area Studies, 1983).
29. See, for the general case of Africa, Claude Ake, *Revolutionary Pressures in Africa* (London, England: Zed Press, 1981).
30. See Julius O. Ihonvbere, "Nigeria as Africa's Great Power: Constraints and Prospects for the 1990s," *International Journal* 46 (Summer 1991).
31. Ukpabi Asika quoted in *The Punch* (Lagos, Nigeria) (13 December 1983), 16.
32. Lawrence Amu, "A Review of Nigeria's Oil Industry" (Text of Public Lecture Delivered to a Carefully Selected Audience, NIIA, Lagos, Nigeria, 2 August 1982).
33. United Bank for Africa, "Exchange Rate Liberalization: What Impact on Non-Oil Export Development in Nigeria," *UBA Monthly Business and Economic Digest* 14, No. 10 (October 1991), 3.
34. Ibid., 2.
35. See Toyin Falola and Julius O. Ihonvbere, *The Rise and Fall of Nigeria's Second Republic, 1979–84* (London, England: ZED Press, 1985).

36. F. R. A. Marinho, *Nigeria: A Regenerative Economy or Vegetative Existence?* (Lagos, Nigeria: NNPC, n.d.), 3.
37. Editorial, *The Guardian* (Lagos, Nigeria) (24 December 1983).
38. Federal Government of Nigeria, *The Blue Book* cited in Y. Bala Usman, *Nigeria Against the IMF: The Home Market Strategy* (Kaduna, Nigeria: Vanguard Publishers, 1986), 15.
39. See Julius O. Ihonvbere, *The 1983 Elections and the Buhari Coup in Nigeria: Contradictions in/at the Semi-Periphery* (Halifax, Canada: Centre for African Studies, 1985).
40. Larry Diamond, "Nigeria in Search of Democracy," *Foreign Affairs* 62, no. 4 (Spring 1984), 907-8.
41. This section has benefited extensively from the very important work of Y. B. Usman, *Nigeria Against the I.M.F.: The Home Market Strategy* (Kaduna, Nigeria: Vanguard Publishers, 1986), 76-77.
42. See Julius O. Ihonvbere and Eme N. Ekekwe, "Dependent Capitalism, Structural Adjustment and Democratic Possibilities in Nigeria's Third Republic," *Afrika Spectrum* 3 (1988).
43. See Ibrahim Ayagi, *Nigeria: The Trapped Economy* (Ibadan, Nigeria: Heinemann, 1990) reviewed in "Ayagi Shoots at CBN, Bank MDs," *The President* (Lagos, Nigeria), (20 August 1990).
44. See Julius O. Ihonvbere, "Military Intervention in Nigerian Politics: An Analyses of Coup Broadcast Statements, 1966-1990." Mimeo, University of Texas at Austin, 1992.
45. Trevor Parfitt and Stephen Riley, *The African Debt Crisis* (London, England: Routledge, 1989), 53.
46. Ibid., 52.
47. See Julius O. Ihonvbere and Eme N. Ekekwe, "Dependent Capitalism, Structural Adjustment and Democratic Possibilities in Nigeria's Third Republic," *Afrika Spectrum* 3 (1988); and J. Attah, M. Kwanashie, and O. Ojowu eds., *The Nigerian Economy Under (S)Fem* (Zaria, Nigeria: Department of Economics, Ahmadu Bello University, 1987).
48. See Mokwugo Okoye, "A Time of Sadness," *The African Guardian*, (24 September 1990); Ademola Oguntayo, "The Hard Times," *African Concord*, (3 September 1990); "Five Years of President Babangida's Rule: A Tortuous Journey," *West Africa* (27 August 1990); Demola Abimboye, "And the SAP Song is Sad," *African Concord*, (3 September 1990); Olu Awofeso, "Decades of Nightmare," *The African Concord*, (8 October 1990); and Seye Kehinde, "Songs of Woe," *The African Concord*, (3 September 1990).
49. John Odigie-Oyegun, "Leadership Must Be by Example," *The Observer*, (22 November 1991), 3.
50. Joel S. Migdal, *Strong Societies and Weak States—State-Society Relations and State Capabilities in the Third World* (Princeton, NJ: Princeton University Press, 1988), 4.
51. Okey Ndibe, "Jihad and Crusade—Nigeria's Religious Wars," *Emerge* (January 1992), 14.
52. See Timothy M. Shaw and Julius O. Ihonvbere, *Nigeria: The Illusions of Power* forthcoming (Boulder, CO: Westview, 1993).

2

Foreign Policy in a Contracting Economy: Nigeria as Africa's Great Power?

> The defence of the humanity and freedom of the black man is an issue dear to us all. Nigeria has never been and can never be indifferent to the plight of the black man, where ever he may be. This is natural in view of the role which providence has cast for Nigeria in Africa. It has been a cardinal factor in our foreign relations to provide the African continent focus and leadership in the struggle against colonialism, exploitation and racial oppression.[1]

> The Babangida administration . . . has brought us back again to the position that we were before things began to slip away from us, the position of leadership in Africa. . . . We have established that in our sub-region, Nigeria is a country that can not be put away.[2]

> Vast size, and population, and abundance of resources do not guarantee in any automatic way the leadership of this (African) continent. Until we are able to establish a stable political order at home, industrialise, and take-off technologically, and improve the quality of life of our people, no country within and outside Africa will accept our claim to leadership in Africa seriously except to flatter us.[3]

The content and context of Nigeria's foreign policy have always been controversial. True, the fact that the country is blessed with the largest population in the continent, vast oil wealth, abundant mineral resources, a fertile land, and conducive environment has tended to give it some, indeed, several advantages over other African nations. These advantages have enabled it to provide some leadership, dominate initiatives at the subregional and continental levels and play the "superpower" role in the region. But its aspirations have been checkmated by several internal contradictions—dependence, foreign domination, corruption, political instability, poor leadership, inconsistency in policy formulation and implementation, technological backwardness, and a marginal location and role in the international division of labor. Thus, debates on the content and direction as well as effectiveness of the country's foreign policy have generally followed two conflicting paths.

On the one hand of the debate is the Nigerian state, sections of the media, traditional rulers, and some conservative political figures. To this group, Nigeria is a "giant," a "leader," and a representative for Africa. Nigeria is a "distant Frontline state." The "liberation" of Africa from all forms of domination, exploitation and foreign manipulation is, and will remain, dependent on Nigeria.[4] This position has also received substantial support from a large section of the Western media and foreign policy analysts.[5] That government performs the functions for which it was set up in the area of foreign policy is, to this group, interpreted as a "service" to Nigerians for which they must be grateful. Generally, it is difficult to get this group to admit to one single error or blunder in the country's foreign policy; if there was any at all, it was easily attributed to defunct regimes.[6]

In opposition to the group identified above are those who have argued that a neocolonial, underdeveloped, dependent, foreign-dominated, distorted, disarticulated, politically unstable, debt-ridden and crisis-ridden, social formation cannot provide credible leadership or operate a viable, credible, respectable, and consistent foreign policy. It is contended that Nigeria, in spite of its vast human and material resources, cannot make claim to leadership in Africa as long as it is characterized by mindless corruption, mass poverty, gross inequality, mismanagement, waste, and social, political, and economic tension, contradictions, and conflicts. Thus, to this group, made up largely of critical scholars, popular organizations, students, the labor movement, and sections of the media, Nigeria's assumed "power," "influence," and "credibility" are merely rhetoric, propaganda, and "issue-based" diplomacy rather than evidence of any credible, viable, and consistent basis of foreign policy.[7] This group has received support also from the "radical" section of the international media and Western scholars.[8]

Yet, the debate notwithstanding, many recent developments in the global system will significantly affect Nigeria's policies. These developments include: the unification of Germany; the disintegration of the Soviet empire and the creation of the Commonwealth of Republics under the "leadership" of Russia; the emergence of the United States as the only superpower in the world; the redirection of aid, investment, and interest away from Africa to Eastern Europe and the Middle East; the decline of communist governments all over the world especially in Africa; the release of Nelson Mandela and the institution of the reform process in South Africa; the rapid increase in the number of prodemocracy movements in Africa and other parts of the developing world; the prospects for the creation of a European market in 1992 and the finalization of arrangements for a Canada-Mexico-United States free trade area; discussion between North and South Korea on unification; the ruthless route of Iraq by the so-called coalition forces in the name of liberating Kuwait; the role of the United States and the European Community in the civil war in Yugoslavia; and the increasing global concern for the environment as evidenced in the June 1992 earth summit in Brazil, to name a few. These events dictate a need to review and reexamine the content and direction of Nigeria's foreign policy. This will enable us to investigate Nigeria's past achievements, the basis of the claims to leadership, and the prospects for the leadership role in the 1990s.

Nigeria's Claim to Leadership in Africa: An Evaluation

Arguments in support of claims to regional leadership have always been based on the country's resources—in the 1960s, cash crops, and since the 1970s, oil, population (currently put at 85.5 million by the 1992 census), and size of the economy, especially the market. Right from the early days of the country's political independence in 1960, the political leaders were convinced of the country's "manifest destiny."[9] As the opening quote from Ibrahim Babangida clearly shows, the political leaders believe that Nigeria's leadership role was actually destined by God. Even then, Babangida was merely expressing a view that was common in the official pronouncements of politicians and governments before his own.

In the early years of political independence, the Western media and Western governments contributed immensely to encouraging this highly inflated image among Nigeria's leaders. The country was then hailed by the West as the "cradle of democracy" in Africa and the prime minister, Alhaji Abubakar Tafawa Balewa, was referred to in the Western media as "the golden voice of Africa."[10] It was believed that with its huge and vibrant population, productive agricultural base, and openness to the West in every respect, the prospects of the country were very bright. Such analysts were, of course, focusing on the superficial aspects of Nigeria's power, while ignoring objective realities. They effectively overlooked the distortions and disarticulations of the colonial experience, the limited legitimacy and weaknesses of the state, the domination of the economy by transnational corporations, the factionalization and fractionalization of the dominant classes, the virtually independent and conflicting foreign policy postures of the regions, and the vulnerability of the country to external pressure, manipulation, and exploitation.[11] As John Hatch was to note some decade and a half after political independence was achieved, "The optimism which was expressed in the West over Nigerian prospects was based rather on her commercial and social life than on political realities."[12] These expectations disappeared as the various governments were unable to fundamentally restructure the Nigerian economy toward self-reliance and increased diversified production, and as politics degenerated into warfare culminating in a civil war in 1967.

So much has changed since then. The four regions became twelve in 1967, nineteen in 1976, twenty-one in 1987, and thirty in 1991. A bitter three-year civil war was fought between 1967 and 1970. The federal government was strengthened by the restructuring of the regions, the civil war and the defeat of Biafra, and the oil boom that followed the civil war in the 1970s.[13] As well, the economy has experienced substantial growth; the army, which expanded to 250,000 due to the civil war, has become more sophisticated,[14] and Nigerians have developed more interest in foreign policy issues. In spite of these, and other changes, the Nigerian power elite has not altered its perceptions of the country's manifest destiny. If anything, it has become more convinced that the future of Africa as well as the place of blacks in diaspora in their respective locations are dependent on Nigeria.[15]

It has been possible for Nigerian governments to maintain this view of the country's manifest destiny because of the generally underdeveloped and crisis-ridden nature of the majority of African economies. With declining foreign aid and foreign investments, increasing energy bills, and deepening internal crisis all over the continent, Nigeria has managed, over the years, to keep its "head above water" even while it is drowning like other states. This was made possible in the 1960s because of the relatively diversified agricultural base of the economy; the exportation of cocoa, groundnuts, cotton, palm produce, hides and skin, timber, and other minerals brought in foreign exchange and reduced dependence on foreign sources. However, the oil boom of the 1970s following the oil price increases, which ironically devasted other non-oil producing African states, served to increase the country's foreign profile and influence even while agriculture was being neglected. The oil boom increased the "financial autonomy" of the government, and enabled it to achieve some "influence" and to pursue a vigorous and relatively active foreign policy within and outside the region.

It is precisely the "activism" that followed the oil boom and the civil war that encouraged analysts and the government to constantly restate the country's "power," "influence," "leadership," and "destiny" to lead Africa. Reflective of such perceptions is Olajide Aluko's declaration that "Nigeria cannot readily give up the bid to play a leading role in the OAU."[16] The Nigerian government, in its *Second National Development Plan*, lent support to such interpretations when, at the height of the oil boom, it boasted that "the country is fortunate in having the resource potential in men and material and money to lay a solid foundation for a socio-economic revolution in Africa. The uncompromising objective of rising economic prosperity in Nigeria is the economic independence of the nation and the defeat of neo-colonialist forces in Africa."[17]

In 1976, the Federal Military Government set up a panel under the chairmanship of Professor Adebayo Adedeji to review the elements of Nigeria's foreign policy. The panel submitted its report in May 1976 and it was accepted in June of the same year by the government. Among other fundamental elements of national interest identified by the panel were (1) the creation of the necessary political conditions in Africa and the rest of the world that would facilitate the defense of Nigeria's sovereignty, independence, and territorial integrity; (2) the creation of the necessary economic and political conditions in Africa and the rest of the world that would foster Nigeria's national self-reliance and rapid economic development; (3) the achievement of collective self-reliance in Africa and the rest of the developing world; and (4) the promotion and defense of world peace.[18] As well, in the 1979 Constitution, the Nigerian government further enshrined commitment to playing a leadership role in Africa when it declared that

> the state shall promote African unity as well as total political, economic, social and cultural liberation of Africa and all other forms of international cooperation conducive to the consolidation of universal peace and mutual respect and friendship among all peoples and states, and shall combat racial discrimination in all its manifestations.[19]

From the above official positions, it is clear that the Nigerian government has never had any doubts as to its leadership role in Africa even in the developing world.

As I pointed out earlier, such claims have received support from analysts and scholars outside the country. According to the *Times* of London,

> Nigerians, justifiable see themselves as the giants of Africa. It is the one element they are agreed upon. And they are now seeking to use their oil and emerging industrial muscle to influence opinion and guide events. . . . It is Nigeria's foreign policy, more than that of any other black African country, that most determines Africa's collective future . . . Nigeria is determined not just to play its natural leadership role in Africa, but to also build upon it.[20]

Oye Ogunbadejo, in his study of Nigeria's foreign policy between 1966 and 1979, also writes glowingly of the country's "international role in Africa" and its "economic leadership . . . evident at the regional level."[21] Finally, a 1981 publication of the Nigerian Federal Ministry of Information bragged about the fact that

> Nigeria now enjoys more international *influence* than ever before. This is based partly on her position as the most populous country in black Africa, and one whose military forces, although in numbers they have been considerably reduced since the civil war, are still black Africa's biggest, with their equipment constantly being improved. It is based, too, on her recognition of her responsibilities to her neighbours and her ability, at least until recently, to afford to other African countries considerable financial help, and to invest in their enterprises. . . . Above all Nigeria has been, and is, the moving spirit behind the Economic Community of West African States (ECOWAS) . . . with a population expected to exceed 200 million by the century's end . . . Nigeria also belongs to a wide range of regional bodies in West Africa. . . . In wider continental problems, African countries always look to Nigeria.[22]

To be sure, the country's *influence* has increased over the years, especially in its foreign policy postures in the West African subregion, toward southern Africa and to some extent in its relations to extra-African powers. In spite of deepening internal crisis and constraints in the global system, Nigeria's political leaders are still convinced that the country's foreign policy should remain directed at "upholding the dignity of the African, safe guarding his interests and promoting his well being and protecting him from all forms of oppression and exploitation."[23] The government, in spite of current constraints, which have necessitated the implementation of a harsh stabilization and adjustment program, remains convinced that "the support which Nigeria gives for the struggle for human dignity and eradication of all racialism and colonialism in Africa and our determination to pursue these goals will continue to be intensified until the whole of Africa is free from the stain of degradation."[24] Even with the recent obvious surrender to the dictates of the World Bank and the IMF and to the dictates of so-called market forces, the Nigerian government continues to emphasize its preparedness to "munster efforts to win the other aspects of independence: the economic decolonization of Africa."[25] In the face of popular opposition to the country's financial commitments to other African states in a period of deep socioeconomic decay and dislocation in Nigeria, the Nigerian president in a nationwide broadcast on 27 August 1991 argued that there is a "strong link between our domestic and foreign policies," that the country was "building a new socio-economic and political order in which the country will not live in isolation from the rest of Africa and the world," and that

> it is this context rather than the narrow framework of 'economics' and 'opportunity costs' that our strategy in the Organisation of African Unity (OAU) and the Economic Community of West African States (ECOWAS), as well as our economic diplomacy and stance in the politics of self-reliance and change in South Africa will be understood and appreciated.

He went on to assure Nigerians that the country was "better equipped than before to interact with other countries" and urged that "popular and informed attitudes towards the 'new foreign policy' strategy . . . must transcend the sacrifices which it entails."[26]

In spite of these assertions and hopes about the country's power and commitment to Africa and the world, it has faced challenges to its aspirations and foreign politics from countries such as Zimbabwe, Zaire, Ghana, Zambia, Cote d'Ivoire, and Kenya. As well, the government has been unable to carry the populace along with it in most of its foreign policy actions and pronouncements. Hence, it has been wise enough to keep its commitments to financial contributions, "shuttle diplomacy," the contribution of materials and diplomatic support to liberation movements. Let us now examine aspects of Nigeria's foreign policy.

Nigeria's Leadership Claims and Roles in the 1970s and 1980s

In the first decade of political independence, Nigeria's foreign policy was severely constrained by the neocolonial inheritance and the conservative and opportunistic character of leadership. The regions were virtually independent of the federal government in their foreign policy actions. In fact,

> Each of the three regions had its embassy in London. Western Nigeria had a consulate in New York. Regional Premiers spoke freely on foreign matters and sent delegations on goodwill visits and to hunt for foreign investment. It led to a great deal of confusion abroad especially when a region follows another in quick succession. There was little co-ordination.[27]

Today, there is general agreement that Nigeria's foreign policy in the early years of political independence was characterized by timidity, defensive radicalism, large-scale confusion, opportunism, political posturing, rhetorics, gradualism, opposition to communism, competition between the center and the regions, and subservience to the West.[28] The postcolonial government rejected all forms of foreign assistance from the Eastern bloc, banned Nigerians from traveling to socialist countries, opposed all militant anticolonial moves in the continent, especially those initiated by Kwame Nkrumah of Ghana and Sekou Toure of Guinea, and interpreted the problem of apartheid in purely racial and moral terms. For instance, when Nkrumah advocated a Union Government of Africa, Balewa spoke out strongly against it, casting aspersions on Nkrumah's motivations. In addition, while allowing complete freedom for Western diplomats in the country, officials of the Soviet Embassy were controlled and monitored; very generous incentives were provided to foreign investors even where such investors were likely to weaken local entrepreneurs; and the Balewa government took sides with the West on practically every issue at the United Nations.[29] Along with the position of Middle Eastern countries Nigeria refused to recognize Israel and remained aloof from subregional issues regarding the other West African states as too small, too weak, and of little consequence to the country's growth and development.

This pro-Western, gradualist, and weak foreign policy position did not win Nigeria any substantial influence in the continent. Without doubt, in spite of the country's size, population and resources, Ghana easily overshadowed Nigeria in influence. Kwame Nkrumah was certainly more articulate, more militant, ideologically committed, and enjoyed greater global prominence than Balewa. Added to this was the fact that Nigeria was hardly in a position to advance alternative policies given the corruption, factionalization and largely unproductive disposition of the country's dominant classes as well as institutional and structural weaknesses that increased the country's vulnerability to foreign manipulation and domination. Of course, at this time, Nigeria, like other countries in the region, was dependent on Western markets for the sale of a narrow range of cash crops, relied on foreign aid substantially and had no political or economic basis on which to hinge a relatively independent foreign policy position.

The civil war and the oil boom that followed altered all these. The rebels in Biafra had received support from African states like Tanzania, Cote d'Ivoire, and Gabon; employed South African weapons in the war; and enjoyed diplomatic, military, and financial support from Portugal, France, and foreign oil companies. In addition, until the entry of the Soviet Union into the conflict on the Nigerian side, the United States and Britain refused to provide the federal government with needed aircraft and weapons. They regarded the war as an "internal affair." When the war ended, the postcivil war regime recognized the dangers of an "isolationist" foreign policy and decided to become more "interventionist" in the affairs of the region. It decided to oppose the minority regimes in southern Africa in every way; to resist superpower interference in the region; to strengthen the OAU; to support the creation of a subregional economic scheme which it would dominate; and to increase its defense of the interests of blacks in the diaspora.[30] The pursuit of these renewed foreign policy postures was greatly aided by the oil boom that followed the civil war. With the 1973 Middle East crisis, oil revenues accruing to the Nigerian government increased substantially (see chapter 1).[31] The government moved to increase its participation in the oil sector, joined OPEC in 1971, created a major national oil company—the Nigerian National Oil Corporation (NNOC), which later became the Nigerian National Petroleum Corporation (NNPC)—and declared its preparedness to use oil as a weapon of foreign policy by putting pressure on the great powers over African issues, assisting African states, and supporting liberation movements. The country came to depend less on foreign aid to keep development projects afloat and with the economic boom, foreign investors flocked to the country from all corners of the world to take advantage of the increased opportunities. With its increased financial power, increased investor confidence, and substantial economic growth, at a time when the majority of African states were groaning from the burden of energy bills, Nigeria was in a new position to make further claims to being a regional power.

Specifically, Nigeria single-handedly sponsored the creation of the Economic Community of West African States (ECOWAS) in 1975. To achieve this objective it constructed a highway linking Idi-Iroko in Nigeria to Porto-Novo in the Republic of Benin at a cost of N1.8 million, advanced a N25 million interest-free loan to Benin, and agreed to take over 30 percent of the equity and invest N7.2 million in a joint cement venture in Benin. It invested N20 million in a joint sugar project and donated printing machines worth N42,000 and N20,000 for cultural development to Benin; N50,000 was donated to the ruling party in Guinea; and while electricity was scarce in Nigeria, it agreed to supply Niger with electricity from Nigeria's Kainji Dam at a maximum rate of 30,000 kilowatts. At virtually every stop on his numerous visits around the continent, the Nigerian leader, General Yakubu Gowon, made very generous donations.[32] This generosity was possible only because of the oil boom and the economic adversity as well as the drought in the subregion that forced the other countries to accept all available aid.

In southern Africa, Nigeria declared itself a "distant frontline state," moving to dominate the OAU's Liberation Committee, providing scholarships to youths from southern Africa, and making provisions for them to be absorbed into Nigerian schools. It provided financial, diplomatic and material support to the liberation movements. It took some steps against foreign investments in Nigeria to pressure their home governments to impose sanctions on South Africa and hasten negotiations for the end of apartheid. It prohibited all forms of contact between Nigerians and South Africa and took initiatives in securing the recognition of African liberation movements. The language of its condemnation of Western powers for their "collusion" with South Africa took a militant and daring tone. Nigeria declared South Africans as "prohibited immigrants" in the country, imposed a total trade embargo, stopped the harassment of liberation leaders who succeed in smuggling themselves into Nigeria, gave open support to the armed struggle, and, in 1978, withdrew from the Commonwealth Games to protest New Zealand's sporting contacts with South Africa.

In its relations to nations of great power, Nigeria abandoned all its previous gradualist and timid positions. It served as the representative for the African continent in the negotiations of the Lome Conventions, made vigorous demands for the implementation of a new international economic order, and initiated nationalistic economic policies through indigenization decrees to increase local participation and influence the pattern of foreign investment in the country. Nigeria also opposed great power support for South Africa and attempts by foreign powers to influence the direction of African politics and tried to replace France as the dominant country in the subregion. Lagos even boasted in 1977 that it was "compiling information on all enterprises who depend on our raw materials and markets but continue to help our enemies. Such enterprises must decide now to chose between us and our enemies and all that goes with that choice. . . . Foreign contractors who are known to have links with South Africa are already barred from taking part in tenders of any kind."[33] The government tried to break the traditional dependence on Western markets and suppliers by opening a new window to the Eastern bloc both in commercial and military trade, condemned the linkage politics introduced by the United States over Namibian independence, and sanctioned the presence of Cubans in Africa arguing that "in every case where Cuba's intervention was established they intervened as a consequence of the failure of Western policies and on behalf of legitimate African interests."[34]

In spite of these rather militant postures, trade with the West continued to increase and the United States remained the single largest market for the country's oil. In fact, Nigeria continued to threaten the West with its oil power: "Oil has become a weapon in international politics. I am on record as saying that we shall use all weapons at our disposal, including oil if it becomes unavoidable, to pursue and fight for the interests of Nigeria."[35] Pushing the threats a bit further, Nigeria declared its preparedness to confront any power, regardless of size: "Nigeria's new foreign policy abhors any form of confrontation with any super powers, big or small, but if challenged by any foreign power on matters of interest to the nation, Nigeria would stand its ground and would not flinch."[36]

Thus, in spite of regime changes, novel developments in the region, and pressures from the global system, the period of the 1970s and 1980s was generally the high point of Nigeria's "new," "activist," and "interventionist" foreign policy.[37] Without doubt, it emerged the most important, most prominent, and most *influential* power in Africa. The West courted it; liberation movements relied on its diplomatic and financial support; African countries relied on it for financial assistance; and international organizations looked up to it as the most credible and solvent country in Africa. Nigeria, unlike most African countries, could be relied upon to pay its dues on time. Most importantly, foreign investors saw Nigeria as another "Brazil" and investment opportunities seemed endless. Nigerian analysts were convinced that Nigeria had become "the natural leader of the African continent and the black race."[38] As Stephen Wright has rightly noted, "diplomatic successes in bringing ECOWAS into existence (over French hostility), Angolan independence (over American opposition) and British petroleum nationalization affair contributing to Zimbabwean independence all served to bolster the image of a dynamic and powerful foreign policy."[39] But these images were merely one aspect of the picture.

Nigeria's *influence* relied on its oil wealth and large market. The oil sector was largely dependent on the information, investment, technology, and marketing opportunities in the West. The West was the only viable market for its oil. Its large market was dominated by foreign supplied goods and services. These facts reduced the efficacy of foreign policy pronouncements and postures. Threats to use the oil weapon were hardly taken seriously by the West. It was obvious that the various governments were merely being rhetorical. As well, the country's technological backwardness meant that it was absolutely reliant on the West for military and other technological input supplies. This meant that militarily Nigeria was not a threat to either South Africa or the West. Radical pronouncements did not scare the West, notwithstanding half-hearted nationalizations and a weak indigenization program. After all, Nigeria did not have a leader like Libya's Muammar al-Qaddafi. Nigeria's dominant class was, and remains, rabidly antisocialist and pro-West. Stephen Wright has in fact suggested that it may be "more accurate, however, to see the achievements in the sphere of foreign policy in the 1970s and early 1980s as separate or sporadic successes rather than as linked events in a constant chain of political power. These successes were also partly assisted by favourable external factors."[40]

With the oil boom came the near total neglect of agriculture and a new dependence on food imports. The food supplies came almost exclusively from the West. This heavy dependence on foreign food supplies to urban residents served to mortgage political stability in urban centers. Since Nigeria's early generosity and financial support to liberation movements were largely dependent on the collection of oil rents from Western markets and royalties from Western oil corporations, it followed that any reversal in oil fortunes could affect the ability to continue to support other

African states financially. Given that oil wealth was not used to build a productive economic base, Nigeria remained a dependent country like other African states. Thus, in spite of its generosity, it could not replace France in the subregion or the United States as an aid donor. The Francophone states, therefore, refused to transfer their allegiance to Nigeria.[41] Beyond all these conditions were the continuing problems of political instability, coups and countercoups, lack of policy continuity, mass poverty, inflation, unemployment, foreign domination, rural decay, urban dislocation, crime, widespread corruption, mismanagement, and the inability of the government to provide for the basic human needs of the majority, promote self-reliance, and regulate the presence and participation of foreign interests in the economy.

In 1981, the International Labour Office issued a report that showed that Nigeria had made very little progress inspite of huge expenditures, an oil boom, and its growing influence in the world system.[42] These conditions made foreign investors cautious, led to a mounting foreign debt, created severe contradictions between bourgeois and nonbourgeois forces, and mediated the ability of the state to contain popular pressures and take advantage of concessions in the global system. It is from this perspective that we can better appreciate the view of Nigeria's onetime federal commissioner for external affairs, Brigadier Joseph Garba, that

> a nation's foreign policy is as successful as its internal policies are equally successful. In other words no nation can successfully pursue its foreign policy objectives without comparable success in its domestic policies.[43]

Garba's position is also supported by *Africa Events*, which, in a review of Nigeria's foreign policy in the 1980s, argued that "a nation with a sound economy, stable polity and a contented citizenry is better placed to assert itself in the international community."[44] In the period under review, Nigeria's internal policies can hardly be described as moderately successful. The inability to use its oil wealth to lay a solid foundation for self-sustaining growth and development, promote science and technology development, encourage the strengthening of the market and productive base of the economy, and create conditions for political stability, democratization, and governmental accountability to the people substantially weakened the effectiveness and influence of Nigeria during that time. Oil wealth was squandered; agriculture, rural areas, and rural producers were neglected; corruption reached unprecedented proportions; politics became warfare; coups became a recreational activity for the armed forces; the elites reveled in decadence and waste; the poor majority became alienated from the state; and the country's foreign policy became one of rhetoric and propaganda more than any consistent, systematic, and well-articulated program for advancing Nigeria's foreign interests and achieving declared commitments to the liberation of Africa;

> Our foreign policy also seems to be in desperate need of repairs. In Chad, as in Namibia and the abortive OAU Tripoli Summit, we did not seem to have asserted ourselves enough to ensure that the interests of Africa prevail over those of imperialists.[45]

Whatever the achievements of the 1970s up to the 1980s, a new realism has dawned on Nigerian leaders. Since the last quarter of the 1980s, which brought with it a glut in the world oil market and the imposition of OPEC quotas on oil production, panic has come to grip Nigerian leaders. The generosity of the oil boom era has stopped. The vitriolic propaganda about liberating Africa and the black race all over the world and working for world peace has been toned down. Corruption, mismanagement, misplaced priorities, and waste have bled the country dry. It has suffered several challenges to its influence from several countries in the region and has experienced "constant harassment (from its) neighbours, especially Benin Republic, the Cameroon Republic, Niger, Chad and even Equatorial Guinea."[46] Mounting foreign debt, rising food import bills, inability to service foreign debts, increasing internal instability and alienation, as well as increasing marginalization in the global system have had a significant impact on Nigeria's efforts to redefine its internal economic and political relations and foreign policies. Given that resolving its current crisis would rely heavily on Western support, attacks on Western policies have completely disappeared from foreign policy pronouncements. The country has come full circle, from timidity and a total pro-Western position to a militant and radical pro-Africa posture, and back to a timid and pro-western position. Paradoxically, given the generally dismal conditions of the African continent, Nigeria has managed to remain Africa's most influential, if not Africa's most powerful, country.

Nigeria in the Mid-1980s and 1990s: Economic Diplomacy or Economic Subservience?

As Nigeria entered the last quarter of the 1980s it was obvious that its foreign policy was going to experience a fundamental shift both in terms of its content and focus and in terms of the government's ability to carry out policies without internal reaction. This era was characterized by the return of the military to power, massive human rights abuses, decline in oil rents, border problems with Cameroon, and internal economic and political tensions and conflicts. Ironically, this era also witnessed Nigeria's increasing *influence* in the area of foreign relations. Caught in the oil burst, the country could not keep development projects afloat, nor could it meet its internal and external contractual commitments. It was unable to service its foreign debts and its credit rating dropped substantially. Creditors closed credit lines and forced it to reach a stabilization agreement with the IMF. A full structural adjustment package was introduced in 1986 as the only condition for further credit, loans, and supplies.[47] The military officers who had terminated the second democratic experiment in 1983 were overthrown in 1985. Since then there have been two attempted coups, scores of riots by students, workers, and religious fanatics, and violent demonstrations and strike actions by workers (see chapter 6). The imposition of harsh adjustment policies of devaluation, desubsidization, deregulation, commercialization/ privatization, trade liberalization, and the rolling back of the state have deepened alienation, poverty, and generated/accentuated social contradictions and conflicts. As Mohammed Adam has noted:

> Nigeria could well be described as a country of lost opportunities. Once upon a time, Nigerians used to think of their country as the dominant black nation in Africa. South of the Sahara Nigeria was the unchallenged leader and for many years nothing happened in black African politics without its involvement or knowledge. . . . In the leading capitals of the world, particularly in the West, Third World policy makers were constantly tuned in to the Nigerian wavelength. The view point in Lagos was always the most important in Africa . . . Nigeria in the mid-seventies was a regional power in its own right. . . . A very serious side effect of the economic collapse was that it undermined Nigeria's ability to pursue the high profile foreign policy that had become its trade mark.[48]

The later part of the 1980s saw the gradual decline of ECOWAS. It could not pay rents, its checks bounced and the Francophone members redirected their interest and commitments toward the French-sponsored

West African Economic Community (CEAO). With deepening economic crisis all over the continent, the Economic Commission for Africa(ECA) came to replace the OAU as the dominant organization in Africa, leading the debate against the World Bank over the social cost of adjustment and proposing alternatives to the World Bank/IMF package.[49] Interestingly, the Nigerian government took sides with the World Bank and IMF in this debate, arguing that there was no alternative to adjustment as prescribed by these organizations.[50] In addition, Nigeria's expulsion of so-called illegal aliens, in spite of the ECOWAS protocol on the free mobility of persons, and increasing support for the World Bank and the IMF in Africa became indicators of changing foreign policy positions. Yet, economic crisis, a high foreign debt profile, dwindling oil revenues (save for the brief period of the Persian Gulf crisis), and deepening internal contradictions did not in any substantial way reduce Nigeria's influence in Africa.

Though Nigeria's Ibrahim Babangida, in an unprecedented development, retained the chairmanship of ECOWAS for four years, Nigeria's impact was hardly felt. The Nigerian government was accused of being involved in the assassination of the radical and flamboyant president of Burkina Faso, Thomas Sankara. This allegation was given credence when Blaise Compraore visited Nigeria a few months after Sankara's death, his first visit outside Burkina Faso, and when Ibrahim Babangida made way for him to become ECOWAS chairman in 1988. The Technical Aids Corp (TAC), introduced by Bolaji Akinyemi to assist African states, did provide jobs for some Nigerians but made very little impact on the country's influence and power.[51] The so-called Akinyemi Doctrine introduced the concept of "reciprocal consultation": to obtain Nigeria's political, diplomatic, and other support, Nigeria must first be consulted by other African states prior to taking any major foreign policy action. This policy was advanced by Akinyemi to rationalize Nigeria's failure to criticize the American attack on Libya. At the 1986 National Foreign Policy Conference in Kuru, Nigeria, Akinyemi, then as foreign minister, stated that

> there is no disputing the fact that we have responsibilities to Africa. There should be no disputing the fact that Africa has responsibilities to Nigeria. If when we say that Africa is the centre-piece of our foreign policy, we mean that Nigeria should identify with and defend the legitimate interests of Africa, collectively, and each African state, individually, then I submit, that it also means that Africa and African states should identify with and defend Nigerian interests. . . . If we owe a responsibility to stand up for and respond to Africa, we are owed an obligation to be consulted when the

> situation allows for consultation and a lot of situations allow for consultations. . . . We must not and cannot allow states which of their own free-will adopt policies that lead to crisis to assume that Nigeria will automatically be dragged into that crisis. That is not the position of leadership, that is a position of subservience. Because of what we are and who we are, Africa expects us to do right by her . . . Nigerians also expect Africa to do right by Nigeria.[52]

The Akinyemi Doctrine not only served to widen the gulf between Nigeria and other African countries, which already perceived Nigeria as a bully, but further demonstrated growing common grounds between the West and Nigeria. Within the country, the minister's position served to widen the gulf between the opposition groups and the government. To the former group, it was a clear case of selling out to the West by refusing to make direct and very critical statements on the downing of Libya's plane over the Gulf of Sirte by the United States. Even when, days later, the United States bombed Tripoli and Benghazi, the government's statement reflected the "new realism" in its foreign policy; it lacked the expected bite and hard condemnation of an attack on another member of the OAU.

The country's economic crisis imposed severe constraints on the ability to pursue a radical foreign policy and resources and attention were redirected toward deepening internal problems that threatened the very foundation of the state and society.[53] With declining resources, Nigerian leaders and officials of the Central Bank of Nigeria(CBN) have roamed the world signing all sorts of loan agreements. A few recent examples will suffice here. In 1989 alone the government obtained a N14 million UNDP grant to boost water supply and sanitation in rural areas, a $270 million World Bank loan at an interest rate of 24.6 percent to finance small- and medium-scale industries, $230 million was obtained from the African Development Bank (ADB) and $150 million from the government of Czechoslovakia for the same purpose, and a $110 million World Bank loan was obtained for the rehabilitation of oil palm and rubber plantations as part of a $350 million loan to be disbursed in three years. In 1990, N89 million was obtained from USAID to promote health programs, a N3.4 million facility loan from ITT and N16 million from the World Bank to establish 20,000 digital telephone lines, $10 million from the ECOWAS Fund to aid the Nigerian Agricultural and Commerce Bank (NACB), $20.8 million from the International Fund for Agricultural Development (IFAD) on behalf of the NACB to promote fisheries in some states of the federation, $2 million FAO grant for the development of wheatless bread, $150 million World Bank loan to develop the NNPC/Mobil Condensate Project, and $20 million from the International Finance Corporation(IFC) to develop the Nigerian Liquified Natural Gas Project. In October 1991 Edo, Delta, Ondo, Kebbi, and Sokoto states obtained a loan of $6 million for fish production and the World Bank granted a $3.5 million loan for the implementation of the Nigerian Tropical Forestry Action Plan. It is clear that Nigeria, in spite of its vast resources, had become like any other poverty-stricken African country seeking loans from all possible sources for fish production, to repair highways, to rehabilitate plantations, to repair schools, in fact, to do anything.

The direct implication of this development was that Nigeria was compelled to restructure its "international behaviour" in order to be considered for many of these loans and grants. This of course meant supporting Western initiatives, opposing militant regimes identified by the West to be against its interests, accepting the dictates of the IMF, the World Bank, the London and Paris Clubs, and other creditors without debate, service its debts regularly even at the expense of national survival, and refrain from making radical and condemnatory statements on international issues. The net result has been a bloated external debt of $37 billion and an internal debt of N85 billion. Negotiations about the country's debt has become a major issue in the nation's foreign policy as ministers for external affairs, finance, and planning, and top military leaders roam around Western capitals seeking one concession after another.

To be sure, and paradoxically, these constraints did not prevent Nigeria from seeking to "hunt" for top positions in international organizations and to provide financial assistance to other African states, even if the regularity and size of such assistance have declined steeply over the years. This new aspect of Nigeria's foreign policy of course contradicts the so-called new focus of "economic diplomacy" (see below). This is because when a nation hunts for top positions in virtually all international organizations it needs to spend heavily, make concessions and promises, some of them dangerous and dubious, and it has to tailor its foreign policy to reflect that of a "mature," "responsible," "friendly," nonmilitant, and "neutral" country. What is now referred to as "post hunting diplomacy"[54] a cardinal aspect of Nigeria's foreign policy under the Babangida regime, started in 1988 "when the government sounded bitter that fewer

Nigerians were occupying important posts at the international level."[55] When Uthman Yola was not reappointed as under-secretary to the United Nations by the UN secretary-general, Nigeria expressed "grave concern" and complained that "smaller" countries like Ghana had more representation in the UN than Nigeria. When it realized that Adebayo Adedeji, the only UN under-secretary, was due to retire at the end of 1991 as executive secretary of the ECA, Nigeria initiated an "intensive lobby" and the president started a "one-to-one diplomacy with some key world leaders" to increase Nigeria's representation in international bodies.[56] Consequently, Rilwanu Lukman become the president of OPEC for six terms; Hassan Sunmonnu, the first president of the Nigeria Labour Congress (NLC), became the secretary-general of the Organization of African Trade Union Unity (OATUU); Major-General Joe Garba (rtd) also became the president of the 44th Session United Nations General Assembly after serving as chairman of the General Assembly's Sub-Committee on Apartheid for five years; Gorbon Bristol was elected to the post of vice-chairman of the UN Fourth Committee on Decolonization in October 1989; Emeka Anyaoku became the first black secretary-general of the Commonwealth, and Ibrahim Babangida became the twenty-eighth chairman of the OAU in June 1991. As well, Babangida, after serving as chairman of ECOWAS for four years consecutively made way for Blaise Compraore of Burkina Faso for one year and returned to the position for the fifth time in July 1991. The country's attorney-general and minister for justice, Bola Ajibola, was "presented" to replace Talsim Elias at the International Court of Justice[57] and Nigeria's former head of state, Olusegun Obasanjo, who had served as cochair of the Eminent Persons Group (EPG) was sponsored for the position of secretary-general of the United Nations in 1991.[58] In spite of Nigeria's intensive lobbying on behalf of General Obasanjo, it was strongly opposed within the African continent by Egypt, Sierra Leone, Zimbabwe, Gabon, and Ghana. The Egyptian candidate eventually won the UN seat.

These successes certainly demonstrated that Nigeria still had the resources and influence to sponsor its nationals for important positions in international organizations even if they did not always succeed. But not much should be made of them because most of these positions were won at great cost. It will take years before the unknown concessions made by the government begin to show. The country's international behavior since this "position hunting diplomacy" started has been that of a sleeping giant with no capacity to defend the interests of Africa. We see Nigeria siding with the IMF and the World Bank and pretending to be "neutral" on several critical intenational issues. More important is the fact that the contest for these positions faced serious challenges at home and abroad. At the level of ECOWAS, the poverty-stricken and debt-ridden West African states are willing to let Nigeria keep the position forever if it so wishes. After all, the Francophone states have their CEAO and Nigeria pays about 40 percent of the ECOWAS budget. In any case, it was Nigeria's creation, and in these difficult days it makes sense to let Nigeria bear the burden of the organization.

At the OAU level, it was actually not easy to find hosts for the summit in 1991. Hosting the OAU Summit can be very expensive. Many African leaders were unwilling to further anger their peoples, especially the irrepressible prodemocracy movements, by spending hundreds of millions of dollars on the gathering of despots, who are legendary for their waste, mismanagement, dependence, irresponsibilty, and corruption. It took a government that was interested in the position of chairman, that was not accountable to anyone, that was capable of shrugging off criticisms, and that was willing to host such a jamboree irrespective of internal opposition to agree to host the summit. Till this very day, the government has not had the courage to reveal how much it spent on hosting the OAU Summit in spite of several public demands for some accounting. As Onome Osifo-Whiskey has noted,

> The OAU conference for heads of state and government is another sore point among critics who see the government as unjustifiably profligate. The centre of the anger is the new Abuja Conference Centre which, with Mercedes Benz limousines specially imported for the occasion, is said to have wiped off more than one billion naira from government's accounts. This, critics say, is unwise for an economy where use of the industrial sector's installed capacity is a mere 40 per cent and unemployment remains ungovernable.[59]

Femi Falana, a radical Lagos lawyer and member of the Committee for the Defence of Human Rights (CDHR) reflects the popular position on the summit when he declared:

> How can a country waste over a billion naira on a jamboree like this meaningless and useless OAU which the press in Nigeria out of ignorance and self-serving thing is now saying was Nigeria's finest hour? You are praising Nigeria for hosting tyrants that litter the African continent? People who are on their way out of power? You are hosting that kind of nonsense?[60]

It is, therefore, clear that Nigeria has not carried its populace along in this quest for international prestige and has created more problems at home with its approach to African politics.

The beginning of the 1990s saw Nigeria working for dialogue in Angola and South Africa. In fact, President de Klerk of South Africa visited Nigeria in 1992 just as Nigeria was intensifying efforts to establish diplomatic and economic relations with the apartheid state. On the recent Gulf crisis, in spite of strong pressures from powerful Muslim interests in the country, Nigeria maintained a neutral posture while insisting that Iraq must withdraw from Kuwait.[61] The Nigerian president called for "reason and maturity" in the "search for a peaceful settlement. Consistent with our foreign policy, Nigeria unreservedly condemns the use of force to settle disputes in inter-state relations." The government expressed its conviction that "the sanctions already imposed by the United Nations Security Council on Iraq as a sequel to its invasion of Kuwait can generate a reconsideration of the Iraqi position . . . Nigeria calls for an international conference to resolve all the outstanding questions on the Middle East."[62] Of course, when the United States shot down peaceful proposals from France and the former Soviet Union, and without consulting the secretary-general of the United Nations, proceeded to ruthlessly bomb Baghdad and Kuwait killing over 100,000 Iraqis (according to American estimates), Nigeria was silent and actually turned around to support the American agenda in the Middle East. If Nigerian troops had not been engaged in war in Liberia, the government would have contributed troops, notwithstanding the pressures from the powerful Islamic lobby in the country that was in favor of open declaration of support for Iraq. As part of its own contribution to the war effort, Nigeria indicated its preparedness to assist African countries that were affected by the increased oil prices during the war. Countries like Tanzania and Benin Republic immediately took advantage of the concessions extended to OAU member states by Nigeria.

Nigeria joined the Organization of Islamic Conference(OIC) in January 1987 as the forty-sixth member in a bid to strengthen its ties with the Arab states. This has led to several religious riots and tensions between Christians and Muslims in the country. The tensions arising from Nigeria's membership in the organization has today created a situation where Christians are leaving parts of the northern states because of insecurity and the Christain-Muslim, north-south issue is back on top of the nation's political agenda. If not properly handled, a religious issue might destroy the political fabric of the nation.[63] Though Nigeria continues to support the Palestinians, it moved to normalize diplomatic relations with Israel in 1992 to the amazement of strong pro-Palestinian interests in the country. Ironically, though the OAU had not collectively lifted the break in relations with Israel, Nigeria under Babangida went ahead to normalize relations while he was serving as chairman of the organization. The leader of the Palestine Liberation Organization (PLO) visited Nigeria in March 1986 and in June 1989. Though Nigeria is not supposed to have any diplomatic relations with Israel, the Babangida administration signed a security agreement with Israel and received security agents to work with the presidency.[64] Israeli companies were already doing very profitable business in Nigeria especially in the oil industry and in construction even before the normalization of relations.

In spite of Britain's very ambiguous position on South Africa, Nigeria has moved to strengthen relations with Britain in its search for foreign investments. The former British prime minister, Margaret Thatcher, visited Nigeria twice toward the end of the 1980s; Prince Philip, Duke of Edinburgh, visited Nigeria in February 1989; Babangida visited Britain in May 1989; Prince Charles and his wife visited Nigeria in 1990; and Nigerian trade delegations have been visiting the United Kingdom regularly.

It is interesting that though British dignitaries are received in Nigeria with all possible publicity, Babangida's visit to the United Kingdom was hardly given any recognition in the British media. As well, British investors continue to refuse to invest in Nigeria claiming that corruption, political instability, and bureaucratic bottlenecks are impediments to investment. Of course, this is mere rationalization because British investors contine to invest in the Middle East, a region much more unpredictable and politically unstable, where religious fanaticism and political extremism are highest and where corruption is equally very pronounced in business dealings. British investors are right now investing in the politically fragile countries of Eastern Europe, even Yugoslavia, which is being rocked by a terrible ethnic and religious war. Of course, there are hundreds, perhaps thousands of young Nigerians in British jails for all sorts of offenses, in particular, drug-related offenses, and like other countries in the world, Britain treats all Nigerians wishing to travel to the

United Kingdom for whatever reasons as potential drug pushers, criminals, and economic refugees.

On Nelson Mandela's release, Nigeria declared a public holiday, and when Mandela visited the country shortly after his release, he was welcomed with pomp and pageantry even though the country was just recovering from the bloodiest coup attempt in its political history. About forty thousand people gathered to welcome Mandela and his wife, Winnie, as well as leading anti-apartheid musicians—Sonny Okosuns, Onyeka Onwenu, Chris Hanen, and Chrity Essien-Igbokwe "all rendered songs on the evils of the apartheid system."[65] Nigeria conferred its second highest honor—The Grand Commander of the Order of the Niger (GCON)—on Nelson Mandela and pledged to "continue to support the South African struggle for a free, democratic, and egalitarian society." Nigeria also pledged to continue to support the calls for sanctions against South Africa "as long as the vestiges of the hated apartheid system remains."[66] It is interesting that in spite of Nigeria's total commitment to the liberation of South Africa, its huge financial contributions over the years, its prominent role in the anti-apartheid committees of the UN and OAU, and the significance of the release of Nelson Mandela, only the "second highest honor" was conferred on him. As well, though Nigeria delared its commitment to ensuring a "free," "democratic," and "egalitarian" South Africa, it is ironic that Nigeria itself is neither free, egalitarian, nor democratic.

Financial assistance continues to go to the liberation movements and other African states even if the regularity and amounts donated have somewhat been reduced. When South Africa invaded the Frontline States on 9 May 1986, the Nigerian President "despatched Professor Bolaji Akinyemi who was then minister for external affairs to the frontline states. He also sent a N10 million aid comprising N7 million in materials and N3 million cash. A further N50 million was . . . pledged in aid to the frontline states and liberation movements in that part of Africa."[67] Nigeria also "bankrolled the reconstruction of damaged buildings in Botswana and Zambia;" contributed N3 million to the OAU toward Namibia's independence, N1.2 million to the UN Transition Assistance Group (UNTAG), 50 policemen and 50 civilians to help supervise the Namibian elections.[68] At home, the government launched a Namibia Fund to which it contributed N5 million and realized N3.9 million from the public. When the Non-Aligned Movement set up the Africa Fund for southern

Africa, Nigeria pledged a contribution of $15 million and donated $1 million to Zimbabwe in 1986 to assist it with hosting the Non-Aligned Summit in Harare. In 1988, Nigeria moved to get the government of Equatorial Guinea to expel South Africa from its territory mainly for security reasons as Equatorial Guinea was only "40 Kilometres away from her territory." The Nigerian president paid the very first state visit by a Nigerian leader to Equatorial Guinea and, in order to replace the enticement offered by South Africa, made "money, food and clothing available to the country . . . [and] established schools and hospitals."[69] When Ghana hosted the Non-Aligned Summit, Nigeria assisted by providing cars and also helped resolve a row between Ghana and Togo in 1988. In 1986, Lake Nyos in Cameroon emitted deadly gas fumes that virtually wiped out a whole community. Nigeria, like France and the United States, rushed science experts there as part of an international monitoring team. Its involvement in the civil wars in Liberia and Sierra Leone have also drained its resources in no small way (see below).

Relations with the United States remain cordial, though there is still a lingering quarrel over Nigeria's ban on wheat imports that has affected the United States in some way. Though the United States wrote off some of Nigeria's official debts in 1990, it remains unimpressed with the economic restructuring, the breakdown of fiscal discipline, the country's involvement in the international drug business, and the poor management of the Nigerian economy.[70] When Bolaji Akinyemi was foreign minister, he tried to put in place his pet idea of a Concert of Medium Powers (The Lagos Forum), a sort of duplication of the Non-Aligned Movement to advance the interest of nonaligned countries under the leadership of Nigeria. The forum was supposed to serve a mediatory role in "international dialogue with the generalized aim of strengthening co-operation, peace and security."[71] At its first meeting in Lagos, held 16–18 March 1987, the forum attracted senior foreign diplomats from Algeria, Argentina, Brazil, Egypt, India, Indonesia, Malaysia, Yugoslavia, Mexico, Senegal, Switzerland, Sweden, Venezuela, Austria, and Zimbabwe. Of course, the country lacked the economic base with which to put such a movement in place. The Lagos Forum died with the unceremonious removal of Akinyemi as foreign minister in 1987.

With deepening economic crisis and increasing pressures from credit clubs and creditors, Nigeria has tried to make a shift in the content and direction of its foreign policy by emphasizing economic issues almost at the expense of political issues. Though the government has tried to make much of this "new" policy, there is nothing essentially new or original about it. In reality it is a mere response to declining foreign exchange receipts from oil, the growing marginalization of Africa in the world economy, increasing competition for available assistance with other regions of the developing world, and an urgent need to increase the level of contacts and dialogue with creditors, investors, and suppliers. Rather than wait for investors to come to the country, the new policy emphasizes going to meet with the investors and plead with them to come by offering all sorts of incentives. This has become necessary because foreign investors are spurning the Nigerian economy and are reluctant to do business with Nigerians, many of whom have developed reputations as crooks in the international market. The Central Bank of Nigeria recently took paid advertisements in international papers to warn the international business community about these dubious business persons.[72]

International awareness of the depth of Nigeria's economic and political crisis, external flamboyance notwithstanding, has had a direct impact on the inability to attract investors in spite of countless trips to virtually all countries in the world in search of investors and other opportunities. In any case, Nigeria has only two things to offer: a large market, which investors can also find in other parts of the world, and oil, which is also available, even at cheaper prices, in several parts of the world. In any case, Nigeria has no choice but to sell its oil as it is totally dependent on oil sales for survival, and its population is so impoverished that it can no longer be an asset in its negotiations. The poverty, disillusionment, anger, and restlessness of its population, which have encouraged coups, riots, and other forms of violence at best, are a liability in the efforts to use foreign policy to attract investors. As the *African Concord* has noted,

> Nigeria's economy is unhealthy, despite five years of the Structural Adjustment Programme (SAP). Nigeria's finances are in terrible shape, and international creditors who Nigeria owes an estimated $35 billon in debts, are unsatisfied with Nigeria's niggardly repayments. Nigeria's debt service commitment is currently put at 3.5 billion dollars a year. But the country's oil receipts are falling, first from N26 billion in 1980 to $9.4 billion in 1989, and down again to 7 billion dollars presently. In effect, there has been a corresponding drop in per capita GNP from $1,090 in 1980 to about $250, which places Nigerians high on *World Suffering Index*.[73]

The *Financial Times* of London has also noted that the Nigerian economy, in spite of all the noise about its growing international profile and the struggles to capture all top positions declared vacant in international bodies, is in deep crisis and is simply not attractive to investors:

> Unemployment is growing, and the country's infrastructure and social services are deteriorating; the telephone system is unreliable; power supply is erratic; the transport fleet is ageing; many industries need re-equipping; schools, universities and hospitals are poorly equipped; and environmental problems in northern Nigeria are mounting as desertification gathers pace. Today, the country still battles with an unstable exchange rate, credit squeeze, escalating unemployment and rapid inflation.[74]

Nigeria's foreign minister, Major General Ike Nwachukwu, does not recognize these limitations; until there is a fundamental internal restructuring based on local efforts with local resources, the economy will be unattractive to investors, local and foreign. Nwachukwu has argued that this "new" foreign policy emphasizes "using foreign policy to achieve Nigeria's economic development"[75] and that with this policy, "this country would take off if only one could collaborate with countries that have advanced technologies or better resource base at their disposal."[76] However, as Olu Awogbemila has rightly noted, "Without doubt, the shift in the focus of Nigeria's foreign policy has been largely a result of the dire straits in which the domestic economy finds itself. The shift has been dictated by an empty purse, debilitating debt and attendant social consequences."[77] Though Nwachukwu firmly believes that the policy "is working very well for us," it might be more a reflection of the narrow, even shallow understanding of the critical issues of global power and economic relations as well as the unfortunate belief that by associating a country with an advanced country, growth and development might just rub off on the dependent, vulnerable, and underdeveloped actor. The experiences of Latin American countries and the theory of dependent development demonstrate clearly that such associations do not fundamentally alter a nation's location and role in the periphery of the global system; they merely replace old relationships with more sophisticated ones. In the emerging unipolar security and multipolar economic order dominated by protectionism, high tech, and trade blocs, such expectations are not only pedestrian but futile. In a rather unfortunate development, the Nigerian government has decided to measure the success of its ambassadors "in terms of the amount of business investments they are able to bring into our country or how much they are able to open up room for Nigerian investments in their country of assignment."[78] So far, "economic diplomacy" has involved junketing around the globe, at great cost to the economy, by the minister and selected members of the Nigerian bourgeois class. The minister has visited Brazil, Japan, Indonesia, Argentina, Malaysia, and Korea, to mention just a few. He has traveled with businessmen such as Adeluyi Adelusi, Aminu Dantata, Chief Adekoya, and Chief M. K. O. Abiola. Other top members of the regime have also been busy traveling from one foreign capital to another.[79] For instance, the minister for information and other top political figures were in New York to attend a conference on "Nigeria's National and Foreign Policy" in August 1992. The conference was hardly noticed by the Nigerian community and was completely ignored by the American media. The policy of "economic diplomacy" has also focused on the renegotiation of debts, attracting foreign investors, seeking foreign aid, and trying to win concessions from the World Bank. Such moves have so far hardly convinced investors and donors.[80]

It is quite true that "Babangida within the sub-region, . . . has become the natural leader of the 'conservative regimes' in the 16-member ECOWAS."[81] Perhaps the most far-reaching demonstration of this "natural leadership" as well as of Nigeria's ability to take foreign policy initiatives and provide required leadership in spite of its own economic crisis was the 1990 formation of the Economic Community of West African States Monitoring Group (ECOMOG) and the direct intervention in the Liberian crisis. Against opposition from Burkina Faso, Cote d'Ivoire and several other countries in the subregion, without financial support from the OAU, the United Nations, and the West, and without reaching any status-of-forces agreement with all the warring parties, Nigeria arranged for Ghana, Guinea, Sierra Leone, and Gambia to contribute forces that intervened in Liberia and eventually stopped the massacre though it has not brought peace and stability to the country.

The intervention was executed at great cost to Nigeria. Public opinion was heavily divided in Nigeria with the majority arguing that internal problems should take priority and that only the OAU had a mandate to carry out such an intervention. As well, it was argued that the ECOWAS Treaty had no provisions for the ECOMOG, intervention ought to be preceded by an agreement between all the parties, and that Babangida's rush to intervene was borne out of his personal friendship with the late Samuel Doe.[82] Furthermore, popular opinion in Nigeria was that Liberians were quite capable of handling their own problems and that

Nigeria had no business in determining who should rule or not rule Liberia.

Nigeria, in fact, initiated the idea, contributed over thirty-five hundred soldiers, about half of the troops involved in the operation, provided most of the combat equipment, and practically financed the operation alone. When it was decided that ECOMOG should be transformed from a "monitoring group" into a "combat operation," Nigeria sent in Major-General Joshua Dogonyaro to replace Ghana's Lt.-General Arnold Quianoo who had expressed reservations about such a transformation. Of the troops contributed by Nigeria, it lost seven hundred fifty soldiers and an "average of one vehicle per day."[83] Because the Nigerian government, in wanting to give credibility to the Doe government in Liberia, delayed in evacuating Nigerians out of the war-torn country, "hundreds of Nigerians were massacred by Liberian rebels."[84] Two Nigerian journalists, Dayo Awotusin and Krees Imodibe, were also killed in Liberia allegedly by Charles Taylor's forces in retaliation for Nigeria's open support for Samuel Doe. By mid-August 1991, Etim Imisim estimated that the government had spent "N313.5 milion" on ECOMOG "to liberate Liberia from itself."[85] William Keeling of the *Financial Times* of London estimated that as of 27 June 1991, Nigeria had spent between $250 million and $500 million on the Liberian operation. The Nigerian government did not like the report since it did not plan to reveal to the Nigerians the cost of its operations in Liberia; consequently, it deported the British journalist from Nigeria. In a statement that was issued on the deportation denying the figures quoted by Keeling, the government cleverly refused to mention what the actual or correct figure was.

Though Nigeria has to some extent succeeded in stopping the blood bath, installing an interim government led by Amos Sawyer and working out a transition program for political and economic recovery, its victory has only been partial. The ECOMOG forces succeeded only in securing the capital city, Monrovia, while most of Liberian territory is still under the control of Charles Taylor. In several instances ECOMOG has complicated the Liberian situation by taking sides in the war rather than being neutral. As well, the war extended to Sierra Leone where the struggles by rebels to bring down the government culminated in a coup d'etat in 1992. The rebels had received full military and financial support from Charles Taylor (among other internal and external sources) in retaliation for Sierra Leone's contribution to ECOMOG. Naturally, since ECOMOG was Nigeria's idea, Sierra Leone, under President Momoh, had turned to Nigeria for a solution to the crisis. Nigeria quickly moved five hundred soldiers from its ECOMOG troops to Liberia and followed this up with an additional one thousand soldiers directly from Nigeria. In addition, it sent four alpha jets, one helicopter gun boat, and three Charlie transporters to assist the troops of Joseph Momoh. Today, Nigeria maintains about seven thousand soldiers in the West African subregion, specifically in Liberia and Sierra Leone, and ironically, the government's praise singers see this as "giving the country thc visibility it has often denied itself, as the greatest power in the West African subregion."[86] The reality is that "such a big diplomatic expense" was not "previously thought-out"[87] and the Nigerian government, having gotten itself into the Liberian tangle, does not know how to extricate itself from it without seriously losing face. Yet, it lacks the military, economic, and diplomatic power to resolve the crisis decisively.

In spite of these limitations, the intervention in Liberia was a clear attempt by Nigeria to demonstrate its leadership capacity and claims in the region. It showed that it was capable of taking the initiative and could execute a major foreign military operation with its own resources. In the context of the "new world order" and the emergence of regional powers and trading blocs, it was necessary for Nigeria to move and assert its leadership in the sub-region. Since the end of the Liberian operation, the Nigerian government has moved to resolve the divisions within ECOWAS and to recommend the ECOMOG experience and example to the OAU.

Conclusion: Foreign Policy in the 1990s

The 1990s will be challenging for Nigeria. Its structural adjustment program has not achieved much. The world oil market, which recovered only briefly during the Gulf War, has fallen once again. Dependence on the oil sector for revenues is still extremely high. The foreign debt profile is still very high.[88] The agricultural policies introduced under the adjustment program have yet to yield positive results. The Nigerian state is still weak, unstable, and enjoys very limited legitimacy. The unequal distribution of the pains and "gains" of adjustment has further eroded the legitimacy of the state. The elites remain largely corrupt, unproductive, dependent, and undisciplined. They remain concentrated in real estate, politics, import-export activities, and transportation, as against *production.* The economy, in particular, the oil sector on which the state is dependent, remains under foreign control. The recent revocation of the indigenization decrees and the introduction of a "new industrial policy" will only further foreign domination of the economy and the consolidation of the peripheral location and role of Nigeria in the global system. Yet, the transition to civil rule planned for January 1993, if it does come to pass, will make very limited difference to the conditions of the majority. In spite of institutional changes to the political processes, the content and patterns of political competition, the objectives and the actors are still the same; politics, to the Nigerian bourgeoisie is still simply a matter of economic calculation follwed by political struggle to attain the power to corner projected profits and investments.[89] With the introduction of structural adjustment the society has been plagued with riots, violence, prostitution, crime, corruption, inflation, poverty, unemployment, institutional decay, and the general delegitimization of the state. Clearly, a viable, credible, and consistent foreign policy cannot be built on such foundations of crisis, uncertainty, and instability. Dan Agbese, writing on the growing cynicism and disillusionment among the populace, has noted that:

> A few years ago, *The Guardian* newspaper asked its readers to list ten good things the country could crow about. Good, positive achievements all Nigerians could justly be proud of. There was some evidence many Nigerians have a serious problem with counting up to ten. Either that or they felt crowing should be left to the cock. But the depth of cynicism among the respondents was bottomless. Many of them simply took the country to the cleaners. The howl of personal disgust could be heard above the chaotic, ear-splitting sound of Lagos. . . . It would seem nothing has changed in the attitude of Nigerians to their country since the newspaper threw the challenge at them. Or, perhaps, it would be correct to say that attitude has even deteriorated and hardened into this: see no good, speak no good, hear no good about Nigeria.[90]

Agbese goes on to capture the mood of the nation and the reason why the populace distrusts, even hates their leaders so much:

> Is there nothing to make Nigerians proud of being Nigerians? In so many years of independence, has this country done nothing for its people to win their confidence, their loyalty? Why is there so much negative feeling about this country despite the vast opportunities it has provided. . . . Cynicism is of course an endemic disease in our country . . . Nigerians are cynical about their country. They are negative about their country. . . . The tribes of cynics and the sceptics in our country are multiplying at an alarming rate. . . . There is despair and cynicism in this country. Both are

> consequences of personal disappontments. Many . . . talk of hypocrisy and corruption. . . . There is some anger that hopes have been betrayed or dashed.[91]

As mentioned earlier, the devaluation of the naira and the introduction of a "new industrial policy" have failed to attract foreign investment to the country. This is very serious because the whole adjustment package, in particular, the policies of devaluation, deregulation, and liberalization, were aimed at attracting foreign investors. Yet, though the Nigerian government has declared that its "doors are wide open," investors are claiming that it has "not liberalized enough."[92] At a meeting in London between the Confederation of British Industry (CBI) and a Nigerian trade delegation, British investors refused to be lured by these concessions pointing out that "there is still too much corruption and bureaucracy. With three military coups in five years, the investment climate is not as stable" as the Nigerian government claims.[93] If investors do not come in, and the foreign debt and debt-servicing obligations continue to increase, Nigeria will be unable to build the required economic base for an effective role as a regional power in the 1990s.

Without doubt the West has, to a considerable extent, lost interest in Africa. Documents from the Economic Commission for Africa (ECA), the United Nations Africa Recovery Programme, and the OAU show very clearly that the West has redirected its aid and investments to Eastern Europe.[94] The relative irrelevance of Africa in the international politics of the current era is shown by: the response to the recent Gulf crisis compared to the lackluster responses to the crises in Liberia, Sudan, and Somalia; the refusal of the United States to impose comprehensive sanctions on South Africa and its enthusiasm not only in imposing sanctions on Iraq but in blockading it; and the postwar concern for economic recovery in the Gulf. In the case of Somalia, the UN and the United States waited until over two hundred fifty thousand Somalis, mostly women and children, had died, and the media brought frightening pictures to American homes before organizing a response. During the Liberian crisis, the United States simply evacuated its citizens from Liberia and left the warring factions to massacre themselves. The United Nations did the same thing. Thus, any country that aspires to act as a regional power in Africa in the 1990s must have the political and economic capacity to influence the new world order, redirect some interest toward the continent, and promote an environment that will attract donors and investors. Ibrahim Babangida recognizes the implications of these developments:

> The international economic system continues to present difficulties for Africa. . . . While many of the Western European, Japanese and American multinational companies have rushed to the "greener pastures" of potentially more profitable investment which Eastern Europe presents, some of these companies have commenced a process of massive disinvestment from Africa. In fact, the economies of many of the countries of the South have deteriorated further with the heavy debt burden pulling them further into stagnation. A clear evidence of the plight of African countries lies in the fact that within the last decade, six African countries have lost their position in the middle income group and have fallen to the low income category. Nine African countries have now joined the league of least developed countries bringing the number to twenty eight. Unless a major improvement occurs in the international economic system, the number is likely to increase.[95]

Babangida goes on to note that in the new priorities of the great powers, "Africa is falling lower and lower in the list. We are no longer of crucial strategic interest to the great powers, therefore, African events may not receive the type of attention which they used to get in the past." His conclusion is that "the picture that is evolving is one of rapid disengagement from Africa."[96]

While this recognition is important, is Nigeria prepared to bear the burdens of the region? Can it encourage, compel or attract the great powers to review their current stance toward Africa? It is interesting to note that in his one year as chairman of the OAU, Babangida achieved very little. The crises in Liberia, Somalia, Sudan, and other areas continued. Resource flows to the region did not improve. There was no open and visible support for prodemocracy movements. The violence in South Africa increased to unprecedented levels. Africa remained a marginal actor in global relations. In the interim, however, is Nigeria in a position to provide economic and political support for the impoverished African states? It should be kept in mind that Nigeria is one of those countries that has lost its middle-income status as a result of general socioeconomic deterioration. Without doubt, a politically unstable, debt-ridden, and generally backward country cannot be suited for such a role.

Within the *continent*, Nigeria will continue to face challenges to its regional power aspirations. Countries like Egypt, Zaire, Ghana, Cote d'Ivoire, and Zimbabwe will continue to assert influence and challenge Nigeria's claims to leadership in Africa. A huge population, it is now widely known, does not make a nation powerful, especially when that population is plagued with unemployment, poverty, and uncertainty. In

1989, Zaire "outsmarted" Nigeria in hosting the Angolan peace talks after Nigeria had initiated them. The greatest challenge, however, will come from a majority-ruled South Africa. Right now, Nigeria's foreign policy revolves around the issue of apartheid. Angola, Zimbabwe, and recently Namibia have become free. The release of Mandela and the ongoing reforms in South Africa, fueled by the changes in Eastern Europe and the end of the cold war, mean that there are reasons to anticipate majority rule in South Africa in the very near future. South Africa is more developed than Nigeria in every respect. It is also of greater strategic importance to the Western powers than Nigeria. Its economy is more developed and more integrated. Its military organization is stronger and much better equipped. Its agricultural system is more developed and productive. Its science and technology program cannot even be compared to Nigeria's because the latter lacks any such program. This means that an independent, majority-ruled South Africa might easily replace Nigeria as the "representative" of Africa. Nigeria might, under this circumstance, be forced to restrict its influence to the West African subregion, where it will easily remain a "giant." Even then, unless concrete policies are initiated to check the country's deepening crisis and the dominant classes begin to take *production* seriously, Nigeria is likely to face major challenges to its *influence* in the subregion in the 1990s. The new world order, whatever its limitations, will have no room for political posturing, rhetorics, and flamboyance not concretely supported with a sound economic base and a high degree of social defense.

Notes

1. Ibrahim Babangida, "Major Contemporary Issues Facing Nigeria, Africa and the Rest of the World," *The Sunday Magazine* (9 June 1991), 32.
2. Ike Nwachukwu, "Our New Policy Thrust," *African Concord* (10 June 1991).
3. Olajide Aluko, "Necessity and Freedom in Nigeria's Foreign Policy," *Nigerian Journal of International Studies* 4, nos. 1-2 (January-June 1980), 13-14.
4. See Olajide Aluko, "Oil at Concessionary Prices for Africa: A Case Study in Nigerian Decision-Making," *African Affairs* 75 (October 1976) and Ibrahim Gambari, "Nigeria and the World: A Growing Internal Stability, Wealth and External Influence," *Journal of International Affairs* 29, no. 2 (Fall 1975).
5. See Daniel Bach, "Nigerian-American Relations: Converging Interests and Power Relations," in Timothy Shaw and Olajide Aluko eds., *Nigerian Foreign Policy: Alternative Perceptions and Projections* (London: Macmillan, 1983); Jean Herskovits, "Nigeria: Africa's Greatest Power," *Foreign Affairs* 53, no. 2 (January 1975); Jean Herskovits, "Dateline Nigeria: A Black Power," *Foreign Policy* 29 (Winter 1977-78).

6. See, for instance, Major General Ike Nwachukwu's interview with the *African Concord* "Our New Policy Thrust," and "Nigeria's Foreign Policy: An Overview," *The Sunday Magazine* (9 June 1991). The latter was more of a public relations job for the Babangida administration than a serious and objective analysis of the country's foreign policy.
7. See Toyin Falola and Julius O. Ihonvbere, eds., *Nigeria and the International Capitalist System* (Boulder: Lynne Rienner, 1988); Y. B. Usman, *For the Liberation of Nigeria* (London: New Beacon, 1979); and Timothy M. Shaw and Orobola Fasehun, "Nigeria in the World System: Alternative Approaches, Explanations and Projections," *Journal of Modern African Studies* 18, no. 4 (1980).
8. See Stephen Wright, "Nigeria: A Mid-Term Assessment," *The World Today* (March 1982); Bill Freund, "Oil Boom and Crisis in Contemporary Nigeria," *Review of African Political Economy* 13 (May–August 1978); and Richard Joseph, "Affluence and Underdevelopment: The Nigerian Experience," *Journal of Modern African Studies* 16, no. 2 (June 1978).
9. See Gordon Idang, *Nigeria: Internal Politics and Foreign Policy* (Ibadan, Nigeria: Ibadan University Press, 1973); and Bolaji Akinyemi, *Foreign Policy and Federalism in Nigeria* (Ibadan, Nigeria: Ibadan University Press, 1974).
10. See Julius O. Ihonvbere, "Resource Availability and Foreign Policy Change: The Impact of Oil on Nigerian Foreign Policy since Independence," *Afrika Spectrum* 2 (1982).
11. See Ibrahim Gambari, "Domestic Political Constraints on Progressive Foreign Policy for Nigeria," *Nigerian Journal of Political Science* 2, no. 1 (June 1980); and Julius O. Ihonvbere, "The Role of Oil in the Nigerian Civil War, 1967–70," *African Studies* 10 (January 1986).
12. John Hatch, *Africa Emergent: Africa's Problems Since Independence* (Chicago: Henry Regnery Company, 1974), 39.
13. See the contributions to Julius O. Ihonvbere and Toyin Falola, eds., *Oil and Nigeria's Political Economy* (Lagos, Nigeria: Longman, 1993).
14. The armed forces has since been demobilized to about 150,000.
15. This also probably because they know very little of the potentials of other African states, particularly, South Africa.
16. Olajide Aluko, "Nigeria's Role in Inter-African Relations—With Special Reference to the OAU," *African Affairs* 72 (April 1973), 162.
17. Federal Republic of Nigeria, *Second National Development Plan 1970–74* (Lagos, Nigeria: Government Printer, 1970), 32.
18. Report of the Committee on the Review of Nigeria's Foreign Policy Including Economic and Technical Co-Operation, Lagos (May 1976), 59.
19. Federal Government of Nigeria, *Constitution of the Federal Republic of Nigeria, 1979* (Lagos, Nigeria: Government Printer, 1979), Sec. 19.
20. *Times* (London) (16 March 1981).
21. Oye Ogunbadejo, "Nigeria's Foreign Policy Under Military Rule 1966–79," *International Journal* 35, no. 4 (Autumn 1980), 758.
22. Federal Ministry of Information, Lagos, in *West Africa* (London) (5 October 1981), 2318.
23. General Yakubu Gowon, Fourteenth Independence Anniversary Address to the Nation, October 1975, reproduced in *New Nigerian* (Lagos and Kaduna, Nigeria) (3 October 1975), 12.
24. Ibid.

25. "Economic Diplomacy Works—Nigeria's External Affairs Minister", *The Sunday Magazine* (9 June 1991), 34.
26. Ibrahim Babangida, "Consolidating the Gains of Development," Address to the Nation, 27 August 1991, reproduced in *Newbreed* (16 September 1991), 50.
27. "Three Decades of Policy," *African Concord* (10 June 1991).
28. See Gordon Idang, *Nigeria: Internal Politics and Foreign Policy*; Bolaji Akinyemi, ed., *Nigeria and the World: Readings in Nigerian Foreign Policy* (Lagos, Nigeria: Oxford University Press, 1978); and Olajide Aluko, *Essays in Nigerian Foreign Policy* (London: George Allen and Unwin, 1981).
29. See Douglas Anglin, "Nigeria: Political Non-Alignment and Economic Alignment," *Journal of Modern African Studies* 2 no. 2, (June 1964).
30. See James Mayall, "Oil and Nigerian Foreign Policy," *African Affairs* 75 (July 1976).
31. For details on the oil industry see Julius O. Ihonvbere, *The Oil Industry in Nigeria: An Annotated Bibliography* (Montreal: Centre for Developing-Area Studies, 1983).
32. See Julius O. Ihonvbere, *Integration in a Dependent Regional Economy: Goals and Problems of the Economic Community of West African States (ECOWAS)* (M. A. research essay, the Norman Paterson School of International Affairs, Carleton University, Ottawa, Canada, 1981).
33. "Nigeria Moves Against Apartheid," *West Africa* (London) (29 August 1977), 1754.
34. General Olusegun Obasanjo (Address to the 15th Ordinary Session of the Organization of African Unity-Assembly of Heads of State and Government, Khartoum, July 1978).
35. "President Shagari Replies," *West Africa* (London) (24 March 1980), 516.
36. Paul Ahebi, "Nigeria: Relations with the Super-Powers," *Radio Lagos* (18 March 1976).
37. See Bolaji Akinyemi, ed., *Nigeria and the World*; and Ali A. Mazrui, "Nigeria and the United States: The Need for Civility, the Dangers of Intimacy," *Orbis* 25, no. 4 (Winter 1982).
38. P. Edem of the Nigerian Institute of International Affairs, Lagos quoted in "A Lame Giant: Does Nigeria Still Have the Diplomatic Clout it Had in the 70s?" *Africa Events* (October 1989).
39. Stephen Wright, "Limits of Nigeria's Power Overseas," *West Africa* (27 July 1981), 1685.
40. Ibid.
41. This is evident in their continued dependence on France and loyalty to the West African Economic Community (CEAO), which was sponsored and remains supported by France. Francophone leaders usually take common positions at the CEAO level before attending ECOWAS meetings. As well, several Francophone states are yet to pay their dues to ECOWAS even when they have conveniently done so to the CEAO.
42. See International Labour Office, *First Things First: Meeting the Basic Needs of the People of Nigeria* (Addis Ababa, Ethiopia: JASPA, 1981).
43. Brigadier J. N. Garba, "The New Nigerian Foreign Policy," *The Quarterly Journal of Administration* 9, no. 3 (April 1977), 114.
44. "A Lame Giant," 25.
45. *New Nigerian* (Lagos and Kaduna) (1 October 1982). See also Kola Olufemi, "Economic Dependence and Class Contradictions: Constraints on Nigeria's Foreign Policy in the 1980s," *Korean Journal of International Studies* 20, no. 1 (Spring 1988-89).

46. Godson Ofonagoro and Larry Arhagba, "30 Years of Foreign Policy," *Daily Champion* (1 October 1990), 3.
47. See Sam Aluko, *The Burden of Economic Structural Adjustment: The Nigerian Scenario* (Ile-Ife, Nigeria: Convocation Ceremony Lecture, University of Ife, 1987); Yusuf Bala Usman, *Nigeria Against the I.M.F.—The Home Market Strategy* (Kaduna, Nigeria: Vanguard Publishers, 1986); and Adeotun Phillips, *Economic Impact of Nigeria's Structural Adjustment Programme* (Ibadan, Nigeria: Nigerian Institute of Social and Economic Research, 1990).
48. Mohammed Adam, "Nigeria—the Busted Boom," *International Perspectives* (January-February 1987), 17 and 19.
49. The ECA's alternative is embodied in *African Alternative Framework to Structural Adjustment Programmes for Socio-Economic Recovery and Transformation* (Addis Ababa, Ethopia: ECA, 1989).
50. See "SAP: What Alternatives?" *Newswatch* (Lagos, Nigeria) (24 July 1989).
51. The TAC was introduced to aid African states. The young professionals were sent to countries that forwarded requests to Nigeria. Nigeria paid their salaries while they served in other African states.
52. Bolaji Akinyemi quoted in "Three Decades of Policy."
53. *The Europa World Yearbook 1990 Volume II* (London: Europa Publishing Limited, 1990), 1938.
54. "Ruling the World," *African Concord* (17 June 1991), 28.
55. Ibid.
56. Ibid.
57. See *Demand for the Withdrawal of the Nomination of Mr. Bola Ajibola as a Judge of the World Court* (Lagos, Nigeria: CDHR, 1991).
58. See "Eyes on the UN: Can Nigeria, Obasanjo Clinch the Chief Scribe's Job?" *The African Guardian* (20 May 1991); "No Consensus," *African Concord* (17 June 1991); "Battle to Stop Obasanjo," *Newbreed* (1 July 1991); *Why General Olusegun Obasanjo Cannot Become the United Nations Secretary-General* (Lagos, Nigeria: CDHR, 1991) and "Its All Over," *African Concord* (2 December 1991).
59. Onome Osifo-Whiskey, "Noose for Third Republic," *TELL* (7 October 1991), 47.
60. Femi Falana, interview in "Friends of NANS Spite Fire," *Newbreed* (1 July 1991), 22.
61. See Paxton Idowu, "The Oil Factor is Important: Nigeria's Response," *West Africa* (28 January- 3 February 1991); and Seye Kehinde, "Gulf War—Nigeria's Response, Nigeria Treads the Middle Road,"*African Concord* (28 January 1991).
62. Ibrahim Babangida, "Major Contemporary Issues Facing Nigeria," 32.
63. See "The Presidency: North vs. South," *TELL* (15 April 1991); "Bloodbath in Kano—Religious Fanatics Strike Again," *TELL* (28 October 1991); Lewis Obi, "The Kano Massacres," *African Concord* (25 November 1991); and "Religious Fanatics are Back: Death, Destruction in Bauchi," *TELL* (6 May 1991).
64. See "IBB's Foreign Policy Still at a T-Junction," *Newbreed* (1 October 1990).
65. "Red Carpet for Mandela," *Newswatch* (28 May 1990), 20.
66. Ibid., 20 and 21.
67. "Some of Those Who have Gained from Nigeria's Foreign Policy Programme," *The Sunday Magazine* (9 June 1991), 38.
68. Ibid.
69. Ibid., 40.
70. For the views of the American ambassador to Nigeria on these issues see "Between Dreams and Reality," *The African Guardian* (2 December 1991).

71. *West Africa* (30 March 1987).
72. See "419 Business, Nigeria's Image and the Organized Private Sector," *The Nigerian Economist* (9 December 1991); "Boom to Nigerian Crude Oil Fraud," *The Nigerian Economist*; John Odigie-Oyegun, "Leadership Must be by Example," *The Observer* (22 November 1991); Sam Aluko, "We are All Liars", interview with *TELL* (15 April 1991); Emma Akpasubi, "Nigerians and Tricks (2)," *The Observer* (22 November 1991); and John Agbakagba, "A Case for Ten Percent," *The Observer* (22 November 1991).
73. "Ruling the World," *African Concord* (17 June 1991), 30.
74. *The Financial Times* quoted in "Ruling the World," *African Concord* (17 June 1991).
75. "The Mercantile Approach," *Thisweek* (Lagos, Nigeria) (4 September 1989), 8.
76. "Economic Diplomacy Works," 34.
77. Olu Awogbemila, "The Mercantile Approach: Governments' Light Pocket Brings 'Economic Diplomacy,'" *Thisweek* (Lagos, Nigeria) (4 September 1989), 8.
78. Ibid., 35.
79. See "Business Outings of the Federal Government," *The Sunday Magazine* (9 June 1991), 42.
80. "Investment in Nigeria: Open Door Policy," *West Africa* (3-9 December 1990).
81. "Ruling the World," 30.
82. See "When a Giant Limps," *African Concord* (27 August 1990); "Peace by War-ECOMOG Forces Move into Offensive to Contain Rebels' Action," *The African Guardian* (1 October 1990); "Easier Said than Done," *The Nigerian Economist* (3 September 1990).
83. "ECOMOG-Nigeria's Toll—the Unsung Tragedy," *African Concord* (21 January 1991), 35.
84. "Three Decades of Policy," 36.
85. Etim Imisim, "ECOMOG: Vietnam on Our Hands," *Classique* (19 August 1991), 36.
86. "Three Decades of Policy," 36.
87. "Ruling the World," 31.
88. "Nigeria's Debt Stands at $33 Billion," *The Punch* (Lagos, Nigeria) (17 October 1990).
89. See "Nigeria at 29: Trial and Error," *Africa Events* (October 1989); Mokwugo Okoye, "A Time of Sadness," *The African Guardian* (24 September 1990); Dele Alaka, "Nigeria at 30: Growing Older, Not Wiser," *Sunday Concord* (Lagos, Nigeria) (30 September 1990); and "A People in Despair: Nigerians Lose Faith in Themselves as Well as in the Future of the Country," *The African Guardian* (13 June 1988).
90. Dan Agbese, "No Trees, Only the Wood," *Newswatch* (7 October 1991), 29.
91. Ibid.
92. "Investment in Nigeria: Open Door Policy," *West Africa* (9 December 1990).
93. Ibid.
94. See *Africa Recovery* July-September 1990 and October-December 1990; Salim Lone, "Africa: Drifting Off the Map of the World's Concerns," *International Herald Tribune* (24 August 1990); and Julius O. Ihonvbere, "Political Conditionality and Prospects for Recovery in Sub-Saharan Africa," *International Third World Studies Journal and Review* 3, nos. 1-2 (1992).
95. Ibrahim Babangida, "Major Contemporary Issues Facing Nigeria," 30.
96. Ibid., 31.

3

The State and Academic Freedom in Nigeria

> Many Nigerian elites, going by the quality of their contributions to debates, are suffering from acute "intellectual malnutrition." It is now pretty difficult to fight ignorance in Nigeria, a country which the World Bank report for (1991) says is the 13th poorest nation in the world. The per capita income of an average Nigerian hardly permits him the luxury of getting information materials. Not many Nigerians can afford the exorbitant prices of books.[1]

> A crop of Nigerians must be selling off their libraries to survive. . . . Many of the lecturers cannot afford to live well as intellectuals. They cannot afford to travel for conferences. They cannot subscribe to the latest journals. They cannot solve the simplest financial problem of their extended families. The tragedy is that most of them have to depend on their wealthy students to make ends meet.[2]

> It is now clear that the so-called "ivory tower" has collapsed. Most of the lecturers have taken to business, hustling or are engaged in a desperate fight to join the looting class in the Babangida junta. The Left has not been left out of this shameful development.[3]

The quotes above reflect, in large measure, the deepening crisis of the academy in Nigeria and the rapidly declining credibility of academics. The quotes also reflect the changing character of social relations, class alliances, and political constituencies. Though in recent times there have been increased regional and international concerns over the repression of academics in Africa, it is clear that these responses are only coming at a time when the deepening crisis of state and society are engulfing the academy. As well, African academics, in general, do not appear to appreciate the fact that an end to the traditional isolation of the so-called ivory tower from the coalitions, contradictions, and conflicts, which historically engulfed the larger society, was only a matter of time.

In this chapter, we take due cognizance of the relevance and importance of the recent declarations of academic freedom and the social responsibility of academics—the Lima Declaration on Academic Freedom and Autonomy of Institutions of Higher Learning (1988), the Dar es Salaam Declaration on Academic Freedom (1989), and the Kampala Declaration on Intellectual Freedom and Social Responsibility (1990). As well, we take due note of the increasingly important role of regional and international organizations in the struggle for academic freedom—CODESRIA, Committee for Academic Freedom in Africa(CAFA), Association of Concerned Africa Scholars (ACAS), the Economic Commission for Africa (ECA), Africa Watch, and the Pan African Writers Association (PAWA). Furthermore, we acknowledge the continuing struggle of progressive labor and academic unions and associations in the African continent against state repression and the violation of university autonomy and academic freedom. We also highlight their traditional efforts to link the struggle for academic freedom to the struggles of the larger society. In addition, the traditional commitment of sections of the African academic community, which, in spite of repression, intimidation, denigration, and all sorts of insults and deprivations, have remained committed to the struggle for emancipation and empowerment, will also be examined. On the other side of the struggle, we note the determination of the desperate and crisis-ridden African state and international finance capital to ensure that the African academy does not serve as a base for the generation, nurturing and recycling of ideas related to social justice, national autonomy, self-reliance, empowerment, mobilization, and genuine democratization. In order to make our point clearer, we wish to restrict the discussion to the Nigerian experience and reality only.

It is important that we make a few clarifications right at the beginning in order to put our discussions in proper perspective. First, the deepening crisis of the academy cannot be divorced from the deepening crisis of state and society in Africa. The constraints of debt, debt-servicing, drought, marginalization in the global order, the withdrawal of foreign aid, and the diversion of investments to other parts of the world, especially Eastern Europe, have combined with historically determined deformities, distortions, and disarticulations to make the state and its custodians desperate and their politics normless.[4] Under such conditions, the academy and other institutions where ideas are generated and nurtured become easy targets. The second point is that while imperialism, foreign domination and exploitation, social inequalities, state repression, and human rights abuses are still part of the African reality, African academics have spent more time bellyaching about these problems and less time organizing for empowerment and liberation from these internally and externally determined inhibitions to progress. Third, not all African academics contribute directly and/or indirectly to the erosion and subversion of academic freedom. Though I will make bold to say that the vast majority are guilty of this charge, there is a small articulate, organized, courageous, ideologically determined, and politically committed fraction who have over the decades remained above board in every way and committed their time, limited resources, and energy to the cause of academic and national freedom. Unfortunately, this fraction has never controlled any higher institution and they have never been empowered enough to determine public policies. As well, in several countries, their ranks have been infiltrated by opportunists, fifth columnists, ideological adventurists, and agents of the state. Finally, just like other documents produced by the World Bank, the ECA, and the OAU, and in spite of the efforts of CODESRIA, the declarations on academic freedom mentioned earlier are not widely known in Africa and have thus not become part of the discourses on academic freedom and social responsibility of academics. Because these declarations are not widely known, let us take a brief look at them.

Declarations on Academic Freedom: Externalization of the Problem?

The three main declarations that have come out recently all emphasize the critical issues of the importance of higher education, the responsibilities of the state, the role of popular organizations, the need for *relevant* education, university autonomy, and the social responsibility of academics. These are certainly very important issues that are also at the root of the crisis of the academy in contemporary Africa. The basic direction of the analyses and prescription in these documents go against the World Bank's view of the future of academic development in Africa. In its 1991 document, *The African Capacity Building Initiative*, the bank ignores the high rate of graduate unemployment in most African countries and goes on to emphasize the need to build and strengthen "local capacities in policy analysis and development management."[5] The bank only suddenly realized this "new" problem after it had contributed to the deepening crisis of the African economy through failed policies and misguided orthodox adjustment programs.

The efforts of the declarations on academic freedom to respond to the bank have met with limited success because African states, caught in the debt and dependency trap, have preferred to embrace bank prescriptions. However, there is one major weakness in all three declarations. They tend to neglect the ways in which academics contribute to the vulnerability of their respective institutions, their support for the repressive regimes, their deliberate reproduction of the ills and contradictions of the larger society within their institutions, and their generally reactionary, conservative, opportunistic, and pro-status quo postures on major political, social, and economic issues in their respective countries. The declarations clearly recognize the fundamental reasons why repression, human rights abuses, and violations of academic freedom have increased in the past decade. Yet, they pay only scanty attention (at least in the final documents) to the following facts: the repressive governments are in several ways sustained, supported, and given intellectual coloration by academics drawn directly from the universities; there are hundreds of African academics researching, consulting, and working for the IMF and the World Bank who help them reach their conservative and anti-education decisions and prescriptions; most military governments in Africa have academics as advisers, ministers, ambassadors, consultants, special assistants, and commissioners; and without the support of "radical" academics, the repressive regimes would generally not find it easy to penetrate the universities, the academic staff unions, and the students' unions, and break them up while incorporating some members of the opposition.

It is my belief that for now, given the political balances in the African region and in view of the emerging unipolar security and tripolar economic global order,[6] the starting point for the "second liberation" and for a genuine struggle against the new imperialism is a fundamental *internal* restructuring, reconstitution of political relations, and extensive self-criticism. We cannot continue to hide under the traditional complaints against the IMF, the World Bank, transnational corporations and so on, important as these may be, because these complaints are not new. In any case, African academics and politicians have contributed significantly to making it easy for these external interests to penetrate, domesticate, and manipulate the universities and governments. The tendency has been to overly externalize the problem, and once this happens it becomes impossible to advance credible and viable analyses and prescriptions because one of the major "culprits"—academics—has been left out.

To be sure, I recognize that the universities exist within the totality of the social system; that academics are, after all, human beings with their own problems, aspirations, and limitations; that academics have never been empowered as a body in such a manner as to be capable of pursuing an alternative agenda; and that in several ways their impoverishment, the numerous pressures they face in and outside the workplace and the deepening crisis of state and society militate against the ability of academics to serve as the vanguard in the struggles for justice, popular mobilization and participation, empowerment, and human rights. It is, however, my contention that even at the level of university management, academics have been a disappointment in general. In any case, the constraints highlighted above are the exact reasons why academics should be in the vanguard of the struggle for liberation and social justice.

As well, I realize that those academics who collaborate in the erosion of university autonomy and work unrepentantly with the repressive state represent themselves, are appointed due to their respective achievements, and are accountable only to themselves and those they work for. Yet, I contend that for academics who live and work in oppressive, hostile, and exploitative environments riddled with corruption, inefficiency, and ineffectiveness, as well as foreign domination and exploitation, indifference, cold complicity, collusion, fence-sitting, "neutrality," and the recycling of conservative, reactionary, and pro-establishment ideas, are totally inexcusable.

The Lima Declaration defines academic freedom as "the freedom of members of the academic community, individually or collectively, in the pursuit, development and transmission of knowledge, through research, study discussion, documentation, production, creation, teaching, lecturing and writing." It argues that "freedom is an essential pre-condition for those educational, research, administrative and service functions with which universities and other institutions of higher education are entrusted." It specifies the rights of all members of the academic community and insists that higher institutions must enjoy autonomy to be relevant to the needs of society. It advances very important and radical pre-conditions and links academic institutions to the struggles to resolve the contradictions of dependence, underdevelopment, and exploitation.

Hence, it emphasizes the participation of students in the "governing bodies" of universities, free education at the secondary levels at the very minimum, and that all institutions of higher education "shall pursue the fulfillment of economic, social, cultural, civil and political rights of the people and shall strive to prevent the misuse of science and technology to the detriment of those rights." Perhaps the most radical declaration is to the effect that

> all institutions of higher education shall address themselves to the contemporary problems facing society. To this end, the curricula of these institutions, as well as their activities shall respond to the needs of society at large. Institutions of higher learning should be critical of conditions of political repression and violations of human rights within their own society.

The Dar es Salaam Declaration begins by noting that the African continent is caught in the web of socioeconomic crises and that "as budgetary allocations for education become minuscule, education is threatening to become the preserve of a minority of wealthy and influential . . . in society." It attributes the increasing authoritarian character of the African state to desperation arising from deepening systemic crisis. It goes on in part 1 to specify the purpose of education—personality development, "emancipation of the human being and society from oppression, domination and subjugation," overcoming of prejudices, development of critical faculties, and "mak[ing] every person conscious of ecology and the need to protect the environment." Chapter 2 deals with the obligations of the state, and chapter 3 with rights and obligations of communities. Part 2 deals with academic freedom. It outlines the "civil, political, social, economic and cultural rights of members of the academic community" and pays particular attention to the autonomy of academic organizations, security of tenure, obligations of the state, and administration. While part 3 deals with the autonomy of institutions of higher learning, part 4 is devoted to social responsibility of institutions of higher learning and of academics. Section 49, chapter 2 of part 4 of the declaration states that

> No member of the academic community shall participate in or be party to any endeavor which may work to the detriment of the people or the academic community or compromise scientific, ethical and professional principles and standards.

Section 50, chapter 2 of part 4 related the responsibility of academics in Africa (and indeed other parts of the world, especially the underdeveloped world) to the crisis of state and society, conditions of exploitation, and underdevelopment:

> All members of the academic community have a duty to contribute towards redressing contemporary inequalities in our society based on differences of class, beliefs, gender, race, nationality, region and economic condition. Towards this end, all members of the academic community should voluntarily give their time to impart education to disadvantaged sectors of the population.

The Kampala Declaration begins by noting in its preamble that

> intellectual freedom in Africa is currently threatened to an unprecedented degree. The historically produced and persistent economic, political and social crisis of our continent, continued to undermine development in all spheres. The imposition of unpopular structural adjustment programmes have been accompanied by increased political repression, widespread poverty and intense human suffering. . . . The struggle for intellectual freedom is an integral part of the struggle in our people for human rights.

Articulating the holistic background and environment in which repression and the violation of academic freedom occurs in Africa, the Kampala Declaration spells out the intellectual rights and freedoms that all must enjoy without discrimination: the right to form autonomous organizations, the autonomy of institutions, the obligations of the state, and the social responsibility of the intellectual community. In the latter section, the declaration enjoins all African intellectuals to "discharge their role and functions with competence, integrity and to the best of their abilities . . . in accordance with ethical and highest scientific standards; demonstrate a spirit of tolerance towards different views and positions and enhance democratic debates," not "indulge in the harassment, domination or oppressive behaviors towards another group." The declaration insists that the intellectual community *"has the responsibility to struggle for and participate in the struggle of popular forces for their rights and emancipation"* (emphasis added). In addition, the intellectual community is enjoined not to "participate in or be a party to any endeavor which may work to the detriment of the people or the intellectual community," "show solidarity and give sanctuary to any member who is persecuted for his intellectual activity," or to "encourage and contribute to affirmative actions, to redress historical and contemporary inequalities based on gender, nationality or any other social disadvantage."

The problems with these declarations in addition to those mentioned earlier include the fact that they are available in the West but little known and circulated in Africa itself. This is in spite of the laudable efforts of the Dakar-based CODESRIA, which has distributed the declaration and published it in its bulletin. It reminds one of the *Lagos Plan of Action for the Economic Development of Africa 1980-AD 2000* adopted in Lagos, Nigeria in 1980 by the OAU but printed in Geneva and almost completely unavailable in Africa![7] As well, the documents do not contain any sanctions against members of the academic community found to have actively, deliberately, and persistently violated all the terms and spirits of the declarations. If this had been attempted, especially in the Kampala Declaration, it would have generated a different and more critical debate on the ways in which African academics have contributed in no small measure to the current crisis in the continent, the erosion of university autonomy, and in giving legitimacy (however tenuous) to very repressive regimes in the continent. As far as African governments are concerned, these declarations are meaningless. Rather, African regimes have devised comprehensive and very complex ways of containing creativity, innovation, and basic freedoms, and domesticating and incorporating the opposition, especially academics and the broad left:

> Some of the human rights abuses documented (against academics in Africa . . .) include: summary executions of academics and students; torture; arbitrary arrest and prolonged detention without charge or trial; imprisonment under conditions that are cruel and degrading; restrictions on freedom of expression, assembly, association and movement; university closures; banning of student organizations and staff unions; the prohibition of "political activity" on campus; discrimination against students on the basis of race, ethnic or regional origin; censorship of teaching and reading materials and manipulation of curricula. Lesser forms of coercion are also used as a means of intimidation, such as denial of promotions and tenure to outspoken academics; restrictions on travel abroad for research or meetings; refusal to grant scholarships to politically active students; and the requirement that students who have been implicated in political disturbances sign pledges of "good behavior" in order to resume their studies.[8]

The methods of intimidation and control highlighted above have been employed frequently by all African regimes of both right and left persuasions. Nigeria has used all of them to the extreme and more so since the Babangida regime seized power in a palace coup in August 1985.

Though African governments are signatories to the Universal Declaration of Human Rights and the UNESCO Convention Against Discrimination in Education, one will be very hard put to find one African country that has lived up to the terms and spirit of these international covenants. If these are international covenants, African governments have not shown much respect for their own decrees, laws and regulations, development plans, and policy papers. Usually, these are not worth more than the papers on which they are carefully scripted. More than the above is the total failure to implement declarations and charters adopted by almost all member states of the OAU: *Cultural Charter for Africa* (1976), *The Lagos Plan of Action for the Economic Development of Africa 1980-AD 2000* (1980), *The Final Act of Lagos* (1980), *The African Charter of Human and Peoples' Rights* (1982), *Africa's Priority Programme for Economic Recovery 1986–1990* (1986), *The African Alternative Framework for Socio-Economic Recovery and Transformation* (1989), and *The African Charter for Popular Participation in Development* (1990).

If African governments had had the courage and political will to implement half of the prescriptions in these and other such declarations, the question of being coerced or maneuvered into implementing an orthodox adjustment program or having to rely on repression, foreign borrowing, and aid with all sorts of strings, as well as having to practically wage a war against the masses of the people would not have arisen. The point, therefore, is that the mere adoption of declarations does not translate into implementation; they have to be supported by organization, mobilization, education, and political activity. From the condition of the universities, the impoverishment of African scholars, the virtual destruction of these institutions by World Bank and IMF policies, as well as the mismanagement, corruption, opportunism, and reactionary politics of administrators at all levels in African universities, there is some room to be skeptical that these declarations would have the impacts they ought to have. For, rather than organize and mobilize to confront the crisis of the universities and their "invasion" by agents of the state and the World Bank, most African intellectuals have either emigrated abroad, joined in the destruction of the universities, gone into private business, or adopted a position of "neutrality," even general indifference. Some of the leading academics have initiated a new culture, setting up research centers and roaming around the world scouting for funding from all sorts of interest groups and organizations. Some have even accepted "donations" from the mindless and corrupt regimes that they had devoted their active academic years to fighting. The implications of this new trend will become obvious in another decade or so. Other intellectuals have joined in the active looting of national resources while still others have adopted a strategy of victimizing junior workers, younger colleagues, and students as a sort of retaliation for the general decline in their standards of living and general marginalization. The Nigerian situation will throw more light on these issues.

The State of Academic Freedom in Nigeria

It is indeed a misnomer to speak of academic freedom in Nigeria, especially under the military junta led by Ibrahim Babangida. This is because no such thing exists in the country today, in spite of the efforts by the scores of "intellectual rationalizers" who work with the military regime as advisers, consultants, ministers, commissioners, and hangers-on. On all counts, the military regime of Babangida and the World Bank with the full collaboration of some academics who joined the government at various capacities, have succeeded in destroying the foundations of the university system. Institutions are no longer known for teaching and research but for politics, manipulation, ethnic and religious jingoism, petty squabbles, mediocrity, political posturing, opportunism, and the recycling of outdated, irrelevant and useless theories, methodologies, and ideas. While most of these have been forced on the universities by the economic dislocation and decay that accompanied the imposition of an IMF/World Bank-inspired stabilization and structural adjustment program, the traditional commitment of the vast majority of Nigerian academics to irrelevance, conservatism, opportunism, and reactionary political postures have made it easy for the academy to be penetrated and domesticated by agents of the state and international capital.

Nigeria has never really been blessed by leaders who have experienced, and who understand, the true value of education and the dynamic role of higher institutions in the process of national mobilization, development, and emancipation. From Balewa, Ironsi, and Gowon, through Muhammed, Shagari, and Buhari to Babangida, not one of them ever stepped into a university classroom! Of course, stepping into a university classroom is not a prerequisite for effective leadership. Yet, it does have some impact on perceptions, consciousness, awareness, and an appreciation of the place of the academy in national development. True, several of the past leaders have paid lip service to the cause of education and the universities. Others have made concessions to the school system at various levels. But these have generally been part of a political program or have been made in the context of ideological declarations that would be incomplete without such programs. In any case, such concessions have never been sustained. The point, however, is that Nigerian leaders, in the past, and more so under the present military junta, have never seen education as a weapon for national development, liberation, and reconstruction. Thus, the neocolonial content and context of the educational system, its repressive and exploitative character, and its gross irrelevance to the objective needs and aspirations of the Nigerian masses have been reproduced over the years since political independence in 1960.

Of course, the limited education of the vast majority of Nigeria's military leaders is part of the problem.[9] I have heard military officers openly express disdain for the universities and academics for no other reason but jealousy. Many of them simply have no idea as to how important a library or laboratory is to the overall development of ideas and policies in society. The university is nothing more than a place to grab a certificate and come out to become a "big man" or "big madam." One would have expected them to respect the universities and academics and incorporate them in the struggle for development. But conservative military training and the philosophies of mainstream military training institutions abroad have only succeeded in inculcating a suspicion for the academy and academics in the majority of the current generation of military officers in charge of public policy.

This attitude has resulted in: total disrespect for university autonomy; a belief that students' unions are of little or no use in the running of the universities; a belief that students cannot and, in fact, have no business debating national issues; disrespect for research and the place of universities in the development process; and the identification of the academy and academics as obstacles to the strengthening of relations with international finance capital. Consequently, the history of the current regime has seen: the unprecedented massacre of students; the unparalleled detention of students and academics; the frequent imposition of vice-chancellors and unrepentant support for corrupt, inefficient, and unpopular vice-chancellors; massive cuts in university funding; the abolition of research grants, scholarships, and bursaries to faculty and students; frequent and confused changes to the school calendar; the attempt to monitor teaching and research to put it in line with the conservative and reactionary policies of the IMF and the World Bank;

the deterioration of libraries, infrastructures, research facilities, and laboratories; and the incorporation of academics into a programmed system of subservience to imperialism, corruption, manipulation, and waste. Under the military junta, the students' and academic staff unions have witnessed unprecedented attacks, harassments, and proscription. As well, with drastic cuts in funding and in the context of devalued wages, the regime has directly reduced academics to beggars and paupers, less interested in teaching and research and more interested in farming, contracting, trading, and hustling. As Ademola Oguntayo and Gbenga Amusan have noted in a very recent report on the plight of teachers in general: "Reviled by parents, mocked by the society, members of the chalk-and-blackboard tribe have no solace even among their pupils. . . . The reverence once held for them by students is fast eroding."[10]

What is more, the regime has, through its economic and political policies and programs, done everything possible to convince the Nigerian people that going to school is indeed a waste of time because you can become a millionaire faster by joining the army, making friends with some generals, engaging in corrupt and illegal activities, or running some backwater organization and just waiting to get the government to donate millions of naira to it. By devaluing the worth of education clearly evidenced in the hundreds of thousands of graduates who are roaming the streets and in the inability of academics to meet the most minimal expectations of their children, the government has created the impression that the future does not lie in education. As Oguntayo and Amusan have noted, between 1979 and 1983, "School teachers were an object of ridicule. The provision of classrooms was a luxury. They had to buy their own chalk. . . . Already the working conditions of teachers are grim and they are expected to get worse."[11] Interestingly, wives of military officers, friends of generals, traditional rulers, contractors, business persons, drug pushers, currency traffickers, and ex-criminals are doing very well and throwing their ill-gotten millions in the face of hungry, unemployed, and frustrated Nigerians. They are equally smart enough to put their children in special and very expensive private schools or to send them abroad. This has made it easy for military and other regimes to close down these institutions for months without qualms, to cut funding drastically, and to order the police and army to shoot protesting students.

As in other African states, Nigerian academics have contributed in no small measure to the reproduction of the neocolonial educational system by colluding with powerful foreign interests to undermine the national economy and by advising regime after regime in the legitimization, rationalization, and reproduction of Nigeria's crisis-ridden dependent capitalist economy. Hundreds of scholars have been drawn from the universities by literate, semiliterate, and illiterate military and civilian governors in the vain belief that a doctorate degree necessarily equals patriotism, knowledge, commitment, honesty, and the ability to engage in productive and useful thinking. As case after case has shown, most of such scholars, in their arrogance and weakness, have been easily incorporated into the corrupt and wasteful political system in the country and have generally done a huge disservice to the cause of Nigerian growth and development.

Nigerian universities are staffed mostly by people who trained in Western Europe and North America. One clear fact that they failed to bring back home was the social responsibility of the academic especially in the context of poverty, exploitation, inequality, oppression, and dehumanization of the vast majority.[12] Until the recent crisis, the vast majority of Nigerian intellectuals, especially in the humanities and social sciences, stayed away from political activity. They recycled classical and other outdated theories, such as "All fingers are not equal" and "Rome was not built in a day," in order to justify existing inequalities and conditions of exploitation, and to explain why the masses should be patient as a trickle-down magic would redistribute national wealth in the near future. They had no doubts that the sky was the limit for them and their children. Their jobs were guaranteed, they lived in houses for which they paid very little, there was money to attend conferences within and outside the country, they enjoyed fully paid sabbaticals from which they made sure that they returned to the country with Mercedes Benz cars, they enjoyed free health facilities and their clinics were well-staffed, their children attended reputable university demonstration schools, they enjoyed car loans and housing loans in some cases, and their staff clubs and guest houses in the federal capital were usually well-stocked with cheap beer and food. That was life. Nothing could be better and the masses were suffering only because they were not intelligent, lucky, or hardworking enough to go abroad and obtain a higher degree; in any case, "All fingers are not equal!" Added to the above, the university was a fertile hunting ground for governments, especially military governments, for political appointments as ministers, advisers, commissioners, consultants, and to serve on the boards of scores of useless, inefficient, ineffective, and corruption-ridden parastatals that dot the country. It did not matter if the corporations were inefficient; such appointments usually came along with free car, free gas, free housing, and other perks of office, including the opportunity to make other "contacts." Thus, in some way, the universities simply replicated the situation in the rest of the country—just as the politicians appropriated the tastes, privileges, titles, and opportunities of the departing colonial officers, so did Nigerian intellectuals pit themselves against the world outside their institutions.

In most cases, as in Port Harcourt, Ile-Ife, and Nsukka, to take just a few examples, the universities were simply dumped in the midst of poor, wretched villages. But, these universitites were provided with basic amenities that the villages themselves lacked. For instance, until 1976 the city of Ile-Ife had no quality tarred roads. Till this very day, Ile-Ife looks like a twelfth-century hamlet compared to the modern beautiful structures of "Africa's most beautiful university" located in Ile-Ife, (the University of Ife, now Obafemi Awolowo University), at least until it became run-down over the last eight years or so. The university had its own electricity generator so that when the National Electric Power Authority (NEPA), in its more popular performance, cut off electricity to Ile-Ife, the university was easily lit up. The university also constructed its own water dam. So when the rest of Ile-Ife lacked water for up to two or three weeks, the university had water. The university had its own primary and secondary schools, and the transition from the secondary school to the university for the wards of faculty, was easily "arranged" where such wards did not perform well in the entrance examination. It even had its own agricultural farm to produce poultry and other food items to be sold at below-market rates to the university and "the public." Yet, the majority of academic staff at Ife never reflected on the gross inequalities in their life-styles and the standards of living of the rest of the town.[13] They never thought it necessary to wage a collective campaign for the redistribution of wealth (and of course power) or to use their vantage position to pressure the state to improve the conditions of the people. Rather they enjoyed the power and privileges that were visible as they rode their air-conditioned 504, 505, and other Japanese cars on the potholes in the city, meandering around hungry and poverty-stricken citizens of Nigeria. Those who bothered to express concern, such as the Ife Collective, were regarded as "hot heads," "do-gooders," and "people who have nothing else to do." This situation is typical in most university towns in Nigeria.

Yet the university itself, in terms of faculty and committees, has shown very low levels of commitment, democratic responsibility, and progressive consciousness. The only time the academic union can count on the faculty's full support is when wage disputes are on top of the agenda. They have, in large measure, demonstrated that they are as inefficient, corrupt, wasteful, undemocratic, irresponsible, and vulnerable to the exploitation of ethnic, religious, and regional biases in their relations to other colleagues, students, junior workers, and in their interpretation of national political, social, and economic issues. As well, the degree of opportunism, commitment to orthodoxy and irrelevance, subservience to political interests and foreign research institutions in the search for foreign exchange and other benefits, and their preparedness to work with security forces, the state, university administrations, and reactionary forces within and outside the university system is unbelievably high. According to the report of the Congregation Committee at Ahmadu Bello University, set up in 1988 to look into complaints of victimization and harassments,

> The main cause of victimization has been the development over time of academic intolerance and sycophancy which have now gripped the university in the last decade. This academic intolerance is further translated into intellectual terrorism, ideological thuggery, political vindictiveness, administrative high handedness, corrupt and authoritarian culture that now pervade the university.[14]

The Nigerian state has always been a coercive and exploitative one. The masses have always been objects of manipulation and exploitation, and public policies—development planning and so on—have been directed at promoting private capital accumulation and rationalizing the unequal relations with foreign capital while furthering the patterns of capitalist exploitation (see chapter 1). Unfortunately, the country's intellectual tradition has not reflected in any serious sense the implications of foreign domination and exploitation, cultural imperialism, and overall vulnerability to powerful external forces. On the contrary, the majority of Nigerian academics in and outside of government have not demonstrated that they appreciate the implications of national dependence and underdevelopment or that they appreciate the role intellectuals can play in the resolution of the crisis of backwardness. Consider the following points, all of which contradict the terms and spirit of the three declarations discussed earlier:

1. Corruption runs rampant in the universities. Vice-chancellors, registrars, and chairs of departments in several institutions have been disgraced because of monumental frauds and embezzlement of public funds. Even food meant for feeding students (when the country had students' hostels) has been known to disappear into private homes or stores run by university administrators, academic and nonacademic.

2. Discrimination on the grounds of region, religion, or ethnicity, which has grounded national politics and ruined possibilities for consensual politics in the country, is even worse in the smaller world of Nigerian universities. It is so easy to count how many nonindigenes dare go to universities outside their home states—this includes several so-called radicals—to teach. It is as if one's ability to teach and research can only be enhanced when engaged to teach at a university in one's home state or ethnic base. Nonindigenes are routinely discriminated against in hiring, promotion, appointment to administrative positions, benefits such as housing, and firing.

3. That Nigeria is a mismanaged society is a known fact. Development plans, the collection of billions of dollars from the sale of oil, and other policies aimed at national development have only increased rural-urban migration, unemployment, inflation, and general social decay. The universities have not fared better and government officials are often quick to point at the waste and gross mismanagement of resources in Nigerian universities. It is difficult to point to one university that can be excluded from the list of badly managed universities. This is largely because the administrators are not often picked on merit, but on other dubious considerations, the recommendations of traditional rulers who have no ideas as to the purposes of universities, connections with the president or his wife, and so on. When such administrators are selected, they quickly surround themselves with sycophants and mediocre intellectuals, people with nothing to their names and who command no credibility among their colleagues and students. Such persons help them to identify and, if possible, weed out or frustrate the "enemies" of the new administration. All Nigerian universities go through this at one time or an other and in some cases it is permanent: the university is under the full control of a clique of corrupt, unethical bigots whose only claim to intellectualism is the possession of a Ph.D.!

4. Subservience to the political class has contributed in no small measure to degrading the university and academics. In the search for contracts, political appointments, and other favors, so-called academics circulate their resumes to military officers, traditional rulers, contractors, even influential drug pushers, all in the hope of making the "right connection." This strategy easily exposes the banality of the academic and reduces his worth. A military governor in Nigeria once complained to the press that he had received over a thousand resumes within one month of his appointment from people wanting to be made commissioners. The struggle for these positions are of course not unrelated to the hope of corrupt enrichment through the looting of public offices and the vast majority of those who have had the opportunity, and have done very well for themselves. Recently, Mr. Samuel Ogbemudia, who was dismissed "with ignominy" from the armed forces for gross abuse of office by the General Murtala Mohammed administration in 1976, boasted in an interview as to how he influenced the recruitment and promotion of a professor at the University of Benin. In his words, "I brought Professor Ambrose Alli from Ahmadu Bello university. He came to me to complain that they were discriminating against him, I brought him to Benin and made him a Professor."[15] Ogbemudia does not even possess a high school diploma!

5. Generally, there is disinterest in union matters. The Nigerian academic often wants the "radicals," the socialists, and "the hot heads" to do the dirty job, while he reaps the profits. There is hardly a university where a third of the staff ever attends the union meeting unless a strike action is being planned or money matters are to be discussed. But they show up in unbelievable numbers during the staff club parties! When a strike action is to be discussed at union meetings, they would be there to ask if "you have exhausted all peaceful opportunities including contacts with religious leaders and traditional rulers!" When the Babangida regime made membership in the Academic Staff Union of Universities (ASUU) voluntary, many academics rejoiced and promptly stopped their monthly check off-dues. In other universities it is almost impossible to get people to run for offices only because these officers are perceived by vice-chancellors and government as confrontational and the last thing these academics want is to offend the powers that be: "offending" the vice-chancellor had implications for promotion, job security, housing, and other benefits.

6. Hostility to students is not uncommon. When many Nigerian academics express their views about students, they are often so backward you wonder if they teach students at all or if they were ever students themselves. For many, a lecturer has no business fraternizing with students and students cannot have the same struggles with lecturers. So the question of an alliance to defend academic freedom does not arise. In fact, the students are only good when it comes to buying useless and poorly worked out hand outs that they copy in the secrets of their bedrooms from books written by others. They are generally blind to or unsympathetic to the deteriorating conditions in which students live and study. Over 90 percent of Nigerian academics never go near the students' hostels to see for themselves the conditions of squalor, filth, and disease in which their students live and study. Senior university administrators do not identify, in most cases, with the slogans, symbols, and traditions developed by students. At the University of Ife (now Obafemi Awolowo University), while the administration stuck to "IfeVarsity" the students preferred "Great Ife" as their marching and mobilizational slogan. In his 1992 convocation address, the vice-chancellor of the University of Port Harcourt distanced himself from the marching slogan of the students, "Great Uniport," which he referred to as "*their* marching slogan."[16]

7. The sexploitation of students is also not unusual. Female students in Nigerian universities are simply objects of sex in most cases. There exist gangs of lecturers whose jobs are basically to exchange sex for grades. Issues of sexual harassment are hardly addressed and students have no rights in the majority of cases. In fact, given the deepening economic crisis, female students find it more convenient to exchange sex for grades than spend their time reading. In an extremely chauvinistic society, sexual harassment is often taken lightly. Recent attempts to address this problem by the federal government, as usual, have consisted more of publicity and paper work than of concrete action. In any case, in a typical neocolonial manner, the problem has been abstracted from the totality of the contradiction.

8. Collaboration with the government and security agents poses yet another problem. Many academics work for the State Security Service (SSS) with the sole purpose of spying and reporting on their colleagues and union leaders. Some of them do this because of poverty and others because it is payment for offenses they have committed. But many union

leaders have been detained or sacked from their positions as a result of "reports" fabricated and submitted to the SSS by other academics.

9. Low levels of collegial solidarity exist among academics. They show very little or no solidarity even for their union leaders. When leaders are arrested, other academics begin to find excuses why the union should not support them, and arguments are advanced as to the possibility that they were arrested for other political offenses like "planning a Marxist revolution!" Scholars such as Omene, Sagay, and Iyayi at the University of Benin, Bene and Eddie Madunagu at the University of Calabar; Alofojie Unuigboje at the Federal University of Science and Technology Owerri; and Yusuf Bala Usman at Ahmadu Bello University, Zaria, often fight for academic freedom and university autonomy, criticize state corruption and human rights abuses, or challenge the political arrogance of the military. When scholars are dismissed for such actions, other colleagues even arrange to relieve them of their union positions and appropriate their on-campus accommodations and offices even before the state makes its action official. Paying solidarity visits or helping the colleague to survive the hard times are usually not considered, after all, he is no longer a member of the university. The question of giving shelter to persecuted colleagues is considered only by a tiny minority. A colleague who carries out research and publishes becomes an object of ridicule: he is hated by the "old brigade," who have nothing to show for years of hibernating in the universities, and by the "young brigade," who spend most of their time on nonacademic affairs and so, in spite of their brilliance, have very little or nothing to show for their years as academics.

10. As soon as Nigerian academics are given political appointments, they become "big men" and turn their backs on the universities. In other cases, they actively assist the military to destroy the university and the academic staff union. The former and present ministers for education—Jibril Aminu and Babatunde Fafunwa—were drawn from the universities. Jibril Aminu studied at the University of Ibadan, taught at the Universities of Ibadan and Maiduguri, served as executive secretary of the National Universities Commission and as vice-chancellor of the University of Maiduguri before becoming minister for education under the Babangida regime. Yet, he was the greatest disaster ever to occupy the position of minister for education. He waged a determined war against social critics, militant students, and university autonomy. He encouraged

the imposition of vice-chancellors and violated all laid down statutes of Nigerian universities while starving them of funds and wasting millions of naira on his pet nomadic education project. Under Aminu, more Nigerian students were killed by the police than under the ruthless colonial authority and it was during his tenure that the staff union was proscribed. The present military regime, which Festus Iyayi has correctly described as the "most vicious, reactionary, the most deadly kind of regime that has ever occurred in the country,"[17]has thousands of academics working for it. Many of them with "radical" convictions, who have associated and /or continue to associate with it—Ada Ugah, Omolara Ogundipe-Leslie, Adele Jinadu, Ikenna Nzimiro, Jonathan Zwingina, Godwill Ogbogodor, Eme Ekekwe, Ugochukwu Uba, and a host of others—have not made any difference in the regime's regard for the universities. In fact, the regime now seems to find it easier to predict responses from staff, students' unions, and radical activists. It has also drawn on the largest group of elements from the critical liberal camp—Sam Oyovbaire, Tunji Olagunju, Wole Soyinka, Jerry Gana, and Tai Solarin. Yet, it has been the most ruthless in its dealing with academics and the universities. More schools have been closed, academics sacked, unions proscribed, vice-chancellors imposed, budgets cut, and students killed by military personnel under this regime than under any other regime in the country's history, and that includes the colonial period. Yet, the dream of many Nigerian academics today is to make inroads into the administration and take part in the ongoing sharing of the national wealth in the name of a transition to democracy.

11. The vast majority of academics in Nigerian universities have no business being there. They neither teach nor do any research worth the name. Some of them stay for up to a decade without publishing a paper or attending any professional meeting. But they get promoted by playing ethnic and religious politics, obtaining political interference, bootlicking, and using the politics of opportunism and gift-giving. Many have been known to call on illiterate traditional rulers, chiefs, businessmen, and military officers to influence promotion exercises in the university system. Many continue to miseducate students by recycling old and outdated ideas, and others simply allocate grades without reading examination scripts because they do not have the time—they need more time to farm, distribute minerals and cement to stores and shops around town, run their food stalls, sit and drink at the staff clubs, or engage in local politics.

Unfortunately, it is this reactionary, unproductive, and corrupt segment of the academic community that controls political power and makes critical decisions. Given their tenuous relation to teaching and research, their poor understanding of the function of the university, as well as their general insecurity because of their poor intellectual capacities, they are often in the forefront of seeking reasons why students' unions should be banned, why certain academics should not be promoted, why persons from certain ethnic groups should be sacked or not allowed to hold certain offices, and why the vice-chancellor should buy another car even when the libraries and laboratories are empty. One only needs to participate at Senate discussions to see the high level of intellectual fraud and academic dishonesty, as well as how mediocre reasoning triumphs over rational thinking, in the majority of Nigerian universities. Universities that lack chairs for students, whose generators have broken down, and that cannot buy books for the libraries often spend millions to organize graduation jamborees, welcome the president or some semiliterate chairman of council, or send off the outgoing vice-chancellor. Thousands of naira will also be wasted in refurnishing the vice-chancellor's lodge for the incoming vice-chancellor and money will surely be found to buy him or her a brand new unmarked official car.

12. In spite of the ongoing changes in the world and the growing concern over the environment and human rights, the majority of Nigerian academics do not take them seriously. Of course, part of the problem is the result of ignorance and very limited appreciation of the inextricable linkages between environmental issues and the survival of society. There are no environmentally conscious groups in most universities beyond the Nigerian Environmental Study/Action Team (NEST),[18] very few belong to human rights associations or other prodemocracy groups, but the majority of them are active in bourgeois politics, jostling for positions and making the "intellectual" resources available to retired generals, banned politicians, and traditional rulers.[19] Issues of gender are not discussed, and to belong to Women in Nigeria (WIN), the only radical and serious women's organization, is to be in the wrong organization. The ongoing struggles for empowerment, democracy and democratization, human rights, accountability, and social justice are yet to have a serious impact on Nigerian academics, even those in the humanities and social sciences.

The above represent some of the traits of the majority of Nigerian academics, which cannot be ignored or downplayed in any discussion of academic freedom or of the social responsibility of the academic. This is because when so-called academics behave in ways that compromise the essence of the university and adopt political postures that not only make the university vulnerable to penetration and control by the state, but also intensify contradictions, petty jealousies, primordial conflicts, corruption, waste, and indiscipline, any talk of academic freedom will be a mere exercise in futility.[20]

The State of the Academy in Contemporary Nigeria

The state of the universities in Nigeria today is pitiable. Perhaps this is the most visible measure of the crisis of the academy and a clear demonstration of the failure of structural adjustment. It is impossible to capture on paper the very shameful state of universities in Africa's "most powerful black nation!" If current trends continue, the future of higher institutions would be in doubt. As Anthony Oyewole, former chair of the political science department at Obafemi Awolowo University (OAU), noted recently, "The University is finished. Please, quote me, the whole system is finished."[21] For Dipo Fashina, chair of the academic union at the same university, "The situation is devastating . . . in OAU both students and teachers alike are demoralized."[22] To be sure, the World Bank has convinced the Babangida regime that university education is not necessary. If it would be required at all, it should be organized and run like a business, a process that will make it "qualitative" by restricting it only to serious and rich candidates. The implementation of the structural adjustment program has only worsened an already bad situation as facilities are decaying; the real value of wages can hardly carry a professor for two weeks; the very best academics—and this is serious—have emigrated to the Middle East, Europe, and North America; universities are always in turmoil or are closed following clashes between security forces and students; many students are in jail for daring to complain, and for criticizing structural adjustment, corruption, and human rights abuses;[23] libraries are at best five years behind in the relevant literature; students are getting degrees in computer science without touching a single computer or are getting degrees in science subjects when the laboratories are practically empty; and most professors remain on campus only because they pay subsidized rent on their accommodations. For most of the time, they are busy preparing over-priced handouts for their students to buy, or devising several ingenious ways to survive the hard times. As Kunle Ajibade notes, "So desperate has the situation become now that, in outright violation of the copyright law, Nigerian students survive mainly on xeroxed materials for their reading needs. At the University of Lagos for instance, in the faculty of arts, students queue up everyday before photocopying machines to have many chapters of books copied."[24] This can be repeated for all universities in the country.

At the University of Port Harcourt, like in many other universities, the Senate tried to control the use of handouts by faculty as a means for making money. The Summer Sandwich Program is a big business session for selling handouts to Post-National Certificate of Education (Post-NCE) students. In his February 1992 convocation address, the pro-chancellor and chairman of the governing council of the university, Chief Isaac Fola-Alade reflected on the sorry state of this federal institution located in the capital of Nigeria's oil producing state:

> Since 1990 when I first came to this university, the question that has repeatedly bugged me and my council has been why has this Federal University remained so physically underdeveloped? Of the seven 'second generation' universities, Uniport still wears the look of some village primary school. After 17 years of establishment, Uniport's physical features, facilities and infrastructures (with no water, no NEPA [electricity from the national grid] and no phones), are still far less than you find in any average secondary school . . . what has happened to the N20 million special grant to the University of Port Harcourt by Mr President in 1990.[25]

Drawing attention to the fact that the plight of the institution was largely a precipitate of internal mismanagement and a gross disregard for laid down rules and regulations since he became pro-chancellor, Chief Fola-Alade informed the audience at convocation that "your Governing Council spent virtually the whole of last session sorting out problems of academic administration, which were internally generated. These problems needn't have arisen if only the University administrators had followed the University regulations."[26]

Parents are withdrawing their wards from school because the "pieces of paper"—certificates—they bring home from school after huge expenditures now means very little. The unemployment rate is so high that those who graduated six years ago are still roaming the streets in search of employment in spite of the efforts of the National Directorate of

Employment (NDE). Those who dropped out of school and took to pimping for top military officers and bureaucrats, drug pushing, and currency trafficking are already "living the good life." Military governors, ministers, and the president make a show with cooked-up figures on how hundreds of thousands of jobs are being created or are about to be created. But the reality is different.[27] The Federal Office of Statistics (FOS) showed that in the first six months, contrary to the hopes of the Planning Minister who believed that 41,000 jobs would be created in 1991, "the army of unemployed swelled by five per cent . . . urban and rural unemployment in 1990 were 75.5 and 72.5 per cent respectively . . . [and] predicted a 25 per cent jump in 1991."[28] The inability of graduates to find employment has contributed to the erosion of the usefulness of university education and the relevance of academics in the eyes of the public. Unfortunately, many of those in positions of responsibility are out of touch with reality and with the ongoing changes in the global economy. Hence, the pro-chancellor of the University of Port Harcourt offers a rather simplistic solution to the job crisis:

> So much has been said about brain-drain. By the time these brains drain or drift back, this nation will still remain the same. So, I have learnt not to worry about them. My worry is about graduate unemployment. . . . It is not enough to set up an NDE, or DFFRI, where the affected graduates have no answers to their problems due to the influx of retired public servants. I believe that with 30 states and nearly 600 Local Governments, we can employ thousands of graduate hands all over Nigeria.[29]

The pro-chancellor's solution is obviously against current economic realities and reforms taking place the world over. At a time when the size of the state is being pruned down and private initiative is being encouraged across board, he is still advocating a discredited and wasteful strategy of government employment for all in the name of job creation. If the administration were to absorb all graduates, in what ways would that strengthen the productive base of the nation? This is clear evidence of the near total irrelevance of the university to the urgent task of reconstruction, growth, and development in Nigeria.

In universities all over the country, toilets are overflowing with maggots, water and electricity supply is erratic, roads in campuses are full of potholes, many professors lack office space, and students lack chairs on which to sit, forcing them to write examinations on bare floors. Kunle Ajibade describes accommodation in Nigerian universities as "hell" and notes that "a room meant for three at the University of Nigeria,

Nsukka, is occupied by about 13."[30] Scholarships and bursaries have disappeared, especially for students from the southern states. At a time when the government cannot pay salaries, equip libraries, provide equipment and materials for laboratories, and recruit qualified staff, the regime, the president, and his wife, in particular, have been busy squandering public funds on useless donations of millions of naira to all sorts of mundane and frivolous causes. For instance, the president donated N10 million to the Performing Musicians Association of Nigeria during the Nigerian Musical Awards in March 1992. At the same occasion, the president announced: "I don't know where these women got their money from but I've been asked to tell you that my wife, Maryam, and Rebecca Aikhomu [the Vice-President's wife] have donated N250,000 on behalf of Nigerian women."[31] Ibrahim Babangida, on behalf of the federal government of Nigeria, donated N50 million to the Christian Association of Nigeria (CAN) and N30 million to the Awolowo Foundation in early 1992. This was at a time when the country was sinking into economic abyss and the naira had to be urgently devalued by 100 percent, graduate unemployment had reached a peak, crime and violence had become rampant, and assassinations had become a thriving business.[32] As Olisa Agbakoba, President of the Civil Liberties Organization (CLO), has argued, "Public money must only be spent for the common good. When public money is spent in this manner by Babangida and his wife, especially his wife, it suggests . . . there is no accountability, it's to say the least, reprehensive, because we have millions and millions of Nigerians who require money in education, employment, housing, health services, transport, etc."[33] At the secondary and primary educational levels, schooling has become a mere ritual of congregating at the premises in the morning while the teachers disappear into the markets or farms to make ends meet. While Ondo and Lagos States were busy looking for "mad teachers" to be flushed out of the school system (not to receive medical attention), salaries had not been paid in many states, in some cases for up to six months. Yet, the government, which claims to be pursuing an adjustment program, has been busy squandering hundreds of millions of naira on meaningless projects.

Early in 1991, Aliyu Babatunde Fafunwa, the minister of education visited some schools in Ogun State and was himself shocked at the "sad state of neglect of most of the classrooms in the state, with blown-off roofs, cracked walls and broken windows . . . most teachers taught . . .

without teaching aids."[34] If this was the case in the primary and secondary school system all over the country, a situation of which the minister who had been in the education field for over five decades was completely ignorant,[35] the universities were not better. As the *Nigerian Economist* reported in a special survey of the universities, "Exodus, the movement of lecturers away from universities is just like any other plague affecting campuses. There are no chalks and students have had to contribute money both to buy dusters and send tutors on excursions and conferences. Then too, some students as well as tutors who choose to stay have acquired very dangerous habits."[36] The survey revealed that while the Babangida regime spent N6.2 billion on defense between 1987 and 1990, it spent only N3.7 billion on education. In the 1990 fiscal year alone N2.2 billion or 5.6 percent went to the defense sector while education had only N1.4 billion. Though each university student requires about N48,482 "to cater for his feeding, medicare, books (here exchange rate plays havoc) and other sundry needs,"[37]in real terms only N536 is made available by the government. Reflecting on the sad state of the universities under a regime that has busied itself donating billions of naira for all sorts of jamborees, cultural festivals, international meetings, social events, worthless and prestigious projects since 1985, the *Nigerian Economist* wrote:

> While figures are damning, the reality on the campuses themselves are quite scandalous. Physical evidence of decay abound showing overcrowding in hostels and classrooms. A room designed to accommodate two or four students sometimes takes between eight and 12. Consequently, septic tanks overflow and are not collected, shortage of water has become a permanent feature on campuses, classrooms are clogged, small essentials such as chalks and dusters are not available, teachers are few, underpaid and frustrated and students are malnourished, angry and touchy. Few researches are undertaken, books and journals are hopelessly outdated, more students fail, much more take solace in prostitution, drug abuse and occultism and violent secret societies re-enacting medieval antics and strange bestialities which swathe the campus in frightful dark ages togas.[38]

Newbreed, one of Nigeria's leading monthlies, reported in July 1991 that "if the mess, which revolves around accommodation, feeding, admission, teaching and examination arrangements, is not cleared up quickly, it could leave the nation's campuses in a state of ferment for a long time."[39] Following investigations conducted at several of the leading universities in the country, the magazine reached the conclusion among others that "many now blame the proliferation of secret cults on the squalid conditions under which students live and study. The conditions, it is claimed, *are more suited for the breeding of thugs than for intellectual pursuits.*"[40]

Vice-chancellors, imposed by the military regime on universities, take delight in regularly publishing the names of expelled and rusticated students in the newspapers.[41] In most universities, honorary degrees are being sold in an effort to raise money to run the universities. Hence, the Bendel (now Edo) State University, Ekpoma received a donation of N10 million only after it awarded an honorary doctor of laws degree to the vice-president, Augustus Aikhomu. Similarly, the University of Nigeria, whose facilities and infrastructures have hardly been serviced since the end of the civil war in 1970, received N50 million as donation after it awarded an honorary Doctor of Laws to the president's wife, Mayriam Babangida. Traditional rulers, illiterate business men, and persons whose wealth have come from very dubious sources are chased around the country by "university agents" to be awarded honorary degrees in order to raise money.[42] This has contributed to eroding the credibility of the academy and the "public value" of doctorate degrees. Examination leakages and cheating has reached an all time high,[43] in several institutions the female students' hostels are nothing but brothels, and businessmen and military personnel drive in, even in broad daylight, to ferry the female students to all-night parties on weekdays. As Ajibade notes, "The moral depravity of students and teachers has almost reached its peak. There have been cases of theft, assault and fraud involving students who are sons of lecturers and wealthy Nigerians. It is a season of scandals in Nigerian higher institutions."[44] Oguntayo and Amusan also reported that "despite all the plight of teachers, some members of the profession often bring reproach on the body. The nation was shocked last year (1991) when male secondary school teachers . . . fought in public over the affection of a female student."[45] As a reflection of the frustration of all interest groups, universities are now run by ethnic cabals and are dominated by secret cults involving students and staff who confront each other in a battle to the death. George Caffentzis captures the situation very well:

> Student life verges on the catastrophic; with overcrowded rooms, one meal per day, cramped and noisy study conditions and failing water and electricity supply. The police and/or the army is frequently stationed on or near the campus and classes are frequently filled with informers. The faculty lives and works in similar conditions, with drastically reduced below subsistence real wages, which force them to either

> emigrate or find extra-academic employment. . . . No US university students or teachers would consider the lot of their African counterparts remotely acceptable.[46]

Nigerian academics have a direct responsibility for the predicaments of the universities and the national economy today. By refusing to organize and resist the destruction of the economy by the collusion of local and foreign interests, they must take responsibility. By working for the various regimes and governments in all capacities, since Nigeria became independent, they share the responsibility for the deepening crisis of the Nigerian economy and society. By joining in the looting of national resources and providing, in some cases, justifications for existing inequalities, they share responsibility. By creating hostile, uncertain, unsafe, and anti-intellectual conditions within the universities, they cannot deny responsibility. By not consistently and persistently insisting on academic freedom, university autonomy, social justice, accountability, respect for human rights, and national liberation, they must take responsibility for the cold complicity and misplaced belief in neoclassical theories of growth and development. By miseducating their students, not relating their teaching and research to the objectives of national liberation, and causing mental and cultural colonization, they cannot deny responsibility. By not utilizing their vantage position to struggle against the World Bank, the IMF, reactionary military regimes, and oppressive and corrupt university administrators, and by not forging dynamic alliances with other popular groups in the struggle for popular empowerment, Nigerian academics take direct responsibility for contributing in very large measure to the current conditions of decay and decline in Nigerian universities. They have, through their negative politics and misplaced expectations of social mobility, rendered the university wide open for narrow-minded and self-serving military officers and politicians in strong alliance with international capital to penetrate and destroy. To a very large extent, therefore, the new interest in academic freedom comes from their frustrations, poverty, disillusionment, proletarianization, the closure of opportunities for upward mobility, and the fact that the state, which many of them once supported, has now turned against them.

Conclusions: Is There Hope for the Future?

It will be the height of optimism to expect the universities to recover in the 1990s. Even if there is a transition to civilian rule, the politicians are inherently incapable of reviving the universities. In the first place, they will inherit a heavily debt-ridden and mortgaged economy. Second, from their alliances, methods, goals, and pronouncements thus far, they are no different from the politicians of the first and second republics. There is, therefore, no reason to expect much from the politicians.[47] As Biodun Jeyifo noted recently, "Nigeria is on the brink of a literary dark age."[48] Even Chief M. K. O. Abiola, a multimillionaire, argued recently that "the state of the book publishing industry has gone from the merely bad to the intolerably alarming." The chief further argued that the crisis is partly responsible for the "falling standards of education as well as the frequency of student protests, the brain drain and inadequate remunerations." He concluded that the book crisis reflected a "stultifying veil of darkness in the face of our academic community."[49]

Nigerian academics are facing very hard times both at work and in their respective homes. Many can hardly feed their families. Facilities and resources for research simply do not exist except for the privileged few who come from the "right" ethnic or religious groups or who have connections with the vice-chancellors or members of government. Many have no idea as to how a word processor works; yet, they live and work in a country that is not only oil-rich, but also describes itself as the "giant of Africa!" Many can hardly replace worn-out clothes and shoes. For the vast majority of academics, they see their standards of living plummeting as they lose their credibility with their wives and children due to the inability to cater to them. In desperation many have become very short-tempered. Some have taken to drinking, while others have resorted to the most petty form of economic activities. Yet, those who are lucky, with contacts abroad or with excellent publication records, have been lured by foreign governments, international organizations, and foreign institutions. The private sector and the government have also benefited from the collapse of the university system as qualified staff abandon the universities and seek refuge under the better salaries and conditions of service in the private sector, especially in the scores of so-called merchant banks that have emerged in all nooks and corners of Nigeria since the introduction of structural adjustment in 1986.[50] With this development, the quality of teaching and research has declined precipitously and it is no wonder that expatriates have become the authorities on Nigeria's political economy. Books published on Nigeria, even by Nigerians, are not available in the country and the state continues to only pay lip service to the "book crisis."

The responses sketched above—emigration overseas, to the private sector, into politics, and redirection of attention to business—will definitely not solve the problem of the universities and ensure academic freedom in the country. Osieke's suggestion that "the gravity of the situation calls for a more drastic solution, such as closing down the universities until the country is in a position to provide funds and facilities to run them" is rather unrealistic and escapist.[51] This would be like playing right into the hands of the military junta and the World Bank. Though the vast majority of Nigerian universities are grossly underfunded, the real problem is not funding but the ability to manage available funds, reduce excessive dependence on the state as a way of reducing state intervention, and check the very dangerous, corrupt, and intimidating culture of waste, extravagance, promotion of mediocrity, and the enthronement of narrow interests. It is clear that Nigerian (and African) intellectuals must critically insert themselves in the struggles of popular forces and help redress the situation of want, corruption, poverty, foreign domination, repression, and exploitation, which they have helped to nurture in no small way. They must abandon their arrogance and resolve to learn from the people who have historically resisted exploitation, opportunism, collaboration with foreign interests and indigenous bourgeois elements in the looting of the national wealth, and the reproduction of the country's underdevelopment.

In some ways the current crisis of the universities, the explosion of the myth of the doctorate degree as a reliable "meal ticket," the increasing impoverishment and proletarianization of the middle and upper-middle classes, and the closure of avenues for upward mobility have made it inevitable for intellectuals to see their struggles as directly linked to those of other marginalized and disadvantaged groups in society. The ruthlessness of the military regime against workers, peasants, and students have equally been directed against members of the academic community without regard to ethnic, regional, or religious considerations. This has also showed the intellectuals that a desperate state makes no discrimination between its real and imaginary enemies in times of crisis. In any case, the changes in the world system, the breakdown of old orthodoxies, and the restructuring of global economic, political, and social relations dictates an urgent need for the reconceptualization and recomposition of theories, models of planning, political alliances, and strategies. The increasing struggles for democracy, social justice and accountability all over the world, in particular, the African continent, dictate the need to redefine political strategies and join forces with popular movements if intellectuals and the universities are not to become prime targets of attacks by popular forces.[52] In this case, academics must increase participation in and support for their unions and leaders, strengthen relations with students, labor, youths, and women, and make their research and teaching more in tune with the goals of self-reliance, gender equality, national independence, and social justice. They must begin to take issues of gender, ecology, and the environment seriously and rework their theories to emphasize the specificities of the Nigerian (and African) realities.

The World Bank and the IMF must be opposed to the extent that they continue to prescribe policies that have generally failed all over the continent to promote economic recovery, political stability, social harmony, and self-reliance.[53] As the ECA has argued, "Orthodox structural adjustment programmes . . . undermine the human condition and disregard the potential and role of popular participation in self-sustaining development."[54] In the *AAF-SAP* the ECA contends that

> the orthodox adjustment programmes, by their design, assume that the classical instruments of control of money supply, credit squeeze, exchange rate and interest rate adjustments, trade liberalization etc . . . could bring about positive results in African economies characterized by weak and disarticulate structures. However, *there is documented evidence that in many cases sustained economic growth has not materialized, the rate of investment rather than improve has tended to decrease, budget and balance of payments deficits have tended to widen after some temporary relief and debt service obligations have become unbearable.*[55]

Thus, to expect the World Bank, which represents Western and global capitalist interests, to lead Africa on the path of self-reliant growth and development, and to encourage the development of structures, and institutions of empowerment in Nigeria is to misplace the hope and future of the nation.[56]

With respect to education, it is obvious that the World Bank has a very limited idea of what the real needs of Africa are and it is only just beginning to recognize the *real* roots of Africa's perpetual crisis:

> Factually the World Bank's picture of campus life is out of touch with reality. . . . There is an even deeper contradiction between the World Bank's policy and vision. The World Bank peers into the future and prophesies: "To survive and compete in a

> competitive world of the 21st century, Africa will require not only literate and numerate citizens, but also highly qualified and trained people to perform top quality research, formulate policies, and implement programs essential to economic growth and development." Yet, its policy guarantees that this "requirement" will never be fulfilled; for African higher education is *already* on the verge of extinction.[57]

It would be a mistake for intellectuals to expect that academic freedom would be "granted" to them in a society where the state is under all forms of attacks and the economy is in shambles. Institutions devoted to the articulation of alternative ideas, the elimination of myopia, ignorance, and superstition, and the critique of assumed truths and theories are often the prime targets for attacks under conditions of economic contraction, political uncertainty and decay, and systemic crisis. The military junta in Nigeria, for a variety of reasons and more as a precipitate of its total surrender to dictations from the World Bank and the IMF, has never masked its preparedness to violate its own decrees in the process of stifling academic freedom. With collaboration from the inside, the muffling of the judiciary, and exploitation of the frustration and impoverishment of academics and students, the Babangida regime has succeeded in its mission to a very large extent. Patrick Wilmont, who was deported from Nigeria by the military on very strange and incredible charges, has noted that "under Babangida the once healthy universities are now eerily silent. And the regime considers this one of its most splendid triumphs, a noble victory of machine gun over pen."[58] Festus Iyayi, a former president of the Academic Staff Union of Universities (ASUU) who was unjustly dismissed through a retroactive decree promulgated by the Babangida regime, was right when he reflected on the conditions of struggle in Nigerian universities today: "Right now most of the university lecturers are robots, many of them are under their beds and none can come out and speak his or her mind. They are all terrified . . . in a situation where there is no opposition, tyranny reigns supreme."[59] If anything, the struggle now is to join in the looting of whatever is left in the national treasury rather than opposing the military junta.

Finally, academics outside Nigeria need to utilize their relatively more comfortable positions, new "freedoms," access to literature and the world media to support ongoing struggles in the continent, assist with materials and other information, and expose the depths of human rights abuses in their respective countries.[60] They need to join or create associations dedicated to the betterment of their respective countries, for, no matter how long they hibernate outside or alter their immigration statuses, they are still Africans and will continue to be regarded and treated as such. Their credibility and dignity abroad cannot be divorced from the state of intellectual life, quality of research, and pattern of economic and political reproduction in Africa. In any case, it will be futile to divorce the state of the universities and the struggle for academic freedom from the overall struggles to liberate, recompose, and restructure society at large. The truth is that the academic has been demystified, the Ph.D. has lost its worth, and the ivory tower has virtually lost its relevance and is on the verge of total collapse. Perhaps it is this sort of decay, demystification, and crisis the university needs to wake it up from its dreams and compel it to face new realities. Is there hope for the Nigerian reality in the 1990s?

Notes

1. Kunle Ajibade, "Path of Ignorance," *African Concord* (27 January 1992), 34.
2. Ibid., 35.
3. Letter from a graduate student in political science, University of Port Harcourt, Nigeria, December 1992.
4. See Julius O. Ihonvbere, "Economic Crisis in Sub-Saharan Africa: Depth, Dimensions and Prospects for Recovery," *The Journal of International Studies* 27 (July 1991).
5. World Bank, *The African Capacity Building Initiative—Towards Improved Policy Analysis and Development Management in Sub-Saharan Africa* (Washington, DC: The World Bank, 1991), 1.
6. See Julius O. Ihonvbere, "The Third World, Africa and the New World Order" (Paper delivered as part of the African and African-American Lecture Series, Central Connecticut State University, New Britain, 1 May 1992).
7. Organization of African Unity, *Lagos Plan of Action for the Economic Development of Africa, 1980–2000* (Geneva: International Institute for Labour Studies, 1981). Yet this document was supposed to be the blueprint for the socioeconomic and political transformation of Africa!
8. Rakiya Omaar, Introduction to Africa Watch, *Academic Freedom and Human Rights Abuses in Africa* (New York: Africa Watch, 1991), 2.
9. In several ways, this is changing. The Babangida set is probably the last set of poorly educated military generals. The army has over the years expended a lot of funds in training its younger officers. For instance, the leader of the 22 April 1990 coup, Major S. D. Mukoro, has a Ph.D. in criminology.
10. Ademola Oguntayo and Gbenga Amusan, "The Neglected Tribe: The Plight of Teachers, Nigeria's Professional Underdogs," *African Concord* (11 May 1992), 16. The writers also point out that "teachers' salaries are not regularly paid. Teachers are denied of regular promotion, overburdened by work load and poor pay. Teachers epitomize the most unfortunate among civil servants across the country." Yet, the Babangida regime has been busy donating millions of naira to musicians, foundations, social pimps, and purchasing cars for military officers in the hope that such gifts will serve to discourage coups against his regime.
11. Ibid.

12. The Kampala Declaration was emphatic on the social responsibility of the academic. See *CODESRIA Bulletin* 1 (1991), which is a special issue devoted to academic freedom.
13. While I was on the faculty at that university, whenever the small but active and highly articulate group of leftists raised such issues, they were ridiculed and branded "trouble makers who concern themselves with other people's problems."
14. Report of the Congregation Committee into Allegations of Victimization at Ahmadu Bello University, Zaria, Nigeria, January 1990 cited in "Academic Freedom in Nigeria" in Africa Watch, *Academic Freedom and Human Rights Abuses in Africa*, 47.
15. Samuel Ogbemudia, "My Sack, My Memoirs," *African Concord* (8 July 1991), 31.
16. Professor Kelsey A. Harrison, (Paper delivered at the Eleventh Convocation Ceremony for the Award of Degrees and Prizes, University of Port Harcourt, 22 February 1992), 4 (emphasis added).
17. Festus Iyayi, "It is a Question of Justice," *Classique* (2 December 1991), 51.
18. See "Environment: the Dangers Ahead" *Newswatch* 11, no. 24 (11 June 1990); and Julius O. Ihonvbere, "Community Responses to Environmental Degradation in Africa: A Case Study of Koko, Nigeria" (Paper delivered at the SSRC and CODESRIA Workshop, Dakar, Senegal, January 1992).
19. See the membership lists of the Committee for the Defence of Human Rights (CDHR), the Civil Liberties Organization (CLO), and the Constitutional Rights Project (CRP) easily the three most active and most militant civil rights organizations in the country. Beyond the involvement of radical intellectuals, these organizations are scorned by the majority of Nigerian intellectuals.
20. I do not deny that I have been part of the system I have just criticized. I have served as a students' leader; secretary, vice-chairman, and chairman of two different branches of the staff union; chair of a department; patron to students associations and unions; and member of the university senate. I also served in several university committees. Perhaps the important point now is that I do not attempt to sweep reality under the carpet and externalize all the problems of the university.
21. Seye Kehinde, "Education—Empty, Decrepit Towers," *African Concord* special report (13 April 1992), 35.
22. Dipo Fashina quoted in "Education—Empty, Decrepit Towers," *African Concord* special report (13 April 1992), 35.
23. Many of my former students at the University of Port Harcourt, including the president of the Student Union, Mr. Ejike Asiegbu, have been in jail for several months on strange and cooked up charges—belonging to secret cults, disrupting the peace in the university, arson, and so on. In virtually all the major universities in the country, student union leaders are clearly an endangered species. This has had the effect of discouraging articulate, independent-minded, politically motivated, and intelligent students from contesting for union positions.
24. Kunle Ajibade, "Path of Ignorance," 43.
25. Chief Isaac Fola-Alade, (Paper delivered at the Eleventh Convocation Ceremony for the Award of Degrees and Prizes, 22 February 1992) 3–4. Professor S. J. S. Cookey, second vice-chancellor of the university (1982–1989) has, in a very critical response to this address, argued that the university was underfunded by the federal government and did not enjoy some privileges that were available to other "second generation" universities. He also contended that "a comparison of the university with a 'village primary school' and 'an average secondary school' is an unnecessary over-dramatization since it bears no relationship with reality and trivialises a serious

issue." See S. J. S. Cookey, "Some Remarks on the Recent Convocation Address," Department of History, University of Port Harcourt, 4 March 1992.

26. Ibid., 4.
27. At a very personal level, I have two brothers, one with a graduate degree in the social sciences, the other with a bachelor's degree in the humanities. They have both never worked since graduating several years ago. Over 98 percent of my former students who graduated with first or second degrees between 1989 and 1991 at the University of Port Harcourt remain unemployed today.
28. Demola Abimboye, "The Queue Lengthens," *African Concord* (27 January 1992), 42. Abimboye reveals in his piece that "of Nigeria's estimated 40 million workforce, 10 per cent is unemployed. Even the 30 million employed hands are poorly paid."
29. Chief Isaac Fola-Alade, (Paper delivered 22 February 1992), 5.
30. Kunle Ajibade, "Path of Ignorance," 35.
31. Zik Okafor, "PMAN'S Day of Perpetual Glory," *The Sunday Magazine* (22 March 1992), 15. In 1992, General Babangida also spent N500 million in purchasing a car for each military officer in the country! Olusegun Obasanjo, the country's former military leader, has criticized this and other frivolous and wasteful expenditures in an economy undergoing structural adjustment. See Olusegun Obasanjo, "Our Situation is Desperate," *TELL* (Lagos, Nigeria) (23 March 1992).
32. See "An Old Guard's Challenge," *African Concord* (6 April 1992); Adebayo Williams, "At the Barricades," *African Concord* (30 March 1992); "I Knew They Would Fail—Interview with Sam Aluko," *African Concord* (30 March 1992); "IBB's N30m Gift Causes Confusion," *City News* (18 May 1992); Joe Nwokocha, "FG Donates N50m at CAN Lunching," *Sunday Vanguard* (26 April 1992); and "Nigeria: One Death, Too Many," *African Concord* (16 March 1992).
33. Olisa Agbakoba interviewed in "IBB's N30m Gift Causes Confusion."
34. "In Shambles: Poor Financing, Inadequate Facilities and Low Teachers' Education Have Crippled Primary Education," *Newswatch* 11, no. 26 (26 February 1990), 8.
35. According to the report, the Minister said the revelation was "funny" because "all along I thought the problem of blown-off roofs is restricted to the northern parts of the country." "In Shambles," 8.
36. "Decay of Universities," *The Nigerian Economist* 4, no. 15 (29 April 1991), 12.
37. Ibid.
38. Ibid.
39. "Scandal in Universities," *Newbreed* (1 July 1991), 24.
40. Ibid. Reporting on the country's premier university, the University of Ibadan, *Newbreed* notes that "sewage pipes are broken in most halls, and flies in their droves line those pipes. From a distance of 400 metres, on approaching the halls of residence, one is assaulted by a strong stench which forces one to involuntarily cover his nostrils." The vice-chancellor of the institution, Professor Ayo Banjo, admitted to the reporters that "facilities are on their last legs . . . Independence Hall which as the name implies was built around 1960, has not been repainted once in 31 years."
41. See, as a typical example, "University of Benin, Expulsion/Suspension Order 9th September 1991," *The Guardian* (13 September 1991), 6. This expulsion/suspension order covered all departments/faculties of the university and included forty-six names expelled, forty-two names suspended for five academic sessions, forty-two names suspended for three academic sessions, and seven names suspended for two academic sessions.
42. See Olusegun Obasanjo, "The Nigerian Society and the Third Republic," *The Guardian* (14 March 1992); "Maryam, Soyinka Bag UNN Honours Today," *Daily*

Times (14 March 1992); and Kunle Amuwo, "The State of Our Universities," *The Guardian* (14 March 1992).

43. "Exam Fraud Defies Solution," *Newbreed* (2 December 1991).
44. Kunle Ajibade, "Path of Ignorance," 35.
45. Ademola Oguntayo and Gbenga Amusan, "The Neglected Tribe."
46. C. George Caffentzis, "The World Bank and Academic Freedom in Africa" (Paper presented at the Annual Meeting of the African Studies Association, St. Louis, November 1991), 7.
47. See Julius O. Ihonvbere, "Structural Adjustment and Nigeria's Democratic Transition," *TransAfrica Forum* 8, no. 3 (Fall 1991); "The Magic Makers," *African Concord* (25 November 1991); Babafemi Ojudu, "As in the Beginning . . . Money and Ethnic Loyalties Manifest in Third Republic Politicking," *African Concord* (6 August 1990); Emmanuel Efeni, "Warding Off Political Oblivion," *The Guardian* (14 March 1992); "Editorial: Danger Ahead," *Daily Champion* (18 February 1992); and "The Pains of Living in Nigeria," *African Concord* (27 January 1992).
48. Biodun Jeyifo was a former president of the Academic Staff Union of Universities. One of Nigeria's leading progressive scholars and literary critics, he, like many of the leading scholars, is now based at Cornell University, Ithaca. He was quoted in *African Concord* (27 January 1992), 34.
49. Chief M. K. O. Abiola quoted in *African Concord* (27 January 1992).
50. See Ebere Osieke, "Our Unfortunate Universities," *The Guardian* (4 July 1991), 11. Osieke argues that a situation where an editor of a newspaper earns N45,000 per annum and editors-in-chief earn even higher, where managing directors of banks and private companies earn at least N60,000 plus several fringe benefits, it is unfair for full professors to earn N14,280 with the maximum set at N27,000.
51. Ibid.
52. Colleen Lowe Morna, "Africa's Campuses Lead Pro-Democracy Drives," *The Chronicle of Higher Education* (28 November 1990). The role of the universities must not be overstretched. In reality, popular organizations—labor, civil liberties organizations, students, women, NGOs, and VDOs—are in the forefront. Intellectuals, having been rejected in large measure by the state and the elites, have had no option but to join forces with these popular organizations. See Julius O. Ihonvbere, "Economic Crisis and Pro-Democracy Movements in Africa" (The University of Texas at Austin, February 1992, mimeographed).
53. The World Bank, in spite of its pretensions, has no respect for Africa and Africans. The kinds of research it supports in Africa are usually in areas of marginal importance to the pressing needs of African peoples. George Ayittey revealed recently that the "World Bank employs the services of management consultants. About 80,000 expatriate consultants work on Africa alone. Less than 0.1 percent are Africans. In 1988, the World Bank spent close to $1 billion on consultants." See George Ayittey, "Why Structural Adjustment Failed in Africa," *TransAfrica Forum* 8, no. 2 (Summer 1991), 48. It is easy to understand why the bank does not understand Africa. It prefers, in its misguided arrogance, to see Africa through expatriate eyes!
54. ECA, *African Charter for Popular Participation in Development* (Addis Ababa, Ethiopia: ECA, 1990), 19.
55. ECA, *African Alternative Framework to Structural Adjustment Programmes for Socio-Economic Recovery and Transformation* (Addis Ababa, Ethiopia: ECA, 1989), i (emphasis added).

56. Our position is not that structural adjustment is not required in Nigeria as well as in the majority of African economies. On the contrary, we believe that the IMF/World Bank brand of adjustment can never work because it is out of tune with African realities; overlooks serious issues of power, politics, and contradictions; is grafted on a sea of poverty, deprivation, corruption, waste, and mismanagement; and ignores issues of political spaces, room for maneuver, statecraft of leadership, regime credibility, and the distribution of the pains and costs of adjustment. In any case, African economies need, not mere adjustment, but adjustment with transformation. See Julius O. Ihonvbere, "Making Structural Adjustment Work in Africa: Issues and Prospects for the 1990s," *Philosophy and Social Action* (1992).
57. C. George Caffentzis, "The World Bank and Academic Freedom in Africa," 7.
58. Patrick Wilmont, "Homage to Silence" in Africa Watch, *Academic Freedom and Human Rights Abuses in Africa*, 52. See also "No War, No Peace," *Newswatch* (10 June 1991); Dayo Omotoso, "Crime and Punishment," *TELL* (9 September 1991); and CDHR, "Press Release: Wave of Arrests of Student and Former Student Leaders Begins," Lagos, Nigeria, 26 May 1991, and "Press Release: The Students' Protest and Human Rights Violations," Lagos, Nigeria, 3 June 1991.
59. Festus Iyayi, "It is a Question of Justice," 51.
60. For such exposure of the massive scale of human rights abuses in Nigeria see Amnesty International, *Nigeria: A Summary of Human Rights Concerns in 1990* (London: International Secretariat, March 1991); "Human Rights: No Need for Applause—as the Year Saw Gross Abuse of Human Rights," *The African Guardian* (7 January 1991); "Campus Clean-up," *African Concord* (5 November 1990); and CDHR, "Press Release: The Students' Protest and Human Rights Violation," Lagos, Nigeria, 3 June 1991.

4

Economic Crisis and the Politics of Structural Adjustment in Nigeria

> The Naira has weakened, unemployment has grown and inflation has soared. Statutory bans and high prices have thinned out imports into dribs and drabs. Social misery, particularly in towns, is widespread. Office workers, used to paying an average of 3 Nairas [sic] for lunch two years ago have to pay four times as much today. Industry is stalling. Hundreds of apartments and office blocks stand unfinished, their steel frames unwalled like giant multi-storied holes.[1]

> SAP has meant a curse to a majority of Nigerians. It is a string of worries to the low income earners and those who earn nothing. The crisis deepens at the turn of each day. Hapless individuals are at their wits ends, pitted against the efforts of government's self-inflicted devaluation of the national currency, the naira. The eroded naira has brought in its wake teeming crowds at the city's bus stops . . . exorbitant transport fares; a bothersome trend of graduate unemployment and underutilization; and an elusive health-care delivery system.[2]

No nation can make progress when its leaders are corrupt, arrogant, and unwilling to accept their mistakes. Credible, popular, and accountable leadership is a fundamental prerequisite for mobilization, unity, stability, and progress. When leaders manipulate information and statistics, wage a war against popular groups and their organizations, and condone corruption, waste, and inefficiency, the nation is bound to experience socioeconomic and political deterioration. This is the more so in an era of political or economic experimentation, a time when it becomes apparent to all that sacrificies, mobilization, and national harmony are required to reverse conditions of dependence, poverty, social decay, institutional deterioration, and alienation.

The Nigerian experience since receiving political independence has been one of antagonism and mutual suspicion between the leadership and the people. Politicians, within and outside the military, aided by sections of the intellectual class, have generally treated the masses as illiterate, ignorant, and as objects of manipulation and exploitation in the political process. The masses have received the brunt of political mistakes, corruption, squandering of national resources, political intolerance, opportunism, and irresponsibility. The masses have been alienated from the processes of policy initiation and implementation; and the whole process of development planning has been one distant and alien activity to the people of Nigeria. In recent times, this situation has become more pronounced. The Babangida regime has incorporated more elites than any other before it. The regime believes that it has the answers to all the problems of the nation, and hence, it declares that there are no alternatives to its own policies. Even when the regime threw some issues open to national debate, its final decisions were often at variance with the majority decisions. To impose its will on the Nigerian people, the regime has harassed the labor movement, jailed social critics, executed several military officers, eroded university autonomy and academic freedom, violated press freedoms, and relied heavily on bribery, defensive radicalism, lies, the manipulation of official statistics, intolerance of opposition, and other extralegal mechanisms to suffocate civil society while strengthening the military.

Toward the end of 1991, an interesting debate took place in Nigeria. This debate showed very clearly the arrogance of the Nigerian military regime and the ways in which official statistics were being manipulated to give the impression that the structural adjustment program was generating positive results against all visible consequences of the policy since it was introduced in 1986. On the one side of the debate were students, the Nigerian Labour Congress (NLC), the Manufacturers Association of Nigeria (MAN), the Organized Private Sector (OPS), the American Ambassador to Nigeria, intellectuals, and the Nigerian people. On the other side of the debate was the Nigerian military regime, the Central Bank of Nigeria (CBN), and the Federal Office of Statistics (FOS). The issues at stake were the state of the Nigerian economy, the progress made thus far with the structural adjustment program, and the future of the Nigerian economy.

The MAN, in its half-yearly report for 1991, had argued that the Nigerian "economy was getting worse" and that trade liberalization was "making them less competitive."[3] The OPS on its part accused the government of corruption and waste. The American ambassador, Lanon

Walker, in a speech to the Nigerian-American Chamber of Commerce, argued that "the Nigerian economy was badly managed. Inflation, was about 30 percent, contrary to the government's report which put it at 5.5 percent." He went on to argue that "fiscal discipline had broken down" in Nigeria since late 1990. According to the ambassador, "This indiscipline . . . contributed largely to the huge N19.6 billion deficit returned in the first half of this year [1991]. . . . The poor performance is structural and managerial; it is not primarily due to heavy debt service obligation."[4] Supporting this view of the state of the Nigerian economy was General T. Y. Danjuma (rtd.) who said that "no significant private investment, Nigerian or foreign, has been made since the introduction of SAP. On the other hand, the productive capacity in the industrial sector has remained stubbornly low, and the value of the naira in the foreign exchange market unstable and severely undervalued." The general drew the conclusion that "little progress has been made in the fight against inflation, unemployment, under-employment. Consequently, business failures have reached a catastrophic proportion in the past few years."[5] This view coincided with those expressed by the National Association of Nigerian Students (NANS), the Civil Liberties Organization (CLO), the Committee for the Defence of Human Rights (CDHR), the National Association of Democratic Lawyers (NADL), the Campaign for Democracy (CD), the Movement for Democracy and Justice (MDJ), the Academic Staff Union of Universities (ASUU), Women in Nigeria (WIN), the media houses, and other popular organizations.

The unanimous conclusion among these groups was that life had become worse for disadvantaged Nigerians, inflation had increased, and unemployment, prostitution, violence, disease, disillusionment, and corruption had risen to unprecedented proportions.[6] Part of the problem, these groups argued, was due to the poor implementation of the orthodox structural adjustment program and the seeming commitment of the military regime to a corrupt, wasteful, and unproductive status quo.

However, the Babangida regime refused to take a second look at its politics and policies. Rather it attacked these organizations. It accused the civil liberties organizations of receiving financial support from foreign sources. It accused the private sector of not responding to "government incentives" and of being a major part of the corruption plaguing the administration. The Central Bank and the FOS released statistics that showed that the deficit was a precipitate of debt-servicing obligations, that "inflation was gliding, while industrial capacity utilization was on the rise again."[7] Generally, the claim on the side of government was that the economy was recovering fast and the structural adjustment program was making major and far-reaching achievements.

As we shall show in this chapter, the Nigerian government is merely posturing and refusing to face the stark realities of economic decay, social dislocation, deindustrialization, inflation, and systemic crisis, which, if not contained, would subvert its so-called efforts at transition to democracy and militate against long-term growth and development in Nigeria. The recent belated admission by the president that he had not found the answers to the country's economic crisis came only after repressive and corrupt policies had delegitimized the state and its institutions, chased scholars and artists out of academic institutions and the country, demoralized local investors, failed to attract foreign investors, and virtually destroyed the social fabric of the nation.[8] As Babatunde Olugboji rightly notes, "Like true patriots, Nigerians resolved to stand by their leader. Six years after, they are still deep in the dark tunnel, with no ray of light in sight. All the goodies SAP promised are yet to be accomplished. And there are fears that the Nigerian ship may capsize."[9]

It is instructive to note that in spite of the efforts by official and other praise singers of the military regime and in spite of the regime's efforts to suppress information on its poor economic record, particularly as it relates to the structural adjustment program, there is widespread acknowledgment in and outside the country that the program is not achieving its declared goals.[10] This recognition comes from very obvious contradictions, deepening tensions, alienation, marginalization of the poor, proletarianization of the middle class, social decay, a rising foreign debt profile, and instability in the country, to mention just a few of the deepening contradictions and pressures that have been generated or accentuated by the implementation of the adjustment program since 1986. It is true that the SAP cannot be blamed for all the ills of the Nigerian social formation. The program, originally designed for integrated and productive economies with sufficient cushions to absorb the inevitable pains and costs of adjustment, merely accentuated inherited contradictions and problems, while introducing new ones.[11]

Perhaps the most unfortunate part of this development is the extent to which the unequal distribution of the "gains" and pains of adjustment, as well as the unbridled corruption that the government pretends not to notice, have contributed to eroding the already tenuous legitimacy of the state. At the same time, the pains of adjustment, the proletarianization of the middle classes, and the repression of popular forces in the country have created a feeling of alienation, even hatred for the government. The efforts to doctor official statistics and rely on propaganda about the achievements of the SAP have not bought the regime any advantage over its critics because the people feel the direct impact of the SAP in the marketplace and in their homes.[12] Rather than take a critical look at its policies, involve the people in the process of adjustment, curb corruption and waste, and distribute the pains equally among social classes, the Nigerian state resorted to doctoring data, hiring public relations firms all over the Western world to polish its image, and harass all those who dared to criticize its policies.

In contemporary Nigeria, and in spite of six years of structural adjustment under a repressive military regime, tensions within and between classes have become heightened. Industries are closing down. Inefficiency and ineffectiveness in public institutions have risen to new levels. Corruption in Nigeria is at a level never experienced in the country's history.[13] The foreign debt profile has also risen to new levels, almost doubling with adjustment in spite of a general policy of desubsidization and the mass retrenchment of workers. The rural areas continue to be neglected while human rights violations and political tensions have come to characterize relations between state and society.[14]

The IMF and the World Bank have tended to overlook the specificities of African social formations. It was only recently that the bank began to pay some attention to the political dimensions of the African crisis as against its previous economistic interpretations.[15] Thus, the bank appears to have recognized the salient issues of power, contradictions, and the political obstacles to adjustment arising from the suffocation of civil society, nonempowerment of the people and their organizations, and the lack of governmental accountability to the people. Without doubt, the traditional neglect of issues of power, production, class and state, political spaces, ideological discourses, political tendencies, and historical experiences when recommending adjustment packages for underdeveloped and vulnerable economies has contributed in no small way to the failure of such packages. The bank and fund have treated desperate African regimes in a uniform manner with no specific considerations for historical, structural, and other differences. They have paid limited attention to the issues above as well as the degree of legitimacy of the government, depth of pre-adjustment crisis, statecraft of the leadership, strength of opposition forces, room for maneuver in the international system, depth of institutional decay, available resources, and so on.[16]

Nigeria's adjustment program falls into this extreme group that overlooks the character of government and its custodians, the depth of corruption, the depth of pre-adjustment crisis, the credibility of leadership, the ability of popular forces to resist the unequal distribution of the pains of adjustment and the amount of room the military regime has in the global system to seek alternative sources of support for the demands of adjustment.[17] Hence, the fund and the bank expect regimes and class forces, which had presided over the destruction of their respective economies, to suddenly turn around and promote economic growth and recovery even when the corruption and mismanagement of such regimes have become legendary.

When the Babangida regime introduced the adjustment program in 1986, pre-adjustment redistributional programs were either inexistent or very minimal and skewed in favor of the urban-based elites. Until 1986, many Nigerians felt that the deepening crisis of the economy was only a passing phase. This meant that, given the oil boom of the past, Nigerians, unlike the case of Ghana, had not experienced severe economic decline to harden them toward accepting the pains of adjustment within a context of widespread inequalities. Nigeria, unlike Ghana has no national symbols and no culture of mobilization on ideological grounds, and the capacity of the state to mediate contradictions and conflicts was tenuous. Its legitimacy was low. The adjustment program merely increased the process of delegitimization and accelerated the process of institutional decay and incapacity to build hegemony. The adjustment program that removed all the social programs and services previously enjoyed by the poor majority equally contributed to this process of delegitimization and heightened the perception of the "state as enemy of the people."[18] It is therefore quite easy to identify the neglect of the majority and their marginalization in the era of adjustment as one of the major obstacles to the success of the program. This neglect is equally responsible for the widespread opposition to adjustment and thus the inability of regimes to keep adjustment programs on track.

Background to Nigeria's Adjustment Program

Though the oil boom in the 1970s and early 1980s created the impression that Nigeria was a rich nation, the reality was quite different. Today, the country remains an underdeveloped, dependent, and technologically backward economy.[19] In the context of sub-Saharan Africa, the structures of the Nigerian state and economy would appear relatively developed.[20] The fact remains that the economy is dominated by foreign interests and the society is characterized by indiscipline, instability, ethnic, religious, and regional cleavages, and the general absence of basic human needs for the vast majority. Problems of unemployment, a weak production base, a high crime rate, rapid regime turnover, inefficient and ineffective bureaucracy, widespread corruption, waste, mismanagement, rural decay, urban dislocation, and the privatization of public office, especially under military regimes, have plagued the economy since political independence was first achieved in 1960 (see chapter 1). To be sure, the country has experienced dramatic changes since 1960: new states (first twelve, then nineteen, and twenty-one, now thirty with continuing demands for more states!); a new federal capital at Abuja; new national anthem; two new constitutions; two democratic experiments—the West Minster model, which was terminated in 1966 by the military, and the American Executive Presidential model terminated in 1983, again, by the military; a four-year civil war 1967–70, an oil boom; growing influence in world affairs and a generally larger, if not stronger, economy than when independence was first given to Nigeria three decades ago. However, these changes, boom and burst economic cycles, have been mediated by the problems identified above.[21] The indiscipline and weaknesses of the state and dominant elites have combined with other structural contradictions to make the Nigerian economy and society extremely vulnerable to foreign penetration, manipulation, domination, and exploitation.

It was quite easy for Nigeria to paper over the deepening crisis of the economy in the period of the oil boom. Food imports shot up, agriculture stagnated, expenditure constantly overshot income, prestigious projects were initiated, and the country pursued a flamboyant and extravagant foreign policy. Plan and project implementation was measured in terms of ability to expend budgetary allocations rather than in the completion of specified projects. With the oil boom, the country was courted by all sorts of contractors, traders, and business interests of all shades.

The Obasanjo regime (1976–1979), through misplaced priorities, excessive military expenditures, inability to check corruption, deterioration of the bureaucracy, and excessive reliance on the oil sector for foreign exchange earnings, consolidated the country's dependent location and role in the international division of labor. The "belt-tightening" responses to the precipitous decline in oil income in 1977 achieved very little as the regime was unable to check waste and instill some discipline in the ranks of the dominant classes. The Shehu Shagari civilian administration (1979–1983) was a major disaster that set the country back by over five decades. Political irresponsibility and intolerance, corruption, mismanagement, waste, and the privatization of public office weakened the economy and pushed the economy toward total collapse. Though the politicians of the second republic collected more foreign exchange from oil exports in just four years than the country had collected since 1958, it also piled up more debts than all governments before it put together. Thus, a government that earned N43.6 billion from the oil sector alone accumulated a foreign debt of N24 billion in four years. By the time the confused politicians were overthrown by the military in December 1983, workers had not been paid, for up to twelve months in many states, foreign debts were in arrears, credit lines were closed, hospitals became mere consulting clinics, crime had reached unprecedented proportions, and factories were closing down. The belated and post-hoc Economic Stabilization Act of April 1982, which introduced so-called austerity measures, made little or no impact as the economy continued to slide down the path of decline and disaster.

The Generals Buhari/Idiagbon regime (1983–1985) experimented with various forms of austerity packages in response to the deepening crisis of the Nigerian economy. In spite of its petty bourgeois character, it refused to reach a blanket agreement with the IMF, especially on issues of trade liberalization, blanket devaluation, and desubsidization. Unfortunately, the regime inherited a badly damaged economy and an impatient society. Its ethical campaign embodied in the War Against Indiscipline (WAI); countertrade with Brazil, Malaysia, Austria, and Italy involving the battering of Nigerian oil for essential imports; and the repression of all opposition, especially intellectuals, students, and workers, alienated the regime from the populace. The IMF was particularly displeased with the regime for its refusal to implement its conditionalities without question, and in August 1985 the regime was overthrown in a palace coup led by Ibrahim Babangida due to "irreconciliable differences."[22] Ibrahim Ayagi, former chairman of Continental Merchant Bank (CMB) of Nigeria and current chairman of the Kano State Foundation (KSF), recently alleged that "the long, muscular hands of the IMF and the World Bank may have been at play in the ouster of the Buhari-Idiagbon government"[23] as a result of their refusal to embrace the structural adjustment program without questions. At a level, therefore, it can be argued that the Babangida regime had no alternative to a structural adjustment program. The way in which it has been implemented, the policies designed to protect vulnerable groups, and the overall politics of the program itself are issues for debate.

The Babangida Regime and Structural Adjustment

The Babangida administration went ahead and implemented all the conditionalities of the IMF package, but did not take the loan since it had been roundly rejected in an open national public debate by the Nigerian people. The conditionalities included massive currency devaluation, the removal of subsidies, retrenchment of workers to cut the public service, trade liberalization, and the privatization and/or commercialization of public corporations. The public debate was generally opposed to these conditionalities. The consensus was that if the government checked corruption and waste, reduced its expenditure on defense and so-called security, checked the inflation of contracts and irrelevant allowances, especially within the military, and stimulated local production, it would be unnecessary to take the loan or implement the harsh conditionalities. Though the government was to acknowledge the fact that it lost the debate, it was later to ignore the wishes of the public on the matter. The implementation of the program was combined with a policy of defensive radicalism, political posturing (for example, respect for consultations, dialogue, democracy, and human rights), intimidation of popular forces and organizations, the rehabilitation of discredited politicians and military officers, and the incorporation of some members of the broad left, labor, and the media.[24]

This grand corporatist strategy succeeded in its early stages in containing and dividing the opposition and in creating the impression that the regime and its policies had the support of popular organizations, radical scholars, and the media. The regime argued that its recovery package was "homemade" and called on all Nigerians to be prepared to make sacrifices. Babangida criticized the Buhari administration for devoting too much money to debt- servicing and for making very limited improvement on the living conditions of the people. It promised to turn the economy around, revitalize the bureaucracy, revive the schools and hospitals, bring budgetary expenditure under control, promote agriculture, diversify the economy, and promote industrialization.

As a starting point, the Babangida regime announced a fifteen-month economic emergency period beginning 1 October 1985. During this period, the following programs were to be put in place: pay cuts for all workers, the banning of maize and rice imports, a 30 percent levy on all imports, extension of the wage freeze, the removal of 80 percent subsidy on petroleum, and a heavy reduction of subventions to public parastatals and government ministries.[25] These policies were expected to save money, promote government earnings, and compel ministries and parastatals to conserve and manage scarce resources more efficiently. Unfortunately, the burden of these measures, in particular, the freeze on wages and new appointments, fell mostly on nonbourgeois forces, especially the working class. The pay cuts affected workers but had no impact whatsoever on top bureaucrats and military men who, in any case, never relied on their salaries and wages. They continued to collect their generous allowances and kickbacks and engage in other corrupt practices. The removal of subsidy on petroleum products led to sharp increases in transport fares and the cost of food items and services. Again, the brunt fell on the poor as the privileged continued to rely on official vehicles and publicly supplied fuel for their official and private vehicles. By July 1986, a general consensus had emerged that the emergency economic measures were not yielding the desired results,

> Urban unemployment grew and the much needed credit lines to facilitate the importation of raw materials to keep the wheels of industry turning were not forthcoming. Nigeria's creditors could not swallow its rejection of the IMF loan and as a result the nation's credit rating dropped from about 55 percent in 1980 to 24 percent in 1986. All this resulted in Nigeria's inability to reschedule its huge external debt. The stage was set for tougher measures.[26]

In July 1986, the military regime embraced the IMF conditionalities in its entirety. The goals of Nigeria's adjustment program were stated as follows: (1) "to restructure and diversify the productive base of the economy in order to reduce dependence on the oil sector and imports;" (2) "to achieve fiscal and balance of payments viability over the period;" (3) "to lay the basis for a sustainable non-inflationary or minimal inflationary growth;" (4) "to lessen the dominance of unproductive investments in the public sector, improve the sector's efficiency and intensify the growth potential of the private sector."[27]

To achieve these goals of adjustment, the government devalued the currency by over 80 percent, commercialized and privatized several parastatals even lucrative ones, introduced a debt-equity swap program, liberalized the economy and revoked the indigenization decrees passed in the 1970s, outlined a new package of incentives to foreign investors, and retrenched hundreds of thousands of workers. In addition, the government introduced a floating interest rate policy, encouraged an export drive program to earn foreign exchange, introduced new taxes, levies, and user fees on a range of social services, especially health and education, constructed new toll gates on the country's major highways, and put in place a Second-Tier Foreign Exchange Market (SFEM)—later the Inter-Bank Foreign Exchange Market (IFEM) and now the Foreign Exchange Market (FEM)—for the weekly auction of the naira under the supervision of the Central Bank of Nigeria (CBN). Budgetary allocations to ministries were drastically reduced; parastatals were told to go commercial and to depend less on government financing; the importation of rice, maize, wheat, and malt was banned; and up to 45 percent of foreign exchange earnings was devoted to servicing the country's rapidly increasing debts.

These policies in themselves have generated heated debates and disagreements within and outside official circles.[28] Opposition to the adjustment program has been the cause of two attempted military coups d'état in 1986 and in 1990.[29] Workers, students, market women, and the unemployed have demonstrated and rioted against the policies and their consequences in 1986, 1989, 1990, and 1992. On the other hand, opposition and criticisms have forced the government to abandon its human rights pretensions and become outrightly repressive in its bid to maintain some order.[30] Trade unions, students, and other popular organizations have criticized the debt-equity swap program for promoting the interests of foreign capital by allowing creditors to convert their debts to equity shares in strategic and lucrative industries. This is because no foreigner was expected to swap debt owed on foreign exchange for a business outfit that was not making a profit or that had no clear potential for making a profit. The privatization program is opposed by labor because public enterprises are being sold to members of the Nigerian bourgeoisie who in most cases serve as fronts for foreign interests. In any case, the inefficiency of government parastatals as well as their nonprofitability have little to do with government ownership, despite what the World Bank and the IMF lead us to believe. Rather, their poor performances can be traced to the enthronement of mediocrity, favoritism, policy inconsistency, frequent interference in the affairs of the companies by the state, and massive corruption often condoned by the government itself.[31] This means that it is the character of state, the dominant classes, their patterns of politics and accumulation that influence and determine the efficiency of public institutions. After all, public institutions and parastatals in advanced capitalist formations are efficient and profitable, and even the United States has hundreds of public institutions. Policies of deregulation, privatization, desubsidization, and devaluation have had a direct impact on the poor and generally disadvantaged groups as well as local investors.

Local investors, in the face of deregulation of the economy, trade liberalization, and heavy devaluation of the currency, simply find it difficult to remain afloat in the face of foreign competition.[32] This is why the Manufacturers Association of Nigeria (MAN) has been in the forefront of those trenchantly opposed to the *implementation* of the adjustment program. The introduction of the FEM did not eliminate the parallel market. Rather, it strengthened it and restricted the manipulation of foreign exchange to a few banks, top military personnel, businessmen, and bureaucrats. As well, it led to "price rises that were feared by the scheme's detractors. Many traders hoarded goods in anticipation of being able to sell them at high post SFEM prices, and this sent the cost of items such as milk, sugar, meat, soap, detergent, cigarettes and beer soaring upwards."[33] Thus, the FEM, which determines the exchange rate (and indeed, the rate of devaluation) on a weekly basis, has led to inflationary price increases, wiped out several small businesses, and benefited those with foreign exchange outside the country as well as those with connections to the banks. The latter group simply corner the foreign exchange at official exchange rates and sell it off at higher parallel market rates. This is precisely why the naira has continued to fall and new banks, so-called merchant banks, have emerged in all nooks and corners of the country. Business in foreign exchange has become exceedingly lucrative with the devaluation of the naira. Hence, though the banks, especially the merchant banks, are making huge after-tax profits every year, they are not lending money for productive activities. In fact, they are hardly lending money at all or stimulating the economy in any way. Their main business is in the laundering of foreign exchange: buy at official rates and sell in the parallel market while manipulating the books to make it look like a regular transaction. The local bourgeoisie, traditionally known for its unproductive disposition, has thus shifted its accumulative base somewhat to the manipulation of foreign exchange. This foreign exchange business is now so lucrative, especially with the over 100 percent official (and 150 percent parallel) devaluation of the naira, that many of the new banks have traditional rulers, "top military officers," and civil servants behind them.[34] The mushrooming of these "merchant banks" has forced the Chartered Institute of Bankers of Nigeria (CIBN) to urge the federal government to "stop the licensing of new banks."[35]

The above are some of the critical issues of Nigeria's economic crisis. Policies of austerity, indigenization, and now structural adjustment, adopted by different regimes since 1976, have achieved very little in terms of strengthening the economy. The main reasons for the limited achievements of these often post-hoc responses is that they never critically and consistently addressed the fundamental roots of the Nigerian crisis: issues of politics, power, production, and exchange relations. Thus, industries are producing below capacity, foreign investment has hardly picked up, inflation continues to reduce the real value of wages, foreign debts continue to increase, and unemployment, mismanagement, corruption, and instability continue to plague the economy and society. The MAN reported in its 1991 half-yearly report (July–December) that "the economy . . . was poorer in 1991 than in 1990. The Gross Domestic Product (GDP) grew at 4.3% compared with 8.2% in 1990."[36]

Without doubt the adjustment program introduced in 1986 has made some modest achievements. In the first place, it has brought to light the depth of the economic and social crisis and exploded the myth of the oil boom. Nigerians now know that though their country is an oil producing nation, it is vulnerable to the vagaries of the international system and subject to pressures from the internal mismanagement of resources. Second, the program has encouraged the rational utilization of resources while at the same time has promoted local creativity. In the public and private sectors, there is some realization that the boom days are over and that there is an urgent need to be prudent in the use of resources and materials. Third, local industries now rely less on imports for their production processes. In the bakery, brewery, printing and publishing, and pharmaceutical industries, local content has increased to between 40 and 70 percent as producers now use local materials. This has in some measure stimulated agricultural productivity and increased accumulation in the rural areas. Fourth, unlike in the 1970s and early 1980s, there is now a better appreciation of the need for resource management, savings, and investment in productive activities. The usual wild all-night parties often organized by the rich have drastically declined in number, "unnecessary expenditures" are now avoided, and the desire to save for the "rainy day" is widespread among nonbourgeois forces. Fifth, there is a reduced reliance on the government by ministries and parastatals for operations. True, the state and its agencies are still the primary means of accumulation for the bourgeoisie, but these bodies no longer rely exclusively on the government for subsidies and subventions. Finally, the ruthless implementation of the program, the grossly unequal distribution of the pains of adjustment, the growing inequalities in the society, the increased arrogance of power displayed by the military and the rich, the further impoverishment of disadvantaged groups, and the widespread violation of socioeconomic and political rights at an unprecedented level have contributed to the emergence of political opposition groups and several civil liberties organizations. As well, the implementation of adjustment under World Bank supervision has influenced the political consciousness of the masses and encouraged a new drive toward genuine democratization and empowerment of popular groups. This latter "achievement" was obviously unintended, but has turned out to be the most far-reaching precipitate of the implementation of adjustment in the country.

Unfortunately, the gains highlighted above are constantly eroded by the inconsistency, insincerity, corruption, and inefficiency of the government. In addition, the unmediated implementation of the adjustment program with little attention to the specificities and inequalities of the country have tended to erode gains and generate deep-rooted contradictions and coalitions. Furthermore, the apparent neglect of the living conditions of the vast majority and the repression of opposition forces who have criticized or opposed the adjustment program has tended to negate the gains of adjustment and the ability of the state to keep the package on track.[37] One of Nigeria's prominent economists has argued that the failure of the adjustment program to effectively respond to the country's crisis resulted from not taking into account the sociopolitical and economic realities of the country. According to him, government officials "don't understand what SAP is all about. They swallow hook, line and sinker the economic policies from Europe and America which is the second line of slavery . . . the government continues in public to praise SAP but in private they accept that the economy is in more trouble."[38] Furthermore, Sam Aluko criticizes the excessive concern of the government with monetary and financial matters rather than with production and the strengthening of the productive capacities of the people:

> Structural adjustment is not what the government has been doing. The government has been doing monetary maladjustment not structural adjustment. The industries are dying, agriculture is not being productive, people are buying goods at higher prices, standard of living is falling, that's not structural adjustment, that is structural depreciation.[39]

In spite of official propaganda, it has become clear that Nigeria's adjustment program is one of the most poorly managed programs in the developing world. Rather than contract the role of the state and give way to private initiative, it has had the opposite effect. Let us now examine the social costs of Nigeria's adjustment.

Structural Adjustment or Structural Destabilization: The Pains and Costs of Adjustment in Nigeria

It is difficult to capture on paper the depth of the unequal distribution of the pains of adjustment in Nigeria. It takes a direct experience of how silence, fear, hunger, disillusionment, and uncertainty have come to replace what was once a very vibrant, active, creative, and innovative society. The military regime in Nigeria assumes, wrongly of course, that any criticism of its adjustment package is either an attempt to overthrow it or a direct attempt at inciting a popular uprising against it. It therefore shuts its ears to all suggestions and criticisms except those from the IMF, the World Bank, Western nations, and so-called investors. Even then, it has been unable to follow such suggestions in any consistent manner. An analysis of the social costs of adjustment and "criticism of the impact of stabilization measures" do not in any way imply "the unmitigated desirability of returning to an earlier policy regime."[40] On the contrary, such criticisms are aimed at directing urgent attention to the need to protect disadvantaged groups who are in the majority, and who already live on "the margin of life."[41] As we have already indicated, the further impoverishment of already disadvantaged groups has only encouraged political opposition to the process of adjustment, thus creating major problems, tension, waste, and the diversion or abandonment of the adjustment process.

Ironically, though World Bank and IMF officials have conceded that it is the poor and disadvantaged who bear the pains of adjustment and that this poses a fundamental obstacle to the implementation of the program, the Babangida regime in Nigeria refuses to admit that structural adjustment cannot be implemented through repression and an open door economic policy that wipes out local producers and strengthens foreign interests. There is no economy in the world today that is open. Trade blocs, protectionism, subsidization, and the use of state power and influence to extend markets for local businesses seem to be the order of the day. European, Japanese, and American leaders and their trade missions are constantly roaming the world seeking new opportunities for their businessmen and businesswomen. Western governments continue to pour resources into social and welfare programs. In Africa the cry is for desubsidization and the total withdrawal of the state from the economy. Western governments continue to impose tariff and nontariff barriers on exports from underdeveloped, especially African, countries in order to protect local producers. African governments are encouraged to open up their economies and remove all protections previously enjoyed by local producers in order to be competitive. As well, in the West, governments continue to prevent their currencies from falling, the state constantly seeks to protect the economic interests of the elites, it encourages the brain drain from the poor nations, and hardly initiates policies that will impoverish their peoples. Unemployment, inflation, and poverty have become major political campaign issues in the West.

In Africa, governments are manipulated, blackmailed, and pressured to adopt the opposite of these policies in spite of their vulnerability, structural distortions, and general weaknesses. These have created untold hardships in African countries in general. This is why the admission by

IMF and World Bank officials that adjustment programs are generating problems and contradictions that directly militate against recovery and growth, in spite of initial benefits, merely supports a position that many Africans have held for years.

It is, therefore, refreshing to see the renewed interest in protecting the poor within the context of adjustment. Even top-ranking officials of the World Bank and the IMF have come to realize the implications of pursuing an adjustment program that fails to yield concrete short-term or long-term results.[42] As M. de Larosiere of the IMF has noted, "Adjustment that pays attention to the health, nutritional and educational requirements of the most vulnerable groups is going to protect the human condition better than adjustment that ignores them." Similarly, in May 1986, the Thirty-Ninth World Health Assembly Resolution urged member states and financial institutions to ensure that "the health and nutritional status of the most disadvantaged social groups are protected when economic adjustment policies are designed and implemented." The office of the secretary-general of the United Nations, which publishes *African recovery*, noted sometime ago that adjustment programs "do not necessarily work in low-income countries where unemployment and malnutrition are already high and which do not have a resilient industrial base."[43] The UNICEF published two volumes in 1987–88, *Adjustment with a Human Face*, focusing on the disaster caused by the adjustment programs in countries that did not pay particular attention to the deplorable conditions of poverty-stricken segments of their respective societies.[44] A recent document released by the African Development Bank (ADB), the UNDP, and the World Bank notes that the current phase of adjustment programs are designed to "incorporate poverty reduction as a *fundamental objective* of adjustment policy, along with improved efficiency and economic growth." These poverty reduction programs are to be designed specifically to "assist poor and vulnerable groups affected by the adjustment process."[45] The UNDP's *Human Development Report 1990* (May 1990) and the World Bank's *World Development Report* (July 1990) and *Sub-Saharan Africa: From Crisis to Sustainable Growth* (1989) also draw direct attention to the dangers of deepening poverty and marginalization of disadvantaged groups in periods of structural adjustment.[46] Finally, in Africa, the battle for a people-centered adjustment program has been promoted over the years by the Economic Commission for Africa (ECA) through its numerous conferences and publications.[47]

In the foreword to the *African Alternative Framework to Structural Adjustment Programmes (AAF-SAP)*, a document adopted by the OAU, Adebayo Adedeji noted that

> From the economic point of view, the orthodox structural adjustment programmes, by their very design, assume that the classical instruments of control of money supply, credit squeeze, exchange rate and interest rate adjustments, trade liberalization, etc. which may be valid in well-structured economies, could bring about positive results in African economies characterized by weak and disarticulate structures. However, there is documented evidence that in many cases sustained economic growth has not materialized, the rate of investment rather than improve has tended to decrease, budget and balance of payments deficits have tended to widen after some temporary relief and debt service obligations have become unbearable.[48]

As well, in the *African Charter for Popular Participation in Development*, another document adopted by the OAU, the member states recorded their "disapproval of all economic programmes, such as orthodox Structural Adjustment Programmes, which undermine the human condition and disregard the potential and role of popular participation in self-sustaining development."[49] The above comments, then, show that there is worldwide recognition of the peculiarities of developing countries and the need to cater to vulnerable groups in periods of adjustment. They also show that Nigeria, as a member of the OAU, is well aware of the criticisms that have been leveled against orthodox adjustment programs as prescribed for underdeveloped countries. What then, is the Nigerian situation?

It might not be exactly accurate to claim that the Babangida regime has done absolutely nothing to care for vulnerable groups. We can easily mention the Better Life for Rural Women program run by Maryam Babangida, the president's wife. Also, the Directorate for Food, Roads and Rural Infrastructure (DFRRI) was set up to promote development in the rural areas. The recently established National Commission on Women (NCW), under the directorship of Bolanle Awe, is aimed at zeroing in on the specific needs of women in the rural and urban areas. We can also mention the National Directorate for Employment (NDE), which provides jobs and loans to unemployed graduates. Finally, we can mention the Peoples Bank, which, though plagued by scandals and corruption, has so far disbursed over N240 million to about 121,000 beneficiaries in its first year of operation.[50]

Unfortunately, many of these policies are post-hoc, uncoordinated, and cosmetic. The Better Life Program for instance has very little to do with rural women. It is a mere pet program involving elegantly dressed wives of state governors, local government chairmen, the president's wife, and their friends. As Professor Aluko has noted, "The Better Life thing is a slogan which does not achieve much. It's just a campaign slogan to keep people happy. I don't think there is any better life in any rural places that I have seen."[51] The DFRRI has become a gold mine for contractors and bureaucrats and millions of naira have disappeared into private pockets for shoddy jobs, poorly constructed roads, and other shady deals.[52] In any case, the consensus in Nigeria is that DFRRI has not improved the lot of rural people; it has neither provided roads, food, nor any rural infrastructure. Yet, the government has invested well over a billion naira in the program.

It has become clear that the Babangida regime was quite unprepared for the implications of implementing a far-reaching structural adjustment program and that, like Aluko said, the government swallowed hook, line, and sinker all the promises and faulty theoretical premises of the IMF and the World Bank that adjustment would turn the economy around within a very short time. The regime also believed that just because it had committed itself to an adjustment program, foreign investors were going to be falling over one another to invest in the country. Such a misplaced belief only shows that the regime and its advisers were completely out of touch with the realities of the new international deployment of capital and the ongoing restructuring of international economic relations in the context of the decline of the Soviet empire and the end of the cold war. Even more evident is the fact that the regime did not recognize the need to protect vulnerable groups during adjustment; hence, it had no program whatsoever to cater to disadvantaged groups.

The policies of privatization, devaluation, desubsidization, retrenchment, freeze on appointments, and floating interest rates, among others, were pursued without any concern for their possible impacts on the victims of the respective policies. Local producers find it difficult to borrow money in order to function with the floating interest rates. What is more, they now need, at the minimum, twelve times the usual capital outlay to import the same inputs for their production purposes. By the time they add production cost, the goods are no longer marketable, especially with unpaid workers, decline in the real value of wages, and heavy competition from foreign-produced substitutes as a result of trade liberalization. Many of them have been forced to close their factories and take to other lines of work.[53]

In its 1986 first half yearly report, the Central Bank of Nigeria noted that production costs have risen by 77 percent, or in terms of naira, from N364.5 million in the first half of 1985 to N645.2 million in a similar period in 1986. In November 1986, the MAN informed the government that "the economy was still sluggish." Similar complaints were made in 1987, 1988, and 1989. In its 1987 half-year report for instance, the MAN noted that

> Nigeria's economy is still neck deep in the slump . . . three factors (are) responsible for the poor state of the economy . . . weak domestic demand, high cost of business operation and rising cost of living. The weak domestic demand has brought about a very low level of economic activity . . . the consistently high Foreign Exchange Market has been responsible for the high cost of business operations. In response to the rising cost of living, the quality of life of Nigerians has declined considerably while their income has either been static or depressed.[54]

In August 1990, Dapo Fafowora, MAN's director-general, complained bitterly that "we still have problems of lack of new investments, of a high foreign debt profile and unusually high debt service ratio of nearly 40 percent."[55] The country's vehicle assembly plants are virtually closed (eight are closed completely) and the prices of their products have become extremely prohibitive. According to Dotun Phillips, the director-general of the Nigerian Institute for Social and Economic Research, the cost of Peugeot 504 GRAC and 505 Evolution "increased from N165,000 and N240,000 respectively to N278,700 and N415,500 respectively following the March 5, 1992 devaluation of the naira."[56] The Peugeot 504G RAC cost about N8000 in 1983. Demand for commercial vehicles declined from 70,000 a year to less than 3000 in 1989. This has meant a massive retrenchment of workers.

The middle and upper-middle classes have been equally hard hit. In the universities, professors now work more or less as part-time staff, devoting the other half of their time to private business concerns, consultancies, hustling for contracts, and farming. Teaching has suffered and research is hardly conducted. Libraries are five to ten years behind in relevant titles, and laboratories lack equipment. Office stationery and research grants just do not exist. Academic staff no longer attend conferences and the exodus of qualified academics to the Middle East, Asia, Europe, and North America alarmed the government to an extent that forced it to set up the Ibidapo Obe Panel on Brain Drain.[57] The devaluation of the naira has effectively reduced the real value of salaries to less than fifteen hundred dollars per annum.[58] In mid-1992, Nigerian university teachers went on strike demanding to be paid the equivalent of what university teachers in Malawi, Zimbabwe, Cameroon, and Ghana are paid![59] Publishers do not bother about the Nigerian market because a twenty dollar book will cost N240.00, which is more than what most Nigerians earn as net minimum wage each month. To put it mildly, the conditions of higher institutions in Nigeria is pitiable (see chapter 3). The World Bank and the Nigerian state have combined to destroy the country's universities at a time when developed countries are establishing more institutions, providing more funds for research, and attacking illiteracy in all its ramifications.

The truth is that most Nigerian parents, seeing the high level of graduate unemployment and the rapid proletarianization of intellectuals, are simply withdrawing their children from schools since it no longer makes sense to invest in education that is being increasingly commercialized anyway:

> [The] intellectual bourgeoisie is so harassed by hunger and repression that many of its members are escaping to places where they can live at a decent modicum, practice their skills in peace while meeting their human responsibilities. This intellectual class, after all, is so malnourished due to poor or insufficient protein consumption that it cannot engage in sustained intellectual activity.[60]

On the increasing phenomenon of withdrawal of students from schools, a situation unprecedented in Nigeria, Ogundipe-Leslie notes that

> in Imo and Anambra states, those . . . involved in literacy campaigns found that (they) did not need to argue for women to be in school. Only girls were in schools, in the first place. The boys were being trained as apprentice marketmen in Aba, Owerri and Onitsha—in the cities. It was felt that schooling was an unsafe and expensive venture for a boy who was a potential head of a household in a social context which did not promise jobs for his certificates. Sending boys to school which parents could ill-afford was felt to be an unwise investment.[61]

In the civil service, the story is the same—facilities for work have simply decayed or disappeared and inefficiency and ineffectiveness have reached new proportions. The general mood, given the extremely high rate of unemployment, is that it is useless sending kids to school when those with degrees are roaming the streets with "their useless pieces of paper." The rate at which official positions are being privatized has never been higher. Public property is being looted for private use or sale in the underground market more than ever before. Every public official now fixes his or her own private price for performing otherwise official duties. It is not unusual to see government vehicles and military vehicles being used to move food items from the markets or being used for commercial purposes. Thus, we begin to see a society that is not just falling apart but which is rapidly losing confidence in itself and in its own future.[62] As Mokwugo Okoye, one of the nation's early nationalists, put it recently, "I feel betrayed as a patriot. All our dreams . . . have died. . . . The Bible calls it years that locusts have eaten. That's the way one could look at what's happening now."[63]

With the adjustment program and the introduction of toll gates on the highways, user fees for social services, massive retrenchment of workers, and the rise in unemployment, armed robbery took on new dimensions. In states like Delta, Abia, Imo, Anambra, Edo, and Lagos, it is plain suicide to be on the streets after 8:00 P.M. Robbery in broad daylight with the direct connivance of police officers is not uncommon. The celebrated Police Inspector Iyamu and Anini case in the former Bendel State is a typical example of collaboration between some police officers and armed robbers. Such officers supply robbers with weapons, information, and help making arrest difficult if not impossible. Police officers set up illegal road blocks and collect tolls to augment their salaries. In the meantime, the rich are busy building police barracks and buying vehicles and communications equipment that they donate to the police. In the majority of police stations, mere stationery cannot be found and the overcrowded prison cells are among the filthiest in the world. The general impression one gets after a cursory study of the Nigerian reality is that law and order have broken down and the law of the jungle now reigns supreme. Military officers can abduct and detain citizens in their barracks for as long as possible without any repercussions. They can take the law into their own hands and flog civilians, irrespective of who they are, without sanctions from their bosses. For the poor, the court system is out of the question. It is so expensive, and there are no minimum guarantees, that it is a waste of time going to court.

Drug trafficking in typical gang-style boomed in Nigeria with structural adjustment.[64] Nigeria has become a major actor in the international drug business. All over Europe and North America hundreds of Nigerians are in jail for various drug-related offenses as the young, unable to find work and caught in the paradoxically ostentatious life-styles of military leaders, and the new rich take to extralegal means of accumulation. In the United Kingdom, for example, "in 1988, nearly 66 percent of all arrests . . . for the illegal importation of hard drugs were Nigerians. Nigerians also accounted for 33 per cent of total seizures of heroine. The statistics for 1989 were higher—314 Nigerians were arrested while 2,000 kilogrammes of cannabis, 130 kilogrammes of heroine and 7.5 kil-logrammes of cocaine were intercepted."[65] At the end of 1989, there were 1,576 Nigerians in jails around the world for drug-related offenses. At the end of 1990, there were 527 Nigerians in British prisons (excluding those detained for illegal entry) and about 444 are being detained on drug charges. Allegations of the involvement of top military officers and other so-called businessmen in the drug business have never been denied. Rather, apprehended couriers usually die in mysterious circumstances. The celebrated case of Gloria Okon is one such example. Following her arrest for drug trafficking, she promised to reveal the names of the drug barrons. She died a few weeks later in detention. A former Nigerian senator, Chief Adegoke is in jail in the United States following his conviction for drug offenses. At all international airports in the world, Nigerians are regarded as potential criminals and drug smugglers.[66] In the United States, "an average of three Nigerians were being arrested weekly for the past six years for drug-related offences . . . while 55 percent of the heroine smuggled into the JFK airport . . . was alleged to have been brought in by Nigerians."[67]

It is instructive to note that until the advent of the Babangida regime, the introduction of the adjustment program, and consequent devaluation of the naira, Nigeria did not have a notorious international reputation and was not a major actor in the global trading of drugs. People with no really visible means of income build marble houses worth millions, buy expensive cars and private jets, and donate millions to all sorts of causes and the government never inquires as to the amount of taxes they pay or the sources of their incomes. Military officers are known to own a great deal of property, yet the government never bothers to check the sources of their wealth. Chief Arthur Nzeribe announced recently that the chief of army staff, General Sanni Abacha, was constucting a N200 million house and that the president could not pretend to be unaware of it.[68] In August 1990 the *National Concord* revealed that "some foreign bank vaults are bursting with $33 billion stashed away by some wealthy Nigerians." The paper went on to note that "the deposits, an equivalent of Nigeria's huge foreign debt . . . were based on a recent report of the Morgan Trust Guarantee Bank of New York . . . rich Nigerians have accounts in almost every bank and in almost all countries of the world." This revelation was made by a member of the Corps of Signals, Brigadier Ishola Williams.[69] Open allegations of mindless corruption have been made against military governors—Princewill (Cross Rivers), Adeleye (Rivers), George (Ondo), Maina (Borno); the chief of general staff (now a civilian vice president), Augustus Aihkomu; and President Ibrahim Babangida and his wife Maryam. Rather than be investigated and punished, all these officers were either promoted or "cleared" by the miltary itself. As an insult to Nigerians, the chief of general staff once argued that a distinction must be made between "misapplication" of funds and "misappropriation" of funds. The point, therefore, is that with the adjustment program and the devaluation of the naira, the dollar and pound sterling have become "little gods" and corruption has become a way of life.[70]

Currency trafficking has become a very fast lane to wealth with the devaluation of the naira and the near fetishism of the pound sterling and the dollar. A thousand American dollars easily translates into fourteen to sixteen thousand naira, sometimes higher in the parallel market. These amounts are higher than the annual income of the majority of university staff and other civil servants.[71] Prostitution has reached unprecedented proportions as school girls in uniforms line the streets or roam about looking for "customers," at times with the full knowledge of their parents who can no longer feed or clothe them. It is no wonder that over half a million Nigerians now carry the AIDS virus with 20 percent of the carriers in Anambra and 18 percent in Lagos.[72] Teenage pregnancies have become rampant and quack abortion clinics have emerged in every nook and corner of the major cities. Child abuse, cases of divorce, marital violence, murders, vagrancy, wanton destruction of public property, and cases of mental illness have all increased to alarming proportions.[73] Nigerians started rummaging the trash cans and garbage dumps for food, clothing, and other items in their struggles to cope with the pains of adjustment. Mokwugo Okoye, an early nationalist and frontline politician, summarizes the situation aptly:

> Unlike the socio-political crisis of the past, that of today however is based on a visible degradation of economic and social conditions in the lives of a vast majority of the people as symbolized by a runaway inflation and unemployment, lack of confidence

> in the country's future, and a feeling among large sections of the people that they are not wanted. There is a palpable mass apathy and nausea resulting from social insecurity and deterioration in the peoples living standard . . . our infrastructure decayed, and what we have is an unprecedented increase in the prices of all kinds and massive devaluation of the currency.[74]

Ademola Ogunlowo puts the blame for the deterioration of the economy and in the living conditions of the people on the way the adjustment program in being implemented. As he put it, in spite of four years of structural adjustment,

> the fundamental problems of the economy appear to be still very much around. The external debt situation . . . is yet to improve, while chronic unemployment and spiralling inflation remain key features of the Nigerian economy; factories still depend on imported inputs. . . . There is still the problem of continued escalation of food prices. . . . Massive devaluation of the naira as well as an escalating cost of borrowing has created a seemingly permanent cash flow problem for Nigerian industries.[75]

In a very recent review of the adjustment program, Mokwugo Okoye noted that

> it is saddening that, three decades after our independence, Nigeria should be getting poorer, indeed should be descending from a medium to a least developed country, with life expectancy (51 years) lower than that of Togo, Zambia and Zaire and an illiteracy rate (58 percent) higher than that of Ethiopia, Kenya and Uganda . . . our per capita income is the 13th lowest in the world, with a growth rate of the country's Gross Domestic Product having fallen from 6.1 to 0.4 percent between 1980 and 1990. All this has meant a drastic fall in the standard of living of the average Nigeria for which government cannot escape blame.[76]

Okoye pursues the issue further by arguing that the Nigerian government, given its corruption, mismanagement, and reckless policies, particularly under the structural adjustment program, cannot extricate itself from direct responsibility for the poor state of the economy:

> It was the government that directed the reckless expenditure of our massive wealth from crude oil sales in the late 1970s and early 1980s on unnecessary defence and consumption. Unfortunately, the "adjustment programme" which the present government has introduced in the last six years has not improved matters and today poverty is all-pervading, the non-oil sector of the economy is hardly more diversified than it was before it came to power, while the sharing of the country's income and amenities is still marked by great inequalities. Adult education, including the inculcation of skills in the mass of the people, and the creation of jobs, proceed so slowly as to leave much of our vast potential resources untapped or unchannelled into areas of basic human needs like food, shelter, health, public works. Nor does anybody in authority today seem to bother about the ever-rising prices of consumer goods including food, drugs and clothing.[77]

In spite of the unavailability of reliable statistics on any aspect of the Nigerian economy, there is agreement on the fact that inflation has made life difficult for wage earners and small-scale producers. In a 1990 review of the SAP, Adeotun Phillips, the director-general of the government-sponsored Nigerian Institute for Social and Economic Research (NISER), reached the conclusion that the "most visible and widespread result to date is stagflation, characterized by hyper-inflation, rising unemployment, serious capacity under-utilization, decumulation of investment, degeneration of social services, and continued decline in general living standards. The 'gains' of SAP, particularly in the form of rural sector revival, are yet to compensate for the 'loses'."[78] The Nigerian Labour Congress (NLC) argued that by November 1990, inflation stood at 50 percent. In many cases, the cost of food items increased by between 500 and 2000 percent or higher. The country's minimum wage of N125.00 ($10.42) monthly (increased to N250.00 in 1991) was hardly enough to cover the cost of rents and transportation for those on minimum wage. *The African Guardian*, reviewing the state of the economy at the end of 1991 noted that "six years after [the introduction of structural adjustment], Nigerians, particularly those in the private sector, are wondering how to evaluate the economic sojourn. Some of them, who talk, are full of venom for an economic package that appears to be unleashing more pains than relief."[79] The magazine went on to describe the conditions of the Nigerian worker at the end of 1991:

> For the citizens, the chaotic mass transport system appears to be worsening each day, despite guzzling more funds. Food, man's basic need, also appears to be getting more expensive. So are many other items such as housing, health care and even education. Income and cost of living of workers continue to go in opposite direction. Real income had declined sharply, while cost of living had risen astronomically. The Nigerian worker's income in the West African region remains about the least. In impoverished sahelian Niger Republic, the minimum wage is the equivalent of N600 per month. It is N250 in Nigeria. A fresh PhD teacher in the university earns the equivalent of $4,300 in Ghana; his counterpart earns about $1000 in Nigeria. And a toilet soap that sold for about 80 kobo a tablet a few years back, now costs N4. . . . The exchange value of the naira has so diminished, that economic operators are beginning to wonder, whether devaluation will justify the trouble. Only about 65 kobo exhanged for $1 in the early 1980s, it declined to roughly N11.96 to $1 in June this year.[80]

Yet, while wages were held down, appointments and promotions frozen, subsidies removed across board, interest rates deregulated, the currency devalued, and retrenchment of workers pursued with vigor, very little was done to control inflation or increase production beyond the emphasis on cash crop production and exportation in the search for foreign exchange. The so-called Productivity and Income Control Board (PICB) is as useless as several other government parastatals, completely out of touch with market realities and colluding with the CBN and FOS in manipulating statistics in order to satisfy the World Bank. The government continued to pour money into the economy and continued to spend money as if the policy of adjustment was meant only for the poor.[81]

The food shortages, riots, and malnutrition, which accompanied the high cost of food and services, increased migration to the urban centers and the further alienation of the people from the state. According to Salisu Nuhu Mohammed, general secretary of the NLC, "there has been no . . . policy to curb inflation, and unemployment and enhance the purchasing power of the consumer. So far it is fair to say that the total effect and socio-economic consequence of these (SAP) policies on the lives of the working class is, to put it mildly, disastrous."[82] *TELL* magazine, reviewing the state of the economy and the impact of structural adjustment on the working class in mid-1991, argued that though statistics from the CBN and FOS show that the nation "was happily beginning to experience a decreasing inflation rate, . . . *actual market surveys show neither signs of a low inflation rate nor of the abatement of its high incidence.*"[83] The magazine, based on *actual* market survey and comprehensive investigations, revealed that

> over the past five years, prices of food items have taken the wings of rocket, recognising not even the sky as a limit. In 1986, a 100-kilogramme bag of beans cost N200. In 1989, it goose-stepped its way to N600 and now in 1991, it has climbed further to N920. This is a high inflationary spiral of 460%. For rice, the situation appears slightly better. A 50-kilogramme bag of the produce sold for about N230. In 1991, it goes for N400–N450, an increase of some 191%. Even these figures put a fine gloss on the sordid portrait of the nation's wild inflation if the price indices are given a 1981 base. One could buy a Volkswagen beetle car in a little above N3,000; a Passat car, N6,000; a Peugeot 505, some N8,000. Now second-hand models of the first two cars go for N40,000 and N60,000 respectively while a brand new Peugeot 505 may command as high as N180,000. Similar stupendous increases in price are the order of the day in respect of sugar and milk which rose from 1981 lows of 30 kobo and 20 kobo respectively to N7.50 and N4.50 in 1991.[84]

The situation is so bad that many Nigerians now compare the present to the days of the civil war (1967–70) and reach the conclusion that things were better at that time. Others openly complain that the colonial days were much better and that political independence has made little difference in the quality of life of the people. In fact, many now feel that independence has been more of a curse than a blessing as they can hardly see the gains of the so-called freedom from colonialism. If anything, they have seen their incomes diminish, their freedoms curtailed, a handful of politicians, traditional rulers, bureaucrats, and military officers get unbelievably rich, and basic needs enjoyed in the early years of independence disappear.[85]

The poor in Nigeria also confront the harsh realities of life under structural adjustment outside the marketplace. As Ademola Oguntayo notes, a majority of transport vehicles are off the roads due to the high costs of spare parts. Thus, in "all prominent cities in Nigeria, bus stops are fast becoming a passage through hell."[86] The middle classes have been forced to convert their private cars into taxi cabs and the majority of commercial vehicles are nothing but moving coffins with fake spare parts, unserviced and uninsured. Of course, the elites continue to use their official vehicles at public expense. At the hospitals, things have taken a disastrous dimension. The majority of experienced nurses and doctors have emigrated to the Middle East, especially Saudi Arabia, and to Europe. Today, the "general grim conditions of the nation's health care delivery are shocking, if not dangerous. Within the last three years, over 1,500 specialist doctors and about 500 nurses are believed to have left Nigeria."[87] Many Nigerians have resorted to patronizing quack doctors, herbalists, and relying on self-medication more than ever before.

In spite of harassments from the security forces, the media has continued to publish reports of increases in premature deaths in rural areas from curable diseases, increasing cases of insanity, malnutrition, starvation, hospitals without drugs, pregnant women who do not eat meat or take milk throughout the duration of their pregnancies, and increasing suicide rates. The urban centers are full of homeless people and children who beg in order to feed their aged parents. The calm, harmony, and trust that used to characterize the rural areas have disappeared as thieves now ravage farms and harvest food crops even before they are ripe for harvesting. Thus, a general mood of distrust, suspicion, anger, disillusionment, and cynicism has taken over from what was once an active, ebullient, innovative, creative, and productive society. The agents and agencies of the state are viewed with distrust. Atavistic and violent attitudes have taken over where attitudes of harmony and communalist relations used to prevail. Intellectuals, social critics, labor leaders, and students live in fear as security agents continue to harass those who speak out against the adjustment program. This is certainly a very unhealthy and potentially dangerous situation in any developing country:

> Those who perceive themselves as victims of SAP say they are particularly unhappy about the programme because it has helped to widen the inequality between the rich and the poor. They say with the introduction of the foreign exchange market, the banks and others who deal in foreign exchange have grown excessively rich while the devaluation of the naira has caused inflation, inflicting poverty and pain on the lower classes.[88]

Consequently, "hunger and malnutrition have become the lot of the majority of Nigerian urban dwellers. The worst hit are the unskilled, semi-skilled and lower middle class people." The adjustment program is thus seen as "a programme designed to punish Nigerians."[89]

This perception is reinforced by the widespread corruption and individualistic attitudes that accompanied the introduction of the program. Though Nigeria has always been a corrupt and dependent capitalist society, communual bonds and tradition served to mediate the harshness of capitalist exploitation in several ways. However, the difficulties introduced by the program has now forced nonbourgeois forces to devise several complex unorthodox and extralegal ways of survival. In several ways this has increased the level of corruption, waste, and inefficiency in the bureaucracy and individualist behavior among rural people. As mentioned earlier, among the dominant forces, corruption has reached unprecedented proportions. It is now more brazen, more complex, and more widespread: the rich put their children in private schools abroad, buy their own private airlines, establish their own banks, sink their personal water boreholes, watch foreign television stations through their private satellite dishes, and establish their private security units. Since public power has more than ever become an avenue to wealth, this has increased the premium on political power, and the competition to win access to the institutions of state has become normless and violent. At the same time, brazen corruption has continued to erode the credibility of the state while the competition to control it has increased its instability. The construction of "designer houses" in choice locations all over the country, the importation of custom-built cars, and the open flaunting of ill-gotten wealth have contributed in large measure to generating opposition to structural adjustment.[90] Nigeria's former military head of state, General Olusegun Obasanjo, noted recently that

> if Nigerians are not being harried as cocaine traffickers, they are being chased for banking and financial frauds. . . . Corruption exists almost in every society. But in Nigeria and particularly since the advent of SAP, it has become uncontrolled and uncontrollably pervasive. Anything and anybody can now "be settled." Inside and outside Nigeria, people talk of corruption in Nigeria as if it is legalised or as "a way of life."[91]

As Jato Thompson has noted, "the lavish life-style of state governors belies their normal salaries. . . . A new estate which sprouted up in the choicest part of Lagos—Victoria island, has been dubbed by the press as Millionaire's Row. Land sells for N5 million an acre and sports some of the most exotic designer-houses, owned by almost everyone who is worth his office in government and in business."[92] The situation is not helped when the government shows its indifference to allegations of corruption against public officials and, in fact, rehabilitates previously disgraced politicians and military officers.[93] As one of the country's popular magazines, *Newbreed*, has noted, "Rumours of financial misappropriation levelled against public officers and the life styles of those in power, among other things have added to the disaffection of the populace toward the government."[94]

Finally, the unequal distribution of the costs and pains of adjustment has not been soothed by the repressive attitude of the military regime. Given the absence of redistributional mechanisms prior to the introduction of the program as well as the accentuation of inequalities in all forms in the adjustment period, opposition has been high and consistent. The unequal distribution of the pains of adjustment has been the cause of two attempted coups d'etat, six major religious riots, three serious nationwide protests, and several riots and demonstrations by workers, farmers, the unemployed, traders, and other disadvantaged groups. The state has responded with repression: branding critical academics as "extremists," holding people in custody without trials, closing higher institutions, prohibiting trade unions, suspending student leaders, and firing professors. The widespread reliance on repression demonstrates the insecurity of the state and its inability to build a degree of consensus around its public policies, in particular, the structural adjustment program. The military regime apparently does not share the view of General Obasanjo that "for young multi-national developing states, the process of nation-building must be continuous. And like the tendering of a young plant, it must be nourished and watered and protected from the extremes of inclement weather. I believe that honest and open discussions, debates and dialogue are major nourishments for a country in the process of nation-building." Of course, the general was also quite clear that one such "extreme" of inclement weather is the structural adjustment program. As he noted, "I am unrepentant on my stand on SAP. It is heartening to note, though, that the architects of the programme in Washington, D.C. have acknowledged some defects in it. That is enough to convince us that we cannot build a solid edifice with the SAP architectural plan."[95]

Conclusions: Adjustment or Transformation?

Without doubt, Nigeria, like all African nations, needs structural adjustment in order to cut waste, revitalize the economy, stimulate savings, investment, and production, and restructure economic relations with foreign markets. However, for these to take place certain internal and external policies must be in place. First, the fund and bank must recognize that all African countries are not the same. Thus, adjustment packages must be designed to take due cognizance of the specificities of these countries, the character of regimes, the content and context of national political discourses, and the degree of governmental credibility and accountability. No matter how we look at it, these are ultimately the critical factors that determine the nature of public support for adjustment and other policies. Where they are overlooked or downplayed, such policies are doomed right from the beginning.

The second critical point (and this is tricky) is that the bank and the fund must carry out extensive studies of the credibility and capacity of adjusting regimes. There is no way in which a corrupt, nonaccountable, repressive, unstable, and inefficient regime can implement a serious structural adjustment program, regardless of the level of external support. The people will not agree to make sacrifices, the regime will squander its limited resources, especially on survival and in containing popular pressures, and it will be unable to keep development projects afloat. As the bank noted in its 1989 report, "Africa needs not just less government but better government."[96] The bank must take the issue of political conditionality more seriously and deny support in whatever form to repressive and corrupt governments, irrespective of the pleas they make. Under such conditions, the corrupt military regime in Nigeria ought to be denied support, for it has hardly changed its corrupt and wasteful ways.

A third point has to do with a package on how to protect vulnerable groups. In contemporary Nigeria, adjustment is meant only for the poor and disadvantaged. It is impossible to capture on paper the depth of hopelessness and impoverishment, which are not readily visible on the faces of the elites who relate to international finance institutions. Ironically, for the military officers, bankers, top bureaucrats, businessmen, and businesswomen who engage in unproductive but lucrative activities, nothing could be better. It is instructive to note that the World Bank, along with the African Development Bank and the UNDP, is moving in this direction. Such packages should not be limited to a handful of countries or made voluntary. They should be tied to the adjustment package, and there should be serious efforts made at monitoring them to ensure that they are implemented. In contemporary Nigeria, policies to protect vulnerable groups do not exist. What exists are post-hoc responses to mass riots, demonstrations, and coup attempts when some concessions are made to nonbourgeois forces.

At the internal level, it is clear that in spite of ongoing debates at the international level and in spite of campaigns by popular groups in Nigeria, the Nigerian state appears unprepared to make serious changes to its adjustment program. Its repressive postures have encouraged further opposition and the unity of forces in civil society. Policy responses to the protests by popular forces have been uncoordinated and post-hoc in nature. In other cases, they have become avenues for diverting public funds to private ends. The country's foreign debt has more than doubled, from $18 billion in 1986 to $37 billion in 1991. Richard Synge has noted that if a lasting solution is not found, "the debt issue could continue to be a destabilising factor for the economy in the years ahead and deprive Nigeria of the foreign support and investment it sorely needs in the 1990s."[97] The Nigerian government has been unable to maintain an appreciable level of financial discipline. Billions of naira continue to go into prestigious projects, the pursuits of foreign honors, sponsoring of candidates for all sorts of positions in international organizations, playing the role of regional superpower in West Africa, rewarding hangers-on of the president, paying public relations firms abroad, and funding political parties and the scores of institutions created since the adjustment program was introduced. Thus, rather than reduce government expenditures as was expected under the adjustment program, spending appears to be on the increase.

In spite of very generous incentives to foreign investors, responses have been "lukewarm" and very slow.[98] In November 1990, the Confederation of British Industry (CBI) hosted a conference in London on "Investment Promotion in Nigeria." The Nigerian delegation announced that the government had put an "open door policy" in place and had done away with all previous regulations on trade, investment, and foreign exchange. Some of the new incentives included "100 percent 5-year tax free holiday for pioneer industries, 30 percent 5-year tax concession to export-oriented industries that export not less than 60 percent of its products, 100 percent tax holiday for companies investing in economically deprived areas and 20 percent cost of providing basic infrastructure such as roads and electricity."[99] Ironically, in spite of these concessions, the Nigerian delegation was spurned by British investors who pointed at the near total breakdown of law and order, widespread corruption that hinders business, bureaucratic bottlenecks, inefficiency, frequent coups, and violent riots, and general economic mismanagement.

Foreign investors also point at the massive decline in the purshasing power of the majority of Nigerians, inefficient supply of electricity, poor communications facilities, and the unstable and weak currency, the naira. Since the country has now become classified by the World Bank as a "Low Income Country," it is now eligible "to receive loans on concessionary terms, reserved for the world's poorest countries" by the World Bank.[100] Youths are deserting the country in thousands and making all sorts of refugee claims at immigration points in Europe and North America. About 13,767 Nigerians made claims for political asylum in Germany by the end of 1991 when there was no civil war in the country.[101] Tensions, regional, religious, ethnic, and other primordial conflicts, continue to mount, posing serious challenges to the country's effort at transition to democracy.[102] What then are the implications for Nigeria?

It is clear that that there is no alternative to the democratization of society and the opening up of democratic spaces in order to build commitment, dialogue, debates, and creativity, and promote an environment propitious for growth, development, and foreign investment. The withdrawal of the military from the political scene is *sine qua non* for the attainment of these goals.[103] The current democratization process is already fraught with problems and the demise of the Third Republic is already being predicted.[104] Yet, some basic indicators of democratization and accountability must be in place before an environment for economic and social development can make any headway. I agree with Adebayo Adedeji on the point that "full democratization of all aspects of economic and social activities and in all stages from decision-making to implementation" must take place before recovery can take place, and that "it is only through the motivation and empowerment of the people as well as the ensuring of the equitable distribution of income that development can take place on a sustainable basis."[105] General Obasanjo is correct in noting that "the worst violation of human rights is poverty. Of what use is the right to vote if you cannot afford the food to sustain you to the point of voting and if ignorance and the pangs of hunger cloud your views on the issues in the election campaign?"[106] The Nigerian government must appreciate these facts:

1. Productivity cannot be expected to improve when producers are virtually dying of hunger with no access to basic facilities. The rural areas remain neglected in spite of vitriolic propaganda and the DFRRI.

2. Accumulation through the market cannot increase when the buying power of workers and peasants is so low due to massive devaluation of the currency, inflation, and unemployment. Policies of rural development, food production, and the mobilization of rural people must be taken more seriously if the rural-urban migration is to be controlled and rural decay stemmed.

3. Local entrepreneurs cannot expand, generate employment, use local raw materials, and strengthen themselves when they cannot borrow, import spare parts, sell their goods, and compete effectively with cheaper imports as a result of trade liberalization. This means that a blanket trade liberalization is a disastrous policy for any dependent and underdeveloped nation to follow in the current global order of trade blocs and high protectionism.

4. With massive corruption and repression of popular groups, the state cannot mobilize support for the adjustment program and get the people to make sacrifices, and thus accommodate the pains of adjustment. Students' unions, trade unions, professional associations, community development associations, and other popular movements are the hub of the mobilizational programs in any society that wishes to involve the people not only in decision making, as advocated by the World Bank, but also in promoting dialogue, sacrifice, and productivity even in the overall context of pain due to adjustment.

5. Conditions of alienation, disillusionment, and impoverishment militate against creativity, innovation, and rationality. Thus, tempers are now very short; prostitution, violence, drug abuse, child abuse, vagrancy, and other social vices and unorthodox business methods will continue to thrive. While these cannot all be eliminated before pursuing a program of reform and recovery, the current situation, in which soldiers, policemen, and security agents terrorize the populace, is antithetical to mobilization of popular support for public programs and governance. Thus, the whole nature of leadership and relationship between state and civil society needs to be reviewed in Nigeria. The judiciary must be truly independent and capable of enforcing contracts and presenting itself to the people as an impartial body. The press must be free in every sense of the word. Political power must be decentralized, the freedom to organize and freedom of expression must be respected, free and fair elections must be the basis for selecting leaders, and basic rights must be enshrined in the constitution, made justiciable, and placed above military decrees.

6. Investors are unlikely to take a renewed interest in the Nigerian market. On the one hand they are yet to be impressed by the country's uncoordinated economic programs, and on the other hand, political tensions, instability, coups and countercoups, as well as general uncertainty discourage investors. In any case, the buying power of the people is so low that investors find very little reason to keep investing new capital. In spite of adjustment, the elites hardly patronize local investors: they carry out their shopping abroad!

7. Conditions of poverty, widening inequalities, and deprivations in society are bound to deepen inter- and intraclass conflicts and tensions. The struggle for state power will become more desperate and political irrationality is bound to weaken the state, distort its restructuring program, generate instability, and further uncertainty. As the state becomes more repressive and diverts resources away from developmental issues toward security, alienation and cynicism will deepen. The only way out here is to demystify the state and its institutions. Politics as a means to accumulation must be redirected to a means of service under the watchful eyes and constitutionally guaranteed power of the people. This is one major way to get the Nigerian elites to redirect their interests away from accumulation through the embezzlement of public funds toward more productive sectors like agriculture and industry.

8. There is an urgent need to redirect attention toward the so-called informal sector and to women. The Nigerian economy today is being sustained through the activities of women and informal producers. Yet, they have never received the attention and resources they need to develop.

9. The proposed transfer of power to civilians in 1993 will become seriously jeopardized by the widespread conditions of disillusionment. The adjustment program is now perceived as "a wrecker"[107] and "a kiss of death"[108] and debates about continuing it have been major aspects of the transition program. The opposition to continuing adjustment arises from the grossly unequal distribution of the gains and pains of adjustment and the widening inequalities, corruption, intolerance, and repression that have accompanied its implementation. The World Bank urgently needs to put in place a program to mitigate the cost of adjustment like the one in Ghana and in line with its agenda drawn up with the ADB and the UNDP. Unless this is done, the masses of Nigeria, already alienated from the program, will remain opposed to it and this will influence their political preferences and postures in the future.[109]

It would seem, therefore, that the Nigerian government must take seriously the recommendations of the World Bank's 1989 document, *Sub-Saharan Africa: From Crisis to Sustainable Growth*, the Economic Commission for Africa's *African Alternative Framework to Structural Adjustment Programmes (AAF-SAP)*, and the *African Charter for Popular Participation in Development*, as well as the Organization of African Unity's *Lagos Plan of Action*[110] and the *African Charter of Human and Peoples' Rights* if it is to effectively respond to its deepening crisis. The basic message of these documents, to which Nigeria is signatory, is the urgent need to put the people first in the growth and development process. The need to strengthen civil society, respect and protect human rights, encourage self-reliance and democratic attitudes, protect the environment and the children, and promote the participation of women, youths, and students in the democratization and developmental processes are emphasized. It is comforting that popular forces have not given up in their quest for accountability, justice, and increased participation in the society. Given that the adjustment program has encouraged the unity of popular forces across ethnic, regional, and ideological lines with emphasis on democratization, human rights, participation, and empowerment, perhaps the adjustment program has some long-term unintended prodemocratic political gains.

Notes

1. Editorial, *Africa Events* (Lagos, Nigeria) "Nigeria at 30," (1 October 1990), 20.
2. Ademola Oguntayo, Kunle Ajibade, and Margaret Ereme, "The Hard Times," *African Concord* (3 September 1990), 46.
3. "Between Dream and Reality," *The African Guardian* (2 December 1991), 28-29.
4. Ibid., 28
5. Ibid.
6. See the various press statements, research reports, and bulletins issued by these organizations.
7. "Between Dream and Reality," 29.
8. Babatunde Olugboji, "Frankly, I've Not Found an Answer," *African Concord* (13 April 1992).
9. Babatunde Olugboji, "Frankly, I've Not Found an Answer," 31.
10. For a view from outside the government see "Interview with Sam Aluko," *Quality* (Lagos, Nigeria) (27 September 1990), 28-35. For a view from the government see "I Have Come, I Have Served—President Babangida Reflects on the Past, Present and the Future," *African Concord* (3 September 1990).
11. See Bade Onimode, *Imperialism and Underdevelopment in Nigeria* (London: Zed Press, 1982) and Toyin Falola, ed., *Britain and Nigeria: Exploitation or Development?* (London: Zed Press, 1987).
12. A typical example of this was in April 1990 when the Central Bank of Nigeria reclassified the export of petroleum products as nonoil exports, against the traditional practice. With this reclassification, the contribution of the nonoil sector shot up from $150 million in the first quarter of 1989 to $546.413 million in the first quarter of 1990, an increase of over 200 percent. See United Bank for Africa, *Monthly Business and Economic Digest* 13, no. 6 (June 1990), 3.
13. See Babafemi Ojudu, "Corruption is Nigerian," *African Concord* (13 April 1992).
14. See, "Where do We Go from Here?", *TELL* (7 October 1991); "Voices of Hope and Anguish," *TELL* (7 October 1991).
15. World Bank, *Sub-Saharan Africa: From Crisis to Sustainable Growth* (Washington, DC: World Bank, 1989).
16. See Eboe Hutchful, "Structural Adjustment and Political Regimes in Africa" (Unpublished paper, Department of Political Science, University of Toronto, 1990).
17. See Mohammed Adam, "Nigeria—The Busted Boom," *International Perspectives* (January-February 1987), 17-20; Adebayo Adedeji, "Transforming Africa's Economies," *International Perspectives* (May-June 1986), 4-8; and Tony Hawkins, "A New Realism in Lagos?" *International Perspectives* (May-June 1986), 73-76.
18. See Mokwugo Okoye, "A Time of Sadness," *The African Guardian* (24 September 1990); Segun Oluwafemi and Isola Omotayo, "A Sober Anniversary at 30," *Times International* (15 October 1990); and Dele Alaka, "Nigeria at 30: Growing Older, Not Wiser," *Sunday Concord* (Lagos, Nigeria) (30 September 1990).
19. See Okwudiba Nnoli, ed., *Path to Nigerian Development* (Dakar, Senegal: CODESRIA, 1981); Claude Ake, ed., *Political Economy of Nigeria* (London: Longman,

1985); and Toyin Falola and Julius O. Ihonvbere, *The Rise and Fall of Nigeria's Second Republic, 1979–84* (London: Zed Press, 1985).
20. For an interesting comparative study of Nigeria, Brazil, and Mexico see Peter Evans, *Dependent Development: The Alliance of State, Local and Multinational Capital in Brazil* (Princeton, NJ: Princeton University Press, 1979).
21. See Julius O. Ihonvbere, "Nigeria as Africa's Great Power: Constraints and Prospects for the 1990s," *International Journal* 46 (Summer 1991), 510–35.
22. See Toyin Falola and Julius O. Ihonvbere, *The Rise and Fall of Nigeria's Second Republic, 1979–84* (London: Zed Press, 1985).
23. "Ayagi Shoots at CBN, Bank MDs," *The President* (20 August 1990), 5.
24. See Julius O. Ihonvbere, "Structural Adjustment, the April 1990 Coup and Democratization in Nigeria" (Paper presented at the 33rd Annual Meeting of the African Studies Association, Baltimore, 1-4 November 1990).
25. See *Newswatch* (Lagos, Nigeria), *Nigeria: From Riches to Rags* (5 October 1987).
26. "SAP: What Alternatives?" *Newswatch* (Lagos, Nigeria) (24 July 1989), 14–15.
27. Federal Republic of Nigeria, *Structural Adjustment Programme for Nigeria July 1986* (Lagos, Nigeria: Government Printer, 1986).
28. See "IBB: In the People's Court," *The African Guardian* (29 August 1988); and Soji Akinrinade, "Is SAP the Magic Wand?" *Newswatch* (Lagos, Nigeria) (5 October 1989).
29. See Julius O. Ihonvbere, "A Critical Evaluation of the 1990 Failed Coup in Nigeria," *The Journal of Modern African Studies* 29, no. 4 (December 1991), 601-26.
30. See monthly reports of the Civil Liberties Organization, the Committee for Defense of Human Rights and the Nigerian Committee for the Defense of Justice. See also Seye Kehinde, "Songs of Woe," *The African Concord* (3 September 1990).
31. See Sam Aluko, *The Burden of Economic Structural Adjustment: The Nigerian Scenario* (Ile-Ife, Nigeria: 1987 Convocation Lecture, University of Ife Press, 1987) and the very critical contributions of Adeotun Phillips and E. C. Ndekwu, eds., *Structural Adjustment Programme in a Developing Economy: The Case of Nigeria* (Ibadan, Nigeria: Nigerian Institute for Social and Economic Research, 1987).
32. See Dare Babarinsa, "Industrialization: Dreams, Sweet Dreams," *Newswatch* (Lagos, Nigeria) (5 October 1990) and Seyi Olu Awofeso, "Decades of Nightmare," *The African Concord* (8 October 1990).
33. Trevor Parfitt and Stephen Riley, *The African Debt Crisis* (London: Routledge, 1989), 61.
34. "Ayagi Shoots at CBN, Bank MDs," *The President* (Lagos, Nigeria) (20 August 1990), 7.
35. "105 is a Crowd," *Newswatch* (Lagos, Nigeria), (8 October 1990), 21.
36. "MAN Reports Low Economic Performance in 1991," *Monthly Business and Economic Digest* (United Bank for Africa, Lagos, Nigeria), 15 nos. 6–7 (June–July 1992), 4.
37. Part of this inconsistency and insincerity is reflected in the very frequent changes in government personnel. The Babangida regime has changed its cabinet more times than has ever been recorded in the history of Nigeria. See Dare Babarinsa, "Like a Revolving Door: A Consummate Wielder of Power, Babangida Uses His Prerogative of Hiring and Firing to Maximize Profit," *Newswatch* (3 September 1990) and Stephen Agwudagwu, "Again, the Musical Chairs Games," *Newswatch* (Lagos, Nigeria), (10 September 1990).
38. "Interview with Sam Aluko," *Quality* (Lagos, Nigeria), (27 September 1990), 28.
39. Ibid.

40. Christopher Colclough and Reginald Herbold Green, "Editorial: Do Stabilization Policies Stabilize?" *IDS Bulletin* 19, no. 1 (January 1988), 1.
41. Robert S. McNamara, *The Challenges for Sub-saharan Africa* (Washington, DC: Sir John Crawford Memorial Lecture, the World Bank, 1 November 1985), 5.
42. M. de Larosiere (Address to the Economic and Social Council [ECOSOC], 4 July 1986).
43. "The Social Costs of Adjustment," *Africa Recovery* 3 (November 1984), 15.
44. See Giovanni Andrea Cornia, Richard Jolly, and Frances Stewart, eds., *Adjustment With a Human Face: Protecting the Vulnerable and Promoting Growth—A Study by UNICEF*, vol. 1 (Oxford: Clarendon Press, 1987). (Volume 2, published in 1988, is devoted to *Country Case Studies.*)
45. African Development Bank, United Nations Development Programme and the World Bank, *The Social Dimensions of Adjustment in Africa: A Policy Agenda* (Washington, DC: The World Bank, 1990).
46. For a discussion, see Richard Sandbrook, "Taming the African Leviathan," *World Policy Journal* (Fall 1990), 673-701.
47. See Economic Commission for Africa, *Economic Report on Africa 1990* (Addis Ababa, Ethiopia: ECA, April 1990); Adebayo Adedeji, *The African Alternative: Putting the People First* (Addis Ababa, Ethiopia: ECA, February 1990); and Economic Commission for Africa, *African Charter for Popular Participation in Development* (Addis Ababa, Ethiopia: ECA, 1990).
48. Economic Commission for Africa, *African Alternative Framework to Structural Adjustment Programmes for Socio-economic Recovery and Transformation* (Addis Ababa, Ethiopia: ECA, 1989), i.
49. Economic Commission for Africa, *African Charter for Popular Participation in Development*, (Addis Ababa, Ethiopia: ECA, 1990), 19.
50. "Tai Issues Report Card," *Newswatch* (20 August 1990), 23.
51. "Interview with Sam Aluko," *Quality* (27 September 1990), 33.
52. See "Man-made Drought, Man-made Hunger," *The Analyst* (Kaduna, Nigeria) 3, no. 2 (March-April, 1988); "The Food Crisis," *Newswatch* (13 March 1989); "Nigeria: Oil Rich, Poor People," *African Concord* 2, no. 18 (2 August 1988).
53. See Abdul Oroh, "Budget '89: Promises of More Pains—Dwindling Oil Fortunes, Naira Value, Paint a Gloomier Year," *The African Guardian* (12 December 1988) and "Nigeria: The Privatization Issue," *West Africa* (9 May 1988).
54. Manufacturers Association of Nigeria in *Business Concord* (12 December 1987), 1.
55. Dapo Fafowora cited in "Five Years of President Babangida's Rule: A Tortuous Journey," *West Africa* (27 August 1990).
56. Dotun Phillips, "Is Experience No Longer the Best Teacher?" *The Guardian* (29 April 1992).
57. Ironically, the panel concluded that the brain drain was good for Nigeria as those who have gone to other parts of the world are bound to bring in foreign exchange and new skills. But the immediate effects on the quality of teaching, research, and administration might negate such long-term expectations.
58. For a very pathetic account of the state of teaching, staffing, and research see Ebere Osieke, "Our Unfortunate Universities," *The Guardian* (4 July 1991). In this piece Osieke revealed that given the current exchange rate, "it will take a whole five and half months salary for a (full) professor to pay the return airfare to London,and there would be nothing left of the salaries." See also Emevwo Biakolo, "The Barracks and the Academy," *The Guardian* (10 November 1990) and his "Other Enemies of the University," *The Guardian* (17 November 1990) and Julius O. Ihonvbere, "The

State and Academic Freedom in Africa: How African Academics Subvert Academic Freedom—Notes from Nigeria" (Paper presented at the Annual Meeting of the African Studies Association, St. Louis, November 1991).

59. See Leke Salau, "ASUU's Litany of Demands," *Daily Champion* (24 July 1992) and "Trouble on the Academic Front: University Teachers Protest Poor Remuneration," *The African Guardian* (8 June 1992).
60. Omolara Ogundipe-Leslie, "Stories of Structural Adjustment: The Human Cost of SAP for Women" (Paper presented at the workshop on "Structural Adjustment and Prospects for Peace in Africa," Park Plaza Hotel, Toronto, October 1990), 9.
61. Ibid., 6.
62. Demola Abimboye, "And the SAP Song is Sad," *African Concord* (3 September 1990); "Ola's Ogre: Ola is One of Millions of City Slickers Who Find Life with SAP a Nightmare," *Africa Event* (October 1989).
63. Mokwugo Okoye, "Death of a Dream," *African Concord* (13 April 1992).
64. See "New Drug War," *Newswatch* (20 August 1990); "Nigeria: The New Rich . . . The Rising Cocaine Profile," *Thisweek* (2 April 1990); and "Nigeria: Britain Questions Drug Decree," *West Africa* (19-25 November 1990).
65. Godwin George-Iroro, "Vice and Visa—Britain Complains that Nigerians are Flooding into the Kingdom by All Means, Keeping the Anti-drug Squad Busy," *TELL* (7 October 1991).
66. "War Against Junkies," *Newswatch* (20 August 1990).
67. Godwin George-Iroro, "Vice and Visa," *TELL* (Lagos, Nigeria) (7 October 1991) and "New Drug War," *Newswatch* (10 August 1990).
68. See Arthur Nzeribe, *Nigeria: Seven Years After Shehu Shagari—Who Next?* (London: Kilimanjaro Publishing House, 1990). See also his other works: *Nigeria: Another Hope Betrayed* (1985); *Nigeria: The Turning Point* (1986); and *Nigeria: I Believe. A Manifesto for the Third Republic* (1988). These publications contain incredible revelations about corruption, mismanagement, and indiscipline in the Nigerian state and society.
69. Uwadiegwu Ogbonnaya, "Nigerians Have $33bn in Foreign Accounts," *National Concord* (16 August 1990).
70. See Pita Agbese and Julius O. Ihonvbere, *The State and the Politics of Structural Adjustment in Nigeria* (Forthcoming); Sully Abu, "Boy George," *The Guardian* (17 February 1991); "Who Will Probe Babangida?" *Newbreed* (1 October 1990); "Drops of Oil on Agreements: Idem Commission in Cross River State Uncovers Irregularities in Lease Agreement of Oil Palm Estates," *Newswatch* (11 June 1990); "Corruption a Nigerian?" *African Concord* (26 March 1990); "Why Governors are Corrupt: Madaki's Insider Account," *African Concord* (26 March 1990); "Million N Tenement Rate Ripoff in Ogun State—N4.4 million Involved," *Probe Magazine* (15 December 1988); "Battle of Nerves: Ex-Governor of Anambra State Locked in a Dispute with Incumbent over Land," *African Concord* (6 August 1990); "An Era of Scandals," *African Concord* (11 February 1991); "The Boats George Bought," *African Concord* (11 February 1991); "The Sack of Sirajo," *African Concord* (6 August 1990); "Nigeria: Fake Debt," *West Africa* (7-13 January 1991); "A Hundred Million Naira Riddle," *African Concord* (18 June 1990); and "Nigeria: 1992—Nzeribe's Fears," *African Concord* (24 September 1990).
71. See "Down Goes the Naira," *Newswatch* (1 October 1990).
72. See Ademola Oguntayo, "The Hard Times," *African Concord* (3 September 1990).

73. See Julius O. Ihonvbere and D. Iwarimie-Jaja, "The Political Economy of Mental Health in Nigeria: A Study of Port Harcourt," *Man and Life* 71, 18051-2 (January-June 1991) 41-64.
74. Mokwugo Okoye, "A Time of Sadness," *The African Guardian* (24 September 1990), 7.
75. Ademola Ogunlowo, *Sunday Concord* (Lagos, Nigeria) (30 September 1990), 37.
76. Mokwugo Okoye, "Abolishing Poverty," *The African Guardian* (2 December 1991), 41.
77. Ibid.
78. Adeotun Phillips, *Economic Impact of Nigeria's Structural Adjustment Programme* (Ibadan, Nigeria: Nigerian Institute for Social and Economic Research, 1990), 3.
79. "Between Dream and Reality," *The African Guardian* (2 December 1991) 28.
80. Ibid., 28-29.
81. See "We Are Behaving Like Father Christmas," *TELL* (7 October 1991). In this interview with Sam Aluko, one of the country's leading economists, he complained that "in a country where 60 per cent of the population cannot produce enough food for us, you are wasting money on sports."
82. Cited in Ademola Oguntayo, "The Hard Times," 46.
83. Onome Osifo-Whiskey, "Workers and the Ravages of SAP," 34.
84. Ibid., 35.
85. See Joy Akanwa, "All these 'Suffer Suffer'," *TELL* (7 October 1991). See also Robert Oteniya, "Unequal Rewards of Freedom," *TELL* (7 October 1991); Samson Makinde, "No Independence Yet," *TELL* (7 October 1991); and Ayo Ajayi, "Inflation, Starvatioon, Oppression," in *TELL* (7 October 1991).
86. Joy Akanwa, "All These 'Suffer Suffer'," *TELL* (7 October 1991).
87. Ibid.
88. *Africa Events* (October 1990), 29.
89. Ibid.
90. See Jato Thompson, "Corruption the Trigger," *New African* (June 1990); "Who Will Probe Babangida?" *Newbreed* (Lagos, Nigeria) (1 October 1990); and "Some People Have Money Like Sand," *The Analyst* 2, no. 1 (1987).
91. General Olusegun Obasanjo, "The Nigerian Society and the Third Republic," *The Guardian* (14 March 1992). See also his "Our Situation is Desperate," *TELL* (23 March 1992).
92. Jato Thompson, "Corruption: A Trigger," *New African* (June 1990), 12.
93. In 1991 the Babangida regime formally rehabilitated all the military officers who had been probed, found guilty of corruption, and "dismissed with ignominy" from the armed forces by the Murtala Muhammed regime in 1976. As well, for the first time in the country's military history, retired military officers were promoted to higher ranks in the armed forces.
94. "Five Years of Strangulation," *Newbreed* (1 October 1990), 35.
95. Ibid.
96. World Bank, *Sub-Saharan Africa: From Crisis to Sustainable Growth*, 5.
97. "Nigeria's Debt Dilemma: Searching for Solutions," *West Africa* (26 November -2 December 1990).
98. See "Investment in Nigeria: Open Door Policy," *West Africa* (3-9 December 1990).
99. Ibid.
100. *The Europa World Yearbook 1990 Volume II* (London: Europa Publishing Limited, 1990), 1938.

101. Thomas Adejo, "13,767 Nigerians Seek Asylum in Germany," *National Concord* (16 June 1992).
102. See Julius O. Ihonvbere, "Structural Adjustment, the April 1990 Coup and Democratization in Nigeria" (Paper presented at the 33rd Annual Meeting of the African Studies Association, Baltimore, 1-4 November 1990).
103. See Pita Agbese, "The Military and the Privatization of Repression in Nigeria," *Conflict* 10 (1990), 239-66 and his "The Political Economy of Militarization in Nigeria," *Afrika Spectrum* 3 (1990), 293-311 see also his "Defense Expenditures and Private Capital Accumulation in Nigeria," *Journal of Asian and African Studies* 23, nos. 3-4 (1988), 270-86; and "Demilitarization and Prospects for Democracy in Nigeria," *Bulletin of Peace Proposals* 22, no. 3 (1991), 315-27.
104. See Pita Agbese, "The Impending Demise of Nigeria's Forthcoming Third Republic," *Africa Today* 37, no. 3 (1990), 23-44.
105. Adebayo Adedeji, Foreword to *The African Alternative Framework to Structural Adjustment Programmes for Socio-Economic Recovery and Transformation* (Addis Ababa, Ethiopia: ECA, 1989), iii.
106. Olusegun Obasanjo, "The Nigerian Society."
107. Ben Olawunmi, cited in Femi Macaulay and Funso Ogunlade, "Winners and Losers," *African Concord* (3 September 1990).
108. Sam Aluko cited in "The Scramble for Alternatives," *Newswatch* (24 July 1989).
109. See *The Economy: Big Threat to 3rd Republic*, *TELL* (Lagos, Nigeria) 26 (7 October 1991).
110. See Economic Commission for Africa, *African Alternative Framework to Structural Adjustment Programme (AAF-SAP)* (Addis Ababa, Ethiopia: ECA, 1986) and *African Charter for Popular Participation in Development* (Addis Ababa, Ethiopia: ECA, 1990); Organization of African Unity, *Lagos Plan of Action for the Economic Development of Africa, 1980–2000* (Geneva: Institute for Labour Studies, 1981); and World Bank, *Sub-Saharan Africa: From Crisis to Sustainable Growth—A Long Term Perspective Study* (Washington, DC: World Bank, 1989).

5

Transition to Democracy or Transition to Civilian Rule? Democratization under Difficult Conditions in Nigeria

It is unfortunate that the parties have been demonstrating a crass inability to rise above pettiness and narrow mindedness by failing to maintain neutrality and ensure justice and fairness among their members. Furthermore, if justice and fairness are not allowed to pervade the conduct of intra-party affairs, what hope is there that the new breed of operators will not subvert the apparatus of government to their private ends if and when they finally accede to power?[1]

With huge external and internal debts, a collapsed naira and high inflation, the economy, which many experts say is in shambles, may sound the death knell for the next civilian regime.[2]

The new breed politicians do not have our mandate to kill the Third Republic.[3]

Nigeria is once again organizing a transition to democratic rule. This will be the second democratic experiment organized by the military in the country's political history. The first republic was unceremoniously terminated by the military in January 1966. This was followed by thirteen years of military dictatorship.[4] The first experiment with returning the country to democratic rule, which was inaugurated in October 1979, was again terminated in December 1983. Since then, Nigeria has been under military rule. Since 1983, the country has experienced one successful coup and two unsuccessful coups.[5] There have of course been several rumored coups in the country.

The reasons for military intervention in politics are varied and have been explored elsewhere.[6] Beyond institutional and personal factors, we can identify, at least in the Nigerian case, the weakness and limited legitimacy of the postcolonial state; the factionalization and fractionalization of the dominant classes; ethnic, regional, and religious pressures and contradictions; mismanagement, indiscipline, and massive corruption among politicians; political manipulation, violence, thuggery, and corruption; the contradictions of underdevelopment and dependence; the marginalization, impoverishment, and pauperization of nonbourgeois forces; and vulnerability to external manipulation. Yet, military intervention in Nigerian politics and the suffocation of civil society must be seen as part of the ongoing class struggles in the country and the efforts by the bourgeoisie to hold on to state power and build some degree of hegemony.[7]

After seizing power, the military in Nigeria has found it necessary to announce a date for disengagement from politics and the transfer of power to civilians. Thus, following the first coup in January 1966, Major Chukwuma Kaduna Nzeogwu announced that "neither myself nor any of the other lads was in the least interested in governing the country. We are soldiers and not politicians. . . . We were going to make civilians of proven honesty and efficiency who would be thoroughly hand picked to do all the governing."[8] In the quest for legitimacy, Major-General J. T. U. Aguyi-Ironsi, who maneuvered Nzeogwu out of power, equally declared on coming to power that "the military has no political affiliation or ambition, it has no desire to prolong its interim administration of government longer than necessary for the orderly transition of the country to the type of government desired by the people."[9]

Following the successful prosecution of the three-year civil war, 1967–1970, Yakubu Gowon declared a nine-point program that was to culminate in the hand-over of power to elected civilians in October 1976. When he reneged on this promise in 1975, he was overthrown. General Murtala Muhammed, who took over the realms of power, promptly promised to return the country to democratic rule in 1979 when he declared that "the present military leadership does not intend to stay in office a day longer than is necessary, and certainly not beyond this date (of October 1979)."[10] His assassination by Colonel Suka Buka Dimka in February 1976 did not change the commitment to the transition to civil rule by that date and General Olusegun Obasanjo succeeded in making that transition in October 1979.

The civilian administration under Alhaji Shehu Shagari barely lasted for three years. Generals Tunde Idiagbon and Muhammadu Buhari, who organized the termination of the second republic, had little time for organizing transitions, though they continued to regard their regime as a "corrective" one. General Ibrahim Babangida, who overthrew the Buhari/Idiagbon regime in a palace coup in August 1985, declared immediately that his "administration will not stay a day longer than is absolutely necessary."[11] It immediately put in place a transition program that was initially planned to culminate in a transfer of power to civilians in 1990, but was later shifted to October 1992, then to January 1993, later to August 1993, and now postponed indefinately following the June 1993 presidential elections. In spite of two attempted coups in 1987 and 1990, several religious, ethnic, and student riots, numerous strike actions by workers, and political opposition to the implementation of structural adjustment program, the regime has so far stuck to the transition program.[12]

The rest of this chapter will examine the dynamics and contradictions of Nigeria's transition program with particular attention to the structures and institutions put in place as well as the overall "environment" of the transition to civil rule being organized by the military.

Structural Reforms in the Transition to Democracy

The structural and institutional reforms toward the transition to the Third Republic began in 1986 with the adoption of a World Bank Structural Adjustment Program (SAP) (see chapter 4). The military regime was convinced that a successful political transition to the Third Republic would be jeopardized in the context of deepening economic crisis and recurring political upheavals. Policies of devaluation, desubsidization, liberalization, retrenchment, privatization, and deregulation were expected to put the economy back on the path to recovery. As General Babangida put it in his 1986 Budget Speech:

> An important lesson of historical experience is that structural adjustment is a very painful process, particularly for a country which had not laid the appropriate foundation for self-reliance. It is therefore important not to postpone the painful corrective measures, because delays can only intensify the consequential hardships. . . . Our structural adjustment involves new uses of wealth, new property relations, new products and new production processes, new attitudes to work, new consumption habits and new interactions with the rest of the world.

The achievements in these areas have already been discussed elsewhere (see chapter 4). Suffice it to note here that achievements have been very limited. As we noted in the previous chapter, corruption has reached new heights, mismanagement and waste continue as usual, the foreign debt profile has more than doubled in less than five years, reaching $35 billion at the end of 1992, and general disillusionment, marginalization of the poor, and cynicism have come to characterize the Nigerian society. Investors have not been attracted, the rural areas remain neglected, local entrepreneurs find it difficult to compete in the context of massive devaluation, trade liberalization, and eroded purchasing power of workers and peasants. Religious and ethnic riots have reached unprecedented proportions and once again, reminiscent of the era just before the civil war, 1967–70, southerners are moving back from the north because of the frequent massacres and government inability (disinterest) in punishing the culprits and maintaining law and order. The air is rendered with cynicism, frustration, greed, corruption, distrust, antagonisms, and deep-rooted opposition to the state's agents and institutions.

In terms of the political and institutional programs, the regime anchored its transition program on four main policies: first, massive financial commitments in order to prevent the transition program from being hijacked by the so-called moneybags; second, the deliberate nurturing of a so-called new breed of politicians who are young, honest, patriotic, and relatively new to the political field; third, the establishment of institutions covering virtually all aspects of the transition process in order to maintain effective control on the formation of political parties, patterns of mobilization, fund raising, and alliances; and fourth, the manipulation, harassment, and domestication of popular and opposition forces through the control of the working classes, incorporation of the left, and prohibition of certain interest groups from participating in the transition process.

Unfortunately, these policies and steps to democratization are not as smooth and well laid out as they might appear. The regime has unilaterally tinkered and tampered with the transition program forty times, at times in direct contravention of its own decrees, to such an extent, that Nigerians really have no idea as to what constitutes an offense against promulgated decrees or what to expect the next day. Today, the government will ban former politicians from politics. The next day they are unbanned. Today, the government will announce that it will not tolerate demands for new states. The next day, nine new states and more local governments will be created. Today, the government will announce its preparedness to sponsor its own two political parties. The next day, it will announce its decision to withdraw support from the parties. The list of inconsistencies can go on and on. Let us, however, examine core policies of the government in the transition program. It should be borne in mind always that these so-called changes are taking place in the context of the painful adjustment program discussed in chapter 4.

Containing the "Moneybags" in the Transition Process

The Babangida regime had no illusions about the role of money in Nigerian politics. Politics in Nigeria has historically been an investment, a business into which someone invested heavily in order to reap huge rewards through access to state power and the control of public funds. The regime, therefore, decided to take the place of money and the place of the bourgeois class in the political transition process. Consequently, after refusing to recognize independently formed political parties and creating its own two political parties (see below), the regime expended millions of naira in the construction of party headquarters in all twenty-one state capitals at a cost of N10.6 million each. It cost the government N1.3 million to construct each party office in the four hundred fifty-three local governments in the country. With the creation of nine new states and forty-seven new local government areas in August 1991, the country now has thirty states and five hundred local governments. The government spent N100 million to construct party headquarters at Abuja, the new the federal capital. It also sponsored all delegates to the national convention of the parties. Thus, each of the 5,876 delegates of the two parties that attended the conventions at Abuja received an allowance of N2000.00 each to cover transportation, food, and accommodation. The registration of members into the two government-created political parties cost the country N44 million. The regime advanced N269.9 million to each of the political parties "to fight the electoral battles." The guidelines for expending the allocations was as follows: N202.6 million for staff salaries at the 5,575 wards, N20.5 million at the local government level, N1.4 million at the state level and Federal Capital Territory (FCT), and N600,000 at the national level. The parties were expected by government to spend N60 million for vehicles and N67.5 million each on office furnishings and campaign expenses in three months, October to December 1990.

The above was just the tip of the iceberg. Financial commitments to setting up the offices of the National Electoral Commission (NEC) also ran into hundreds of millions of naira. Acquisition, furnishing, and running costs for NEC offices in the state capitals and local government offices has been estimated so far at between N150 million and N200 million. Allocation to the NEC in 1988 was N40 million. The same amount was allocated in 1989 and in 1990 its allocation increased to N64 million. The NEC spent N16 million on administration in its first four months of existence in 1987; it spent N100 million organizing the 1987 local government elections and over N500 million organizing the 1990 local government elections. The NEC claimed that this huge sum of N500 million was spent on the construction of 200,000 polling booths at a cost of N500 each. These were actually rickety structures erected with sticks and palm fronds and a few constructed with zinc. The contracts went to politicians and persons, especially women, connected to military governors, chairmen of local governments, and prominent businesspersons. It plans to spend about N2.5 billion on conducting all elections scheduled for 1990–93.

Since Nigeria never had a reliable population count, it was decided that as part of the transition program there should be a national census in November 1991. Like other institutions connected to the transition program, the bottom line of its operations has been huge financial expenditures. In 1988, N5,871,880 was allocated to the National Population Commission (NPC). This increased to N10,423,640 in 1989 and to N47,437,290 in 1990. It is estimated that by the end of the transition program, the NPC would have spent about N2.5 billion. The NPC and the government, in order to justify the huge expenditures, have created the impression that the problems with previous failed attempts at a national census was ignorance and illiteracy rather than excessive politicization as a result of linking population directly to revenue allocation from the federal government. Like Sam Aluko has rightly argued, population should be linked to taxation, so if a region or state or ethnic group inflates its population, it would be bound to collect taxes from the number of registered adults and it would be accountable to the federal government for the specified amount derivable from its inflated population.[13]

The government also created the Directorate for Mass Mobilisation for Social Justice and Economic Recovery (MAMSER) with the sole objective of mobilizing Nigerians in support of the transition program. Of course the MAMSER has nothing to do with "social justice" or "economic recovery" no matter how much the officials and the government might wish to delude themselves. In fact, MAMSER is really not sure as to what its purpose is. It is involved in monitoring elections, just like the police, the army, and the NEC. It is involved in mass mobilization just like the Federal Ministry of Information and the Directorate for Food, Roads, and Rural Infrastructure. It is involved in political education, just like the NEC and the Centre for Democratic Studies (CDS). The list of duplication can go on and on. Again, huge financial expenditure has been the main operative factor in the activities of MAMSER. In its first two years of operation, 1987 and 1988, it received an annual allocation of N500 million. Between 1990 and 1992, it is expected to spend about N2 billion. In spite of vitriolic and suffocating propaganda and self-praise, MAMSER has not made a dent in the attitudes of Nigerians who see it generally as a diversion, a waste of money, and irrelevant to the concrete issues of oppression, deprivation, poverty, and gross inequalities in the Nigerian society.

The Constitution Drafting Committee (CDC), set up in 1987 to fashion out a new constitution for the country, as well as the Political Bureau, which had been set up to harness the views of Nigerians on the country's political future, spent N5 million. The Constituent Assembly, which was set up in 1988 to put final touches on the recommendations of the CDC, cost the nation N145 million. The above does not include expenditures by the police, security services, the presidency, local governments, state governors, and the Transition Tribunals and Monitoring Committee on matters directly and/or indirectly related to the transition to civil rule. Military governors all made a show of donating money, vehicles, offices, and materials to institutions connected with the transition all in the effort to convince the populace that the regime's commitment to the democratization process was unshakable. For instance, each of the then twenty-one state governments as well as the federal capital territory in Abuja received "a government grant of N2 million" during the registration of members into the two government-created political parties. In February 1990, again, each state government received N20 million from the federal government to "supplement" their efforts in the transition program in undefined directions.

While the sole rationale for these and other visible and invisible expenditures by the military regime was to prevent the political processes from being taken over by the rich and powerful in society, it is doubtful that it has succeeded. In fact, while pretending to be interested in keeping the moneybags from dominating the political processes, the regime actually strengthened their role and participation in the political processes by preventing labor, students, radical intellectuals, and other popular organizations from participating in the political transition program. It is precisely this restriction on these groups that has enabled persons like Chief Arthur Nzeribe, Chief Onwuka Kalu, Chief Gabriel Igbinedion, Major-General (rtd.) Shehu Yar Adua, Chief Emmanuel Iwuanyawu, Chief Abel Ubeku, Alhaji Lema Jibrilu, Olu Falae, Olayiwola Balogun, Umaru Shinkafi, Major-General (rtd.) Agbazika Innih, Chief Ifeanyichukwu Okonkwo, and other businesspersons, retired military officers, and traditional chiefs, with no political credentials or records to show, to dominate the political process. The only qualification they have to play these leading roles is their wealth.

In fact, it can be asserted that the Babangida regime has ruined the country's political transition process by introducing the use of money as a major determining factor. The government has erroneously equated the ability to maintain stability and ensure rational politics with the infusion of money into the polity. By taking the place of the rich in the political process, it has promoted corruption and instability as politicians, chiefs, retired military officers, contractors, opportunists, and hangers-on struggle to allocate huge sums of money to the various departments, panels, boards, and countless directorates established by the regime. Tony Momoh, minister for information till his removal in 1990, had defended the huge expenditures on the grounds that it was the only option available to government:

> [Democracy] is not as expensive as people are thinking in relation to the alternative. The alternative is allowing one man to dictate to the whole Nigeria because you don't want it to be expensive. If money is not spent on democracy and a one-man dictatorship emerges . . . it is the same Nigerians who are talking of expensiveness now that will shout that one man is a dictator.[14]

But the regime has not been able to show, in spite of the billions it has pumped into the society, that the influence of money and of "moneybags" has been reduced in any way. Politicians and business persons who were banned from the transition process continued to sponsor political parties, political organizations, and to influence the content and direction of politics. Mokwugo Okoye, reflecting on the nature of current politicking in the country, lamented recently that "politics isn't what it used to be. Looking at politics, from the local government elections, through the state assembly to the gubernatorial elections the key issue was money. . . . It's sad that the issue in Nigeria should be that the highest bidder wins election."[15] In fact, given the degree of mass poverty in the nation today, largely accentuated by the structural adjustment program, Nigerians have become more vulnerable to the influence of money and the so-called moneybags. What the regime has done is to overlook deeper contradictions and the *real* reasons why money has always played a major influence in political competitions. It constructed its straw "moneybag" in order to provide a justification for using the transition program as an excuse to divert public funds to politicians, retired military officers, contractors, and all sorts of petty businesspersons.

In spite of the obvious failure of this "money tactic," the regime has moved to congratulate itself. As General Babangida bragged in a nationwide broadcast on 27 August 1990:

> We have expended an enormous amount of public funds, time, and energy on this program. We fostered the two political parties and during this period, this administration spent a substantial amount of public funds to build party offices and to conduct all the elections to party offices. We believe that the funds were well spent because we are engaged in building fundamental infrastructures for a stable democratic system in the Third Republic. This is the first time since independence from colonial rule that any government has invested heavily and purposefully in the development of democracy and political institutions.[16]

The realities on ground in Nigeria do not support Babangida's claims. At every level money has remained a major, if not the only, factor. Though Decree No. 27 of 1987 banned "old" politicians and certain categories of other Nigerians from participating in politics during the transition period, the banned politicians and retired generals remained visible and very active participants in the political processes. The ban on the old politicians was lifted in December 1991 (see next section).

Available evidence from Nigeria shows clearly that the political stakes have never been higher. Money is still the name of the game. Politics has nothing to do with mobilization, education, rational debates, and the selection of the best candidates for political office. The Babangida regime, by pouring billions of naira into the system in the name of taking the place of the moneybags, by condoning corruption, by lifting the ban on the wealthy old politicians, and by restricting the initial political campaigns to retired generals, millionaires, and traditional rulers, has increased the role of money in Nigerian politics. Let us support this position by referring to some on-the-spot reports from Nigeria. In an extensive report on political developments in Bendel State, Akpo Esajere, of the influential *Guardian* newspaper, noted that

> a Benin multi-millionaire . . . arrived at the polling centres [during the ward elections] of his party with "bags of crisp naira notes" and started an elaborate display with money, announcing: "N100 for one vote." Queues which had formed behind some candidates disintegrated as electors openly and shamelessly switched over to the queues of candidates sponsored by the millionaire. During the June party local government congresses the same millionaire was said to have single-handedly installed more than a third of the members of the executive committee at that level in practically all the three local governments in Bendel North senatorial district. And during the state party congresses, the same millionaire was said to have engineered the installation of his faction as the state part executive committee. The faction was said to have made a clean sweep of the entire executive.[17]

At the national conventions of the two government-created political parties, which were sponsored by the government with the chief of general staff, Vice-Admiral Augustus Aikhomu (now serving as a retired civilian vice-president), in attendance, money changed hands right in his presence on the convention floor as politicians made deals, bought votes, and secured the support of their supporters. In a report by a team sent to the conventions by *Newbreed Magazine*, it was revealed that the convention was run to the dictates and interests of the moneybags. A candidate for the chairmanship of one of the parties confessed that at least "N1 million was spent to 'wet the ground' for his candidature." Another candidate "swore that he spent over N2 million in his own preparation, and in certain cases, he had to pay two delegates from Akwa Ibom a sum of N12,000 each to secure for him nominations."[18] Babafemi Ojudu, who covered the conventions for *African Concord*, reported that the election of Tom Ikimi as chairman of the National Republican Convention (NRC) raised "suspicions that the evils of Nigeria's political past . . . money, blackmail and ethnic nationalism . . . may still be at play." As Ojudu noted, the "bigger cheque won the day" at the conventions as "victory came not only through hard work but what was suspected to be some not-so-hidden powerful hands laden with money." Furthermore,

> in both parties, it appeared the two major factors for victory or defeat in the elections were money and ethnic considerations. Some delegates owed allegiance to some

> candidates because they were ferried to the convention, housed and fed by some candidates. In spite of the N2,000 allowance doled out to each delegate by the Federal Government, most delegates were still beholden to wealthy delegates from whom they could make some money.[19]

Finally, in a special report in *Newbreed*, the Nigerian transition program was described as "the costliest exercise in restoration of democracy ever undertaken anywhere in the world."[20] The report contended that though the government thinks it is promoting grassroots politics, "what is actually on the ground is politics of millionaires and multi-millionaires who buy votes, who would buy party and political offices."[21] Nigeria's leading news magazine, *Newswatch*, reported that during the convention of the NRC, some heads of delegations "paid huge sums of money, ranging from N200,000 to N250,000" to buy votes for certain candidates.[22] Ray Ekpu, one of Nigeria's most credible and leading journalists, revealed recently that at the national conventions of the two parties, "Money—and this includes dollars and pound sterling—changed pockets. Votes were freely auctioned at N1000 or $100 per piece and many of the voters who were carted in mammy wagons from their villages to Abuja smiled home with bulging pockets. One more proof that politics, Nigerian politics, is a high interest-yielding investment."[23] Mokwugo Okoye argued recently that "despite the euphoria in certain quarters regarding the current programme of transition to civil rule in Nigeria, there seems to be an air of unreality about it all." Commenting specifically on the role of money and the rich in the transition program, Okoye noted that

> from all accounts, a majority of those who gathered at Abuja to choose national officers for the two parties were under the pressure of voodoo, money and sectionalism that must have made it impossible for them to exercise their franchise with freedom, a sense of responsibility and full knowledge of what they were doing. . . . Apart from the fear that a cynical, cunning and invisible minority has been able to manipulate the two party congresses to elect the kind of people who would not disturb the old balance of power in the country—and thus give one the impression that they were 'fronting' for some sinister forces we do not know but who obviously intend to replace our traditional *participant* for a *subject-parochial culture* that promises years of instability and exploitation—the strategic objective was classical: everything seemed to have been sacrificed on the alter of ethnicity and religion, *with money-laundering made to disguise the vicious power-play that guided the decisions as to who shall get what, when and how.*[24]

The wealthy in Nigeria continue to "invest" in politics, and such "investments" often lead to political manipulation, political intolerance, and a determination to win elections at all costs. When the government decided suddenly to withdraw its funding of both political parties in January 1991, it was like handing the parties directly to the wealthy since politics in Nigeria always translated into money and the political process up to that moment had been dictated by the exchange of money for votes and positions. As Gani Fawehinmi noted, the lifting of the ban on old politicians shows that the military has no idea of what democracy means; it is arbitrary in its policies and has an agenda unknown to Nigerians because "for five years, Babangida launched a vicious attack against money-bags only to do a U-turn midstream before crucial elections into the state and federal offices."[25] Ojo Maduekwe, the special adviser to the national chairman of the Social Democratic Party, was clear on the implications of the lifting of the ban when he noted that "the withdrawal of funds is like cutting off oxygen from the political parties." Chief Abel Ubeku, a frontline member of the SDP, was even more categorical in noting that the action "will take us back to the politics of the first and second republics because only those who can pay the piper will be able to dictate the tune."[26] What is more, since both parties were created they have been rocked with allegations and counterallegations of bribery, corruption, and the commitment to use money in buying electoral officers, the electorate, and the security officers.

After the primaries for election of gubernatorial candidates by both parties, the chairman of the National Electoral Commission made a nationwide broadcast that showed very clearly that nothing had changed in the content and context of Nigerian politics. He showed that all the vices that had ruined the first and second republics were still very much around and that they had become even more sophisticated and widespread. Among the malpractices perpetrated by the politicians were, in the words of Humphrey Nwosu, NEC's chairman, "blatant corruption and inducement of voters. Instances of bribery involving the use of money to buy votes even right at the polling centres were reported from many parts of the country. Other inducements used by the candidates included provisions of food, drinks and the transportatation of voters to polling centres."[27] In fact, before the election of governors, newspapers were full of paid advertisements containing information on how the use of money influenced the so-called grass-roots delegates and how so many invisible hands directed the campaigns of some candidates and the voting behavior of delegates.[28] The general view about the role of money in

Nigerian politics is that "there is no future for democracy in Nigeria. Money is what speaks. No one cares how you made the money. Even if you just got out of jail, once you have the money, you can aspire to be the President. With the state so corrupt and with criminals of yesterday being honoured by government, what else can we expect? To tell you the truth, we are just wasting our time and money."[29] After these examples from the field of politics in Nigeria, there is not much to be said beyond reiterating the fact that the Babangida regime has not in any way reduced the influence of money in Nigerian politics.

Creating and Nurturing New Breed Politicians: The Magic Makers

Since the Babangida regime had reached the conclusion that the rich and the old politicians were the roots of political corruption, intolerance, and instability in Nigeria, it promulgated Decree No. 25 of 1987, which specifically banned old politicians and other categories of Nigerians from participating in the political transition process. They were, through this decree, prohibited from holding party offices, joining political parties, and contesting for any political positions. The decree also banned those who had been dismissed from their positions, found guilty of corruption through a probe, or found guilty of other official crimes, from participating in politics, holding public offices, and contesting for any positions for the rest of their lives. Politicians of the first and second republics as well as military and police officers who had occupied specified positions were also disqualified from participating in politics during the transition process but could do so after the inauguration of the Third Republic.[30]

The regime did not stop there. It announced that religious and ideological "extremists" were also prohibited from participating in the transition program. The president was against ideological and religious extremists because "they go beyond propriety to advance their cause and they exceed the expected limit of decency in doing that." In any case, according to Babangida's reasoning, these "extremist" organizations and individuals "are not democratic."[31] Though Babangida and his associates have never been able to categorically identify those referred to as extremists and though no political instrument has been enacted to prohibit their participation in politics, it is known that "extremist" is used to refer to the labor unions, the civil liberty organizations, social critics, radical intellectuals, militant student unions, and all those who refuse to buy the faulty economic logic of the government as well as its condonement of corruption, human rights abuses, waste, and misplaced priorities. All those who opposed the IMF and World Bank loans and conditionalities, those who were against the manipulation of the transition program, those who refused to join the government in its diversionary program of government by panels and parastatals, and those who took resolute stands against the abuse of the judicial process, policy inconsistency, and widespread corruption have been branded "extremist" by the regime. On the religious side, the government has been unable to identify the religious extremists. It has taken very little or no steps against Muslim fundamentalists and fanatics who have massacred hundreds of Christians in several parts of the north. It even appointed a self-declared extremist, Alhaji Sani Kotangora, who established a magazine, *Hotline*, to advance the interest of the north and fight the south, into the Constituent Assembly. There is not one policy that demonstrates the government's interest to control religious extremism.[32] Rather, in several ways, such as the illegal and secret enrollment of Nigeria into the Organization of Islamic Conference (OIC), the regime showed its preparedness to condone religious extremism.

Having banned the "old brigade," the regime declared its support for a so-called new breed of politicians—not tainted by corruption, comparatively young, honest, patriotic, committed to new politics and a bright future. In order to facilitate the emergence and survival of this new breed, the government decided to set up several institutions and to pour billions of naira into the political process (see above). The regime also took steps to intimidate the extremists (see below), the old politicians, and other interest groups that did not share its vision of a bright political future dominated by these new breeds. So far, it is clear that, once again, the Babangida regime has misplaced its priorities and ignored the realities of Nigeria's political system. It has gone after the shadow, leaving the substance behind. It has wrongly diagnosed the problem by personalizing it and ignoring the structural and systemic causes of political corruption and instability in Nigeria.

Without changing the socioeconomic and ideological structure of Nigeria's political economy, the regime believed that it was possible to identify a so-called new breed, divorced from the old politicians, unexposed to the cutthroat and divisive nature of Nigerian politics, and uninfluenced by the corruption that pervades the system, and entrust to them the political future of the nation. As well, the regime felt that it could legally prohibit the influence of the old politicians from politics both directly and indirectly. Of course, it was completely wrong. When the ban on politics was lifted, virtually all the leading political associations were directly and/or indirectly created, funded, and manipulated by the old politicians. When Babangida decided not to recognize any of the political associations and created his own grass-roots political parties, the unrecognized associations simply moved into the two parties as blocs and took over. The old brigade influenced the political process, funded the new breed, and the latter consulted them on what to do and what not to do inspite of pronouncements from the government. It was clear that the government's ban was effective only superficially and that the content of the country's politics had not changed in any serious way.

The new breed was as corrupt, confused, ideologically barren, greedy, irresponsible, and even more cowardly than any other political group in the country. It relied on the manipulation of primordial loyalties, on money and political violence; it could not fashion out any credible political alternative; it avoided debates on critical national issues, was scared stiff of the military, swallowed hook, line, and sinker every pronouncement of the military, and relied heavily on all the tactics and strategies of the old brigade, only making them more sophisticated. Mokwugo Okoye has argued that, as for this new breed, "there's nothing new about them at all."[33] Yakubu Mohammed has also commented on the politics of Babangida's "new breed" politicians:

> In this new breed business, people get killed, houses get burnt down. Disturbing reports talk about bomb blasts at opponent's homes. They have become too negatively sophisticated, it is not a laughing matter. The violence in the second republic, which was one of the attractions for the return of the military, did not precede the elections and it was not on this scale though what happened in Ondo was a grotesque dramatisation of people's anger. This one, nobody knows what it is. A man was gunned down in Uyo . . . as opposing factions of NRC abandoned sweet reasonableness in favour of fist cuffs and guns. A man was killed in Okene, Kwara State, last year in a political clash . . . an SDP chieftain in Imo State was trailed from a hotel to his house and mowed down. . . . The new breed politicans do not have our mandate to kill the Third Republic.[34]

Mohammed draws attention to the "intolerance, the immaturity and the impetuousness of many of the so-called new breed politicians. Many of them, mere stooges of the older politicians operating behind the scene, have gone beyond their brief. Where the old politicians would settle for an eye for an eye, the new would go for the eye, the ear, the limbs and in most cases the whole body. Not satisfied, he would visit his wrath on other members of the family."[35]

The new breed has not demonstrated any awareness of changes going on in the world. They are largely ideologically barren and have been scared of straying away from the military regime's structural adjustment program even along the "new" lines advocated by the World Bank. The opportunism, cowardice, and shallowness of the new breed has become a major problem, in fact, an obstacle to the hopes of fashioning a new political environment and agenda for Nigeria's future. As Sully Abu has noted,

> It was bad enough that the familiar political actors, who if nothing else, had the courage of their convictions, all came under a blanket ban. Then the government decreed into existence two political parties which constitutions and symbols were similarly decreed. . . . Such outside intervention in a political process that ought to have some autonomy in order to be credible renders the political atmosphere unduly constraining. Indeed, the only real debate we have had so far was a sterile disputation about one party's foray into the other's exclusive preserve of right wing thinking. . . . Little wonder that cynicism and sheer opportunism inform the present political conduct of quite a number who have ambitions for office pitching their tent not with a political party that necessarily suit their temperament or ideological belief but which, it is perceived, is more likely to be forwarded by the military government.[36]

Abu argues that the political atmosphere has become "so barren of ideas and so bereft of debate or challenge to the present deliberate shift in the country's political and diplomatic posture" that the new breed "deserve all the contempt which their cold complicity invites."[37] The new breed has become so corrupt, irresponsible, and unimaginative that they have been nicknamed "magic makers" for their ability to twist reality, come up with unbelievable figures, and manipulate the electorate:

> Only last month (September 1991), . . . the new breed went through a controversial governorship primaries whose fall-outs have proved so mind-boggling that even the government itself appeared dazed and confused. Among the sharp practices of the newbreed politicians are: a horrendous inflation of votes; preparation of separate voters lists; falsification of election results; allowing underaged children to vote; refusal to supply electoral materials that may favour opposition candidates; harassment of candidates and their agents; abrupt shifting of voting venue; and outright cheating of voters. The new breed, foster children of a military age, are finding democracy irritating.[38]

The *African Concord*, in a comprehensive investigation of the politics of the new breed, revealed also that "in every instance of this fraud, the national and state secretariats of the parties have been very central as mechanisms of the political shame. Perhaps the most disturbing aspect of these developments, however, was evidence, too, that the new breed politicians, weaned within a military sensibility, also have contempt for the courts."[39] In an editorial, the influential *Guardian* newspaper chastized the new breed for its lack of direction, shallow politics, and lack of leadership:

> Since the transition programme started in earnest with the lifting of the ban on politics, we have been watching the performance of our newbreed politicians. We are particularly amazed at the too trusting, almost uncomplaining, even beggerly way they have been receiving the transition programme. Since they are going to administer the post-1992 republic, they have a primary responsibility to help shape the kind of world and system they would like to govern. But they are not doing this. They simply sit and let things happen to them instead of seeking to make things happen. They have become inglorious spectators in a show they are supposed to be major gladiators. How can any class of people be so unfair to themselves? The transition programme is a proposal from government, and it is passing through without any amendment precisely because the new breed have been less than courageous in their attitude to the transition project. They have lacked the courage to persuade the government to enter into public debate on a number of critical issues that would have consequences for the Third Republic.[40]

The editorial went on to note that the new breed politicians have "elevated money politics to a new height unattained before in the history of this country. It is ironic that this evil of money politics which the present regime has sought to excise from our body politic has, in fact, become the grease which oils the new breed political machine." As well, it noted that another negative contribution of the new breed is "their pre-occupation with the politics of sharing power and positions even before those positions are won. They have spent far too much time on ethnic and geographical calculations criteria for sharing power and positions that they have not found time to debate issues." The unfortunate conclusion is that a

> political class that lacks the courage to say its mind on crucial national issues must be a disappointment to the rest of the people it is going to lead. A political class which has no stomach for debates and arguments about national issues probably does not have ideas about governance of its society. A political class which is pre-occupied with sharing power is not likely to know what to do with power when it comes. And a political class for whom money is everything probably does not have any principles in which it believes.[41]

After the "magic makers" gave the government and the public a taste of their art before, during, and after the primaries between September and December 1991, the Nigerian government openly chastised the parties and the new breed. The vice president, Admiral Augustus Aikhomu (rtd.), expressed the government's "disappointment at these strange deeds of the new breed." He catalogued "a long list of irregularities" within the parties which he said "threatened democracy" and agreed with the public that the "irregularities and malpractices of the political process do not augur well for sustenance of democracy in the Third Republic."[42] This looked like a much belated recognition of the mistake by the government, which cannot claim that it was never alerted to these possibilities by the "extremists" in the past. As the *African Concord* noted on this issue, "Government's indictment of its political wards in the heat of the protests arising from the primaries has been seen in political quarters as a vote of no confidence in the new political class, a sense of bewilderment about prodigal sons whose bizarre acts of electoral fraud and roguery have surpassed anything that the old brigade had attempted."[43] Under these conditions in which indicators of "rancorous spirit in politics litter the national landscape especially in terms of the violence it engenders,"[44] it is easy to appreciate Obinna Ayadike's view:

> Ideologically, the SDP and NRC are practically indistinguishable . . . the acquiescence of the parties to the government's wishes has earned them the title of the Yes Party and Yes, Sir Party (in the case of the NRC, which is seen as the government's favorite). The willingness of the politicians to compete on the government's terms has confirmed, for the habitually cynical Nigerian, their opportunism. Ethnicity and religion rather than ideology are the nation's basic political building blocs. . . . The transition program hangs on the emergence of the "new breed." But to most Nigerians, they look very much like the old breed, and a good deal less charismatic. As one leading businessman and former politician scathingly observed: "I'll tell you what the Nigerian new breed is. He is 60 years old, he is a known crook and vagabond, he has no background, he is a wheeler-dealer, and he is a politician. Ever since independence he has been going for election and losing. His people never wanted him in office and he has never served. Today he is a new breed." The "new breed" have also demonstrated a disturbing willingness to jump through whatever hoop the government puts before them.[45]

It is clear from the analyses thus far that the strategy of creating and nurturing a new breed of politicians without creating a new socioeconomic system and without altering existing unequal and ruthlessly exploitative relations of politics, power, production, and exchange has failed woefully just like the strategy of containing the moneybags. As demonstration of this failure, and after expending billions of naira in an era of structural adjustment, the Babangida regime, in December 1991, lifted the ban on old politicians. The process of their reentry into the political process, efforts to reestablish their influence and authority, struggles to displace the new breed and bring them under control, and the desire to recoup their "investments" are creating monumental contradictions and pressures in the political process. It was not surprising, therefore, when, in August 1992, the military regime unilaterally canceled the results of the presidential primaries held by its two foster political parties for gross irregularities, rigging, manipulations, and a total negation of all known principles of democracy.

Restructuring Political Institutions

The third major policy of the regime, in terms of guiding the transition program along lines mapped out by the government, is the creation of specific institutions that are supposed to help mobilize and educate the people in support of the transition program. The belief of the regime was that with institutions covering virtually every aspect of the transition process there was no way it would not be able to keep politicians under control, manipulate public opinion, mobilize the populace, encourage the cultivation of democratic practices and attitudes and lay a solid foundation for the Third Republic. The Babangida regime had in fact promised, while lifting the ban on politics, that it "will watch every step, monitor every move, and follow to ensure that everything is done according to the rule of the game."[46] In line with this belief the following institutions have been created: (1) the Political Bureau to conduct and monitor a national debate on the country's political future; (2) the National Electoral Commission (NEC), which is in charge of conducting all elections, the registration of voters, clearance of political aspirants, and political education; (3) the Constitution Drafting Committee (CDC), which looked into the 1979 constitution and made initial recommendations for the 1990 constitution; (4) more states in 1987—Akwa Ibom in the south and Katsina in the north—and in 1991—Kebbi, Jigawa, Yobe, Taraba, Abia, Anambra, Delta, Kogi, and Osun—to ease ethnic and religious tensions, respond to the calls for more states, reassure some minorities, divert attention from the failings of government, and reduce some pressures on the Third Republic; (5) local government reforms and additional local governments, again to ease local political pressures and open up additional political opportunities;[47] (6) the Directorate for Food, Roads and Rural Infrastructure (DFRRI), to mobilize rural dwellers, provide infrastructures and facilities to the rural areas, and stimulate rural productivity; (7) the Directorate of Mass Mobilization for Social Justice and Economic Recovery (MAMSER), to mobilize Nigerians in support of the transition program through public political education; (8) the Transition to Civil Rule Tribunal, to handle matters arising from the political processes as they affect political aspirants; (9) the Centre for Democratic Studies (CDS), to contribute to the task of mobilizing Nigerians and inculcating democratic attitudes in the people and promoting political education for politicians and public servants; (10) the National Population Council (NPC); (11) the Code of Conduct Bureau; (12) the Code of Conduct Tribunal; (13) the National Commission on Women; (14) the National Planning Commission; (15) the Better Life for Rural Women Programme (BLP); and (16) the National Revenue Mobilization Commission. In place of Shagari's Ethical Revolution and Buhari's War Against Indiscipline (WAI), the Babangida regime introduced the National Orientation Movement (NOM) to contribute to the task of sanitizing the morals of Nigerians. It also set up a Directorate for Movement to Abuja, the new federal capital, with a director-general responsible to the presidency. The regime also put in place an Armed Forces Consultative Assembly (AFCA) comprised of military officers in the middle ranks. This assembly was expected to serve as a forum for buying the support of the officers and thus checking military coups.

These organizations and several others have not made much of a difference to the transition program for several reasons. In the first place, they duplicate one another in several ways. The NEC and the Transition Tribunal have had conflicts with MAMSER. There have been confusing interpretations of the constitution, power struggles, and competition for publicity and access to the presidency. For instance, the NEC and the CDS had announced that no court injunction would stop governorship elections after many candidates felt they had been cheated during the primaries and had gone to court to seek such injunctions. The MAMSER, on the other hand, insisted that the court injunctions must be respected. Though the NEC was later to change its position following public criticisms, it was clear that there was not one organization with clear mandate to speak on the transition program. Second, these organizations and institutions were largely grafted on a sea of cynicism, alienation, distrust, and corruption. Not many Nigerians have much confidence in them and they are generally seen as representing the interests of the rich and privileged in society. Third, many of the organizations, especially the BLP, DFRRI, and MAMSER, appeared to be avenues for, once again, diverting public funds to contractors, friends, and private bank accounts. There is almost unanimous belief in Nigeria that these institutions have achieved very little in the areas promoting rural development or mobilizing Nigerians for democracy in the midst of poverty, hunger, inflation, retrenchment, unemployment, and widespread official corruption. There is little to show given the billions of naira that have been allocated to these institutions since they were created. In Nigeria today, the process of distributing illegally acquired wealth is cynically described on the streets as "MAMSER!" Fourth, many of them have tended to be bogged down in competition with ministries, or have made the established ministries look irrelevant. The DFRRI competes with and duplicates the functions of the Ministry of Agriculture and other departments that deal with food production and rural development. The MAMSER competes with and duplicates the functions of the Ministry of Information, the Ministry of Youth, Sports and Culture, and the respective local governments. The Transition Tribunals compete with the law courts, the Ministry of Justice, and the presidency. Finally, in terms of mobilizing the people and inculcating democratic attitudes, the institutions have hardly made an impact. In several ways they have increased the degree of public cynicism and distrust. They have found it impossible to mobilize a poverty-stricken, hungry, and alienated populace that has come to see the government as an enemy, a populace that barely manages to survive the increasing pressures from the state due to an adjustment program that has no mechanisms to protect the vulnerable. The CDS is headed by a conservative political scientist whose ideas of democracy and democratization do not really go far beyond those set out in bourgeois political science texts, especially those that approximate Western ideas and ideals. That the CDS would have made a pronouncement to the effect that the law courts could not stop elections showed very clearly that, like the new breed politicians, it is so eager to satisfy the conceptualization of democracy as defined and presented by the government that it is prepared to subvert democratic principles.

In spite of the heavy reliance on popular musicians like Sunny Okosuns, Majek Fashek, Chris Hanen, Evi Edna Ogholi, and Christy Essien-Igbokwe to mobilize the public, the MAMSER has made very limited impacts on the task of mass mobilization. Perhaps the greatest inhibition to the ability of these institutions to mobilize Nigerians is the credibility of most of the officers. The majority of MAMSER directors and the Social Mobilization officers hardly understand what social mobilization is and what the implications of a properly mobilized populace can be for politics, power, production, and exchange relations. To make matters worse, and to demonstrate the conservative agenda and perception of the state, as far as mobilizing Nigerians was concerned, a retired inspector-general of police, Alhaji Muhammadu Gambo, was appointed as the national chairman of MAMSER following the resignation of Jerry Gana, who opted for active politics as a presidential candidate.[48] At the CDS, it is unclear as to what sort of *democracy* they are promoting and what sort of democratic attitudes they are inculcating in Nigerians. The rehabilitation of retired public officers, discredited military officers, and disgraced politicians as heads of some of these institutions has further convinced several Nigerians that they were set up in the first place to provide jobs for such persons.

The CDS and MAMSER do not see these actions as capable of sending negative messages to Nigerians, messages that directly challenge the essence of democratic and patriotic ideals.[49] Yet, if they speak on these issues of corruption, abuse of power, mismanagement, human rights abuses, and the impoverishment of the masses at all, it is often in very general terms. Luke Aghanenu of the National Association of Nigerian Students (NANS) has argued that "MAMSER is a World Bank package. When democracy has been abused, certain organs are made to extend some official lies. In Nigeria, that organ is MAMSER."[50] Air Iyare, one of the country's leading social critics, has also argued that government ministries could have performed better than MAMSER in the task of mobilization and "at less cost."[51] Adidi Uyo has also argued that the "setting up of unnecessary structures like MAMSER cannot bring the success of democracy. Government is wasting a lot of scarce resources and we are yet to see the outcome."[52] Eluem Emeka Izeze of the *Guardian*, writing on the confusion being generated by these institutions, has noted that

> we have also ignored a rather important development since the parties took root. Starting with party elections to the ward levels, we discovered that Omo Omoruyi's Centre for Democratic Studies (CDS) has either been teaching the wrong things to its students or has been dragging brightly spotted leopards to the river and attempting to wash off their spots with bare palms. We have not witnessed any change in the attitude of the politicians. Fighting for even party offices has remained a life and death affair. You either win, or you prevent the other fellow from winning. In the process we have been treated to a macabre dance of destruction and disturbance . . . it is obvious to us that the Centre has not changed anything at all. . . . Similar points can be made of the work of Jerry Gana's MAMSER.[53]

The critical point, therefore, is that the Babangida regime seems to take for granted the fact that for institutions to be credible and effective, they must relate to and reflect the objective realities of the society; the people must have cause to accept them and be prepared to work with and for them; their leaders must be aboveboard, untainted, committed, and capable of inspiring the people toward sacrifice and creativity; and the institutions must be able to operate without "bribing" the public to give it support. So far, Nigeria's transition program relies on institutions that generally lack these qualities.

Domesticating Popular Groups and Opposition Elements

The fourth major aspect of the transition program we wish to discuss is the government's strategy of containment, control, intimidation, harassment, and diversions. The purpose of this tactic is basically to control or domesticate opposition forces and keep the transition program in the hands of conservative, pro-IMF and pro-World Bank elements in the country. Since the transition program does not involve a genuine empowerment of the people and their organizations and does not involve the structural transformation of society, it has become inevitable that popular forces, trade unionists, students, civil liberty organizations, social critics, and those Babangida calls "extremists" are kept under control.

The initial human rights posture of the regime was just a front to buy legitimacy, confuse, and if possible divide the opposition, give donors, and investors the impression that a clean break was being made with the past, and open up enough space to lure popular forces into the political trap that was being set for them. Of course, the media, most radical scholars, and labor organizations fell for the trap and were badly bruised by their miscalculations. As Bosah Iwobi has rightly noted, the human rights campaign of Babangida was a trick:

> He abrogated Decree 4 . . . he granted state pardon to two journalists, Nduka Irabor and Tunde Thompson, convicted under the decree. His promise not to rule by force earned him the hearts of many. He raised his public rating when he counselled peace and reason while insisting on dialogue. And he showed an early romance with the press. . . . He granted audience to the *Nigerian Tribune*, an unrepentant critic of government since Nigeria's independence . . . he developed warm relationships with individual journalists. Soon, it was easy to hear of the Presidency presenting gifts to journalists on occasions such as their birthdays.[54]

The only group that did not fall for the "toothy smile" of the president and the tricks of bribery, personal friendship, gifts, as well as the illusions of a democratic and liberal military dictator, were the students and their organization, the National Association of Nigerian Students (NANS). To achieve its goal of control, therefore, the regime did the following: reorganized the National Security Organization (NSO) into the State Security Service (SSS) with more resources, facilities, and power; proscribed popular unions like the Academic Staff Union of Universities (ASUU); fired radical scholars and labor leaders like Festus Iyayi, Itse Sagay and Alofoje Unuigboje from their jobs due to their opposition to the erosion of University autonomy and academic freedom; and detained scholars, journalists, social critics, lawyers, and students who dared to criticize the government and its adjustment and transition programs. Hence, socical critics and scholars like Gani Fawehinmi, Balarabe Musa, Omotoye Olorode, Idowu Awopetu, Femi Falana, G. G. Darah, and a host of others have had their freedoms restricted and have been detained illegally several times.

The Babangida regime also dissolved the Nigeria Labour Congress (NLC), detained all its leaders, and harassed its officers. When the congress tried to organize a sympathy demonstration in support of students that were massacred at the Ahmadu Bello University in Zaria, the army, police, and air force were mobilized against it. On several occassions trade unionists who dared to go on strike were detained without trials. For instance, the leaders of the National Union of Electricity and Gas Workers were jailed for life for organizing a nation-wide strike (the sentence was later reduced to ten years and in 1991, they were set free following relentless pressures from trade unions and civil liberty organizations). To justify its repressive actions, the military junta classifed some Nigerians as "extremists," "confusionists," and persons to be barred from the transition process. The crime of such persons was their refusal to accept official positions on democracy, economic restructuring, and relations with imperialism. The left (using this in a broad sense) was incorported into the government through political appointments at a time when leftists were being harassed and branded as "extremist"—Ikenna Nzimiro, Tunji Olagunju, Sam Oyovbaire, Adiele Jinadu, Godwill Ogbogodor, Omolara Ogundipe-Leslie, Alaba Ogunsanwo, Eme Ekekwe, Jonathan Zwingina, Chidi Amuta, Ada Ugah, Wole Soyinka, Tai Solarin, and scores of others were appointed to serve as consultants and in other capacities in the scores of panels, committees and directorates created by the regime for this purpose. The Babangida regime also refused to register any of the independently created political associations as political parties and created, in their place, two political parties—The Social Democratic Party (SDP) and the National Republican Convention (NRC)—the one "a little to the left" and the latter "a little to the right." To ensure absolute control and continuing direct/indirect influence over their operations, the regime then built their offices, drafted their manifestos and constitutions, appointed administrative secretaries for both parties, sponsored their delegates to their national conventions, named the parties, chose their emblems for them, and provided them with start up funds to cover virtually everything. While pretending to respect human reights and press freedom, the harassment of journalists and media houses was widespread. The regime has the record of detaining more journalists and raiding more media houses than any other government in the country's history.

Under the regime, the very first case of a journalist being murdered by parcel bomb with several fingers pointed at the government occurred in 1986. The *Concord*, *Newswatch*, and *Newbreed* magazines were among the media houses that were closed by the regime.[55] In addition, Tony Ukpong of the *Weekly Metropolitan*, Etim Etim of the *Guardian*, Ikepe Etukudo and Tunde Ogungbile of the *New Horizon*, Femi Aborisade of the *Labour Militant*, Haruna Mohammed, Innocent Oparadike, and Yusuf Ozi Usman, all of the *New Nigerian*, Chris Okojie of the *Vanguard*, Paxton Idowu of *The Republic*, Chris Mamah of *The Punch*, Emma Agu of *The Champion*, Chris Okolie of *Newbreed*, and Mitchel Obi of *Guardian Express* have all been detained for offenses that the government never had the courage to take to the law courts. It also promulgated a Press Council Decree to enable it to promote the domestication of the media.[56]

While the banning of popular groups opened the political arena to domonation by conservative and corrupt politicans, frequent reshuffling of the cabinet, governors, and all sorts of surprise announcements were largely an attempt to live up to the unpredictable "Maradona" image created by the media, and partly, designed to check possibility of entrenched opposition. This has, however, not reduced the degree of popular opposition to the regime.

Given the degree of proletarianization of the middle class, in particular, the intellectuals, the "politics of poverty" has become an effective weapon. Virtually every critic now has a price: political appointment. Such appointments often come with free official car, driver, free housing, opportunity to travel abroad and draw estacodes in foreign exchange, opportunities to make the "right" connections for the future, and more importantly, the chance to eliminate poverty and want permanently from one's family through all sorts of kickbacks and "gifts" from contractors. The regime has used this effectively as a weapon of control, division, and manipulation. The ruthless execution of coup plotters and others implicated in attempts to overthrow the government is often designed as an example to warn others with such hidden agenda of the possible consequences. The regime has executed more Nigerians than all the other governments, including the colonial government, put together!

Yet, these measures, which have served in several ways to divide and weaken the opposition, have not succeeded in preventing the growth of a strong movement advocating the strengthening of civil society. The repressive tendencies of the Nigerian state and its increasingly desperate nature, especially with the burst of the oil bubble and declining foreign exchange, have tended to mobilize political opposition to it. Apart from the general distrust of the people for the state and its agencies, its inability to meet the basic needs of the people, the rehabilitation of discredited elements, and corruption have combined with other forces and factors to erode its legitimacy and credibility. Each dismissal of a critical scholar, each act of incorporation through bribery and sinecure appointments, and all acts of direct violence against students and workers appear only to have strengthened the resolve of nonbourgeois forces and increased the demands for accountability, human rights, and democracy.

Conclusions: Transition to Civilian Rule or Transition to Democracy?

Nigerians have come to reject military rule by refusing to support coups and allowing themselves to be provoked by the indiscipline, corruption, mismanagement, and arrogance of the military into actions likely to encourage the military to remain in power perpetually.[57] The imposition of the harsh conditionalities of the adjustment program on the people has tended to increase the resolve of the people to resist the state and its increasing subservience to the IMF, the World Bank, and international suppliers. The structural distortions and contradictions that have historically generated tensions and conflicts, which have in turn militated against the strengthening of democratic traditions, have not been addressed. The march forward remains plagued by several obstacles.

Obstacles to Democracy and Democratization in Nigeria

The conditions of human rights abuses, poverty, intimidation, and incorporation of critical and opposition elements highlighted above in no way implies that the struggle for democracy, accountability, and empowerment of popular organizations will cease. If anything, given the traditional commitment of Nigerians to democracy, developments in the global system, and internal pressures for accountability, the struggle for democracy will certainly wax stronger. As well, with the widening gap between the rich and the poor, the increasing impoverishment of the people, and the suffocation of democratic spaces by the state and its agents, popular forces and their organizations are certain to develop alternative political positions and programs. The evident breakdown of old orthodoxies and the increasing cooperation among civil liberty organizations, womens' movements, trade and student unions with substantial support from progressive professionals and some liberal members of the armed forces are bound to strengthen the struggle for empowerment, democracy, and democratization. Yet, the ability of the prodemocracy and other popular movements to survive increasing pressures and manipulation and repression from the state would depend on a clear recognition of the obstacles to their objectives in order to initiate adequate responses to them.

The first obstacle to democracy in the country is the *military* itself. In the country's history the military has consistently intervened in politics and prevented the consolidation of democratic institutions. The view that military rule is an abnormality and that the best military regime is worse than the worst civilian regime has become widespread in the country. The numerous "corrective" regimes have been unable to correct much. Yet, the military has been more corrupt than the civilians even if they have been less flamboyant in their corruption.[58] The military has succeeded in taking some far-reaching decisions in the interest of the country; but they have not necessarily always been the best decisions. Military rule has led to the militarization of the society, culminated in a civil war, and laid the foundation for intervention in the political process. Since the current transition program was put in place, there have been at least two major coup attempts. The transition program would have been the first casualty of the coups if they had succeeded. There have been several rumored coups and, to be sure, not all officers believe that the military should leave power. Those who had served as military governors and in other lucrative positions are often angered at being asked to leave office, and try to find a way to get back. The life-styles of ex-governors and ex-ministers in and outside of the active force continue to encourage others who have not had a go at power to make a bid for it. Current governors and ministers are in no way different.

The fact that military officers virtually live above the law in Nigeria continues to promote a culture of military arrogance and domination of the political processes. But more importantly is the fact that the military now sees itself as an alternative to politicians. Many military officers easily take pride in calling nonmilitary persons "bloody civilians." The monopoly of the means of coercion has come to be equated with a right to dominate political power. The military has established its own bank, insurance scheme, war college, university, research institute, and other institutions to promote an *esprit de corps* and demonstrate its unity and common objective. The military has become a route to capital accumulation. It has produced more millionaires than any other profession in the country and now believes that it has full control of the economy and society with the harmony between serving officers and retired officers who get the first shot at all contracts. In most cases, the governors, ministers, and other officers awarding lucrative government contracts are either promoted to their respective ranks by the retired officers or have served in junior capacities under them.[59] It is the retirement of senior officers that paves the way for the younger officers to rise to power. It is, therefore, easy to figure out the background conditions to contract awards in the country. With the current political postures of the so-called new breed, the "popular fear now is whether the new breed can be trusted with any higher moral, cultural or political value for the civil society. Will their excesses not provoke overzealous military hot heads to conclude . . . wrongly as always . . . that handing over power to civilians is unecessary afterall?"[60]

Corruption under the military, in particular, in the current era of adjustment, is unparalleled in the country's history. So far, no civilian regime in Africa has succeeded in probing the military. Any attempt to do that will lead to another military coup by officers interested in protecting their corrupt past. But this is essentially because civil society is fragmented and weak. Thus, so far, the Nigerian military, which has assumed an air of superiority and regards nonmilitary persons as "undisciplined," "disorganized," "irresponsible," and so on, poses the greatest challenge to democracy and civil liberties in Nigeria. Given that the conditions that prompted previous military coups in the country remain in somewhat more prominent dimensions, there is no reason to underestimate the dangers the military pose to democracy in the country. Though Nigerians have said a resounding "no" to the "divine rule of the gun,"[61] the military has convinced itself that it is the only institution that can serve as a "corrective" institution and determine whether civilians were ruling well or not. There lies the real danger.

The second obstacle to democracy is the Nigerian *state*. Under normal circumstances, the state, its institutions, and its agents would be relied upon to promote the democratization process by creating the "enabling environment" for reorganizing social and political relations, articulating political interests, mediating contradictions, resolving conflicts, and ensuring the enforcement of the rules of politics. But the situation in Nigeria is not a normal one, no matter what the IMF and the World Bank, even Western governments think. The limited autonomy of the state, its weaknesses, and its reliance on repression and manipulation of particularistic interests to reproduce its tenuous hegemony means that it cannot be relied upon or expected to generate the required "enabling environment" for the survival of democracy, popular mobilization, and structural transformation. The Nigerian state is critically immersed in the class struggle on the side of the privileged and imperialism.[62] Its history is one of consistent and ruthless opposition to popular forces and their organizations and, in fact, only tenuous disposition to democracy and democratization. Its failure to promote any credible structural transformation of the country since political independence is testimony of its relatively even, clear disinterest in the empowerment of the people and the strengthening of civil society. The Nigerian state has, over the decades, through its massacre of students in Ife, Nsukka, Zaria, Benin, Jos, and Ibadan, its massacre of peasants in Ibadan and Bakolori, its detention of students and other critics of the patterns of indiscipline, corruption, waste, and mediocrity, its neglect of the basic needs of the vast majority, and its alliance with international finance institutions and other external interests to entrench the structures of unequal exchange, demonstrated that it is incapable of supporting the emergence of a mobilized, democratic, and productive society. Today, the state has been very much delegitimized, its rules and regulations are hardly obeyed and its institutions remain corrupt and inefficient. To put it mildly, it is a badly battered state useful only to the extent that it provides an avenue for the stealing of public funds. To the extent that the state remains a predatory, exploitative structure used by the dominant class primarily for accumulation purposes, it cannot be on the side of the struggle for democracy.

A third obstacle to a democratic Nigeria is the Nigerian *bourgeoisie*. It is possible to write about the so-called *productive bourgeoisie* in Nigeria. It is possible to attribute the qualities of a disciplined, patriotic, nationalistic, and efficient bourgeois class to the Nigerian bourgeoisie. We argue that such attempts will constitute a disservice to the cause of the Nigerian people and a major fraud in the interpretation of the realities in the country. We do concede that a *tiny* fraction of the Nigerian ruling class has recently moved into production, especially in agriculture, and are making a bid for state power. This fraction seems to have realized that their ability to survive and expand as well as to effectively compete with foreign capital depends on its ability to control the state and thus preside over the allocation of resources and the initiation of public policy. This is perhaps one way to explain the deep involvement of retired Generals Abgazika Innih, Shehu Yar Adua, Samuel Ogbemudia, Olusegun Obasanjo, Chief Onwuka Kalu, and other retired military officers in the political transition program. Yet, given the unrestricted access to (though not necessarily control of) the state that they already enjoy as well as the unlimited influence they command over state policy, we can only contend that their involvement in politics is part of a strategy to return to power and accumulate through the control of state power. This is the more plausible because of their strategies of political competition—they have relied on the use of money, and ethnic, religious, and regional manipulation to gain influence over other political actors.

Taken together, the Nigerian bourgeois class seems to have a legendary reputation for waste, inefficiency, corruption, indiscipline, reliance on extralegal and irrational modes of political competition, and accumulation through investment in politics and access to state power.[63] Hence, it has been very hostile to all attempts at *genuine* struggles for democracy, empowerment, democratization, justice, equity, and accountability. The ideological character of this class has not changed one bit since political independence. It has learned almost nothing from the experiences of its counterparts in other regions of the Third World. It has resisted every effort at instituting structures of accountability—Ethical Revolution, War Against Indiscipline, Code of Conduct Bureau, Public Complaints Commission, Assets Declaration, and so on. It still wallows in waste, throwing lavish all-night parties, importing all products, and relying on money to get its way through virtually everything including securing university admission for children, clearing goods through customs, and even participating in community activities. In the political process it has continued to manipulate the poverty of the people and regard the masses as objects of manipulation and exploitation. Its investment patterns have continued to be concentrated in lucrative but *unproductive* sectors of the economy—real estate, hospitality services, import-export activities, transportation, and serving as fronts to foreign investors. Recently, the Nigerian bourgeoisie has found even more lucrative ways of accumulation requiring political influence and power and limited investments: currency trafficking, drug running, and importation of toxic waste.[64] It is interesting that Eddie Madnagu's description of the Nigerian bourgeoisie as "extremely irrational and underdeveloped"[65] several years ago, remains valid today. Such a dominant class cannot be expected to support democratization, empowerment, and accountability as such processes will serve to check its immersion in waste, indiscipline, decadence, and suffocation of civil society.

Poverty and the adjustment program, with all their consequences and implications, equally pose serious obstacles to the democratic struggles in Nigeria. The story of Nigeria in the last three decades has been one of squandered opportunities and the further impoverishment of the people.[66] The vulnerability of the Nigerian people to political manipulation is not due to ignorance, illiteracy, or some other superficial explanation often advanced by the Nigerian state. Rather, the explanations must be found in the conditions of deprivation, hunger, unemployment, disillusionment, and marginalization. To be sure, limited popular political education and mobilization are equally part of the problem of vulnerability to political manipulation. The fact remains that an unemployed person is an easy recruit as a thug. A hungry person will succumb to temptations to sell his vote for a bag of rice or food. In a society where the state retrenches able-bodied workers daily and where there is no social insurance to protect the poor and unemployed, it is easy for disadvantaged groups to be vulnerable to ethnic and religious manipulation. A population subjected to severe deprivations and that had become disillusioned and cynical about the leadership and the country can become easily ignited to violence at any time. The numerous religious and anti-tructural adjustment riots in the country are largely precipitates of this anger and frustration.[67] Today, the majority of Nigerians are walking time bombs, ready to take any action in support of their opposition to the government.

In a society where the government's agents and agencies command virtually no respect and confidence, it cannot expect any appreciable degree of harmony between its interests and those of the people. Even the Barclays Bank of London acknowledged the implications of adjustment for the democratization process in Nigeria when it noted recently that the adjustment program has so impoverished the masses of Nigeria that it has become a direct challenge to the planned transition to democracy.[68] Of course, the military might just succeed in managing the political process to a hand over of power to civilians, though the prospects are rather dim. But its economic programs would have laid a dangerous foundation for the survival of the Third Republic. It is clear that poverty becomes a major obstacle to democracy where there are increasingly limited outlets and opportunities for the poor beyond crime, prostitution, scavenging for food in trash cans, and drug abuse.[69]

Finally, we believe that conditions in the *international system* have direct implications for the prospects for democracy in Nigeria. Too often, much has been made of the impact of the demands for political reforms by donors and Western governments as well as the changes in Eastern

Europe. While these are important, they fail to explain the fact that the international system is still basically hostile, undemocratic, and exploitative.[70] There is now only one world system: the capitalist world system. The so-called American Century, implying absolute American hegemony, together with the devastating and ruthless destruction of Kuwait and Baghdad in the name of freeing Kuwait from Iraq, show very clearly the gradual closure of room for maneuver in the "new world order" declared by the American president.[71] Since the Gulf War, the United States has tried as much as possible to dictate and determine the content and direction of international politics, frequently using Iraq as a test case. Yet, the United States cares very little for Africa. With declining foreign exchange receipts from the oil sector, mounting debt-servicing obligations, declining foreign investments, and increasing pressures and manipulations by powerful Western interests, countries like Nigeria are in serious trouble.

It will be increasingly impossible to initiate and implement policies that do not have the approval of the United States. Countries that are of little geostrategic importance to the United States will receive little or no foreign assistance and will be marginalized in the global system. Nigeria has become a dumping ground for toxic waste from the West and has become an important actor in the global drug business. The individualism, greed, and ostentatious life-style encouraged by the military and their hangers-on, which have risen to new proportions since the adjustment program, and the devaluation of the naira have combined with other vices to practically ruin the country's image abroad. The Nigerian passport is now treated as a dangerous document all over the world. Nigerian businessmen are no longer trusted by their foreign counterparts because of frequent attempts to outsmart others and the ease with which they forge documents. Nigerian youths who have fled the economic hardship at home have been known to involve themselves in all sorts of sharp practices abroad. It was disappointing to many Nigerians when a minister, during a press conference abroad, said that "foreigners have no need to come to Nigeria because Nigeria had no system. The system, the minister claims, is confused with everybody doing whatever he likes."[72] To make matters worse, the Central Bank of Nigeria placed advertisements in foreign magazines "warning the international community of the dubious intent of Nigerians."[73] When the central bank of a country begins to destroy the image of the nation abroad, then there is little reason to expect the international business community to regard that country as a serious place for business.

With its inability to resolve its numerous internal and external problems, the West will give no concessions on matters of debt, credit, and other assistance. With the end of the cold war and the disintegration of the Soviet Union, the West does not need to make any concessions to any country that is virtually marginal to its economic interests. Though Nigeria might not be a typical African nation given its huge population and oil resources, increasing difficulty in doing business in the country could scare off serious-minded investors. Yet, increasing pressures from the international system will limit the options available to the Nigerian state and force it into either adopting more repressive measures or making major concessions to democratic forces. The first response will deepen internal coalitions, contradictions, and conflicts and close up existing democratic spaces as well as prospects for democratization. The second response will strengthen ongoing struggles for democracy and democratization as the starting points for a fundamental restructuring of Nigeria's political economy.

Yet, there is some light at the end of the tunnel. Intellectuals are abandoning their traditional concentration in university campuses to join in popular struggles for democracy. Workers, market women, students, and other nonbourgeois forces are coming together to make direct political demands for participation and accountability. People are rejecting traditional political figures and are presenting alternative candidates for election to positions of responsibility. Old ideological orthodoxies and interpretations are being reconceptualized and reformulated to make them more relevant to existing realities. In short, the political culture and the content and direction of political struggles are changing. With the new emphasis shifting from a blanket call for socialism (which is nonetheless still important) to democracy, participation, human rights, employment, basic human needs, empowerment, and basic freedoms, the foundation for new relations of power, politics, production, and exchange are being laid. This basic deconstruction of the socialist ideal is the only way to avoid the pitfalls of the former East European nations.[74] It is only in this context that we can see a positive political future for Nigeria.

Notes

1. "Objectionale Politics," Editorial, *The Guardian* (21 November 1991).

2. "A Noose for Third Republic," *TELL* (7 October 1991), 42.
3. Yakubu Mohammed, "Killing the 3rd Republic," *Newswatch* (5 August 1991), 6.
4. See James O. Ojiako, *13 Years of Military Rule 1966–79* (Lagos, Nigeria: Daily Times, 1979)
5. See Julius O. Ihonvbere, "Coups and Counter-Coups in Nigeria: A Critical Evaluation of the April 1990 Major Gideon Orka Coup." Mimeo, University of Toronto, Ontario, Canada 1991.
6. See Toyin Falola and Julius O. Ihonvbere, *The Rise and Fall of Nigeria's Second Republic, 1979–84* (London: Zed Press, 1985), chapter 10.
7. This argument is further developed in Toyin Faloba and Julius O. Ihonvbere, *The Rise and Fall.*
8. Quoted in *The Nigerian Tribune* (Ibadan) (2 July 1967).
9. Cited in Zainab Duke, *The Revolutionary Potentials of the Nigerian Military, 1966–1986* (Ikeja, Nigeria: Jeromelaiho and Associates, 1987), 71.
10. General M. R. Muhammed, (Text of broadcast to the nation, 1 October 1975).
11. Ibrahim B. Babangida, *Portrait of a New Nigeria: Selected Speeches of IBB* (Lagos, Nigeria: Precision Press, 1989), 33.
12. See "Toward Civil Rule: Why the Changes," *The African Guardian* (10 September 1990); "Nigeria '91: The Danger Spots," *The African Guardian* (7 January 1991); "Parties for Sale," *The African Guardian* (21 January 1991); and "Council Elections: The Hidden Facts," *The African Guardian* (24 December 1990).
13. Sam Aluko, "We are All Liars," Interview with *TELL* (15 April 1991).
14. Austin Oghuma and Sylvester Olumhense, "Interview With Tony Momoh," *Newswatch* (Lagos, Nigeria) 121, no. 22 (28 May 1990), 17.
15. Mokwugo Okoye, "Death of a Dream," *African Concord* (13 April 1992).
16. General I. B. Babangida, (Nationwide broadcast on occasion of the fifth anniversary on assuming power, Lagos, 27 August 1990).
17. Akpo Esajere, "Bendel Governorship Race: Will Money Make the Essential Difference?" *The Guardian* (Lagos) (1 October 1990).
18. Toyin Egunjobi, "Waterloo For the South," *Newbreed* (20 August 1990), 36.
19. Babafemi Ojudu, "As in the Beginning . . . Money and Ethnic Loyalties Manifest in Third Republic Politicking," *African Concord* (6 August 1990).
20. "Transition Programme: Third Republic Lies on Weak Foundation," *Newbreed* (1 October 1990), 27.
21. Ibid.
22. *Newswatch* 12, no. 6 (6 August 1990).
23. Ray Ekpu, "The North-South Divide," *Newswatch* 12, no. 7 (August 1990), 6.
24. Mokwugo Okoye, "Transition Tantrums," *The African Guardian* (1 October 1990), 7.
25. Gani Fawehinmi quoted in "Parties in the Money Market," *The African Guardian* (21 January 1991), 23.
26. Ibid., 24.
27. Humphrey Nwosu, "Parties Breached Rules of the Primaries," (Text of nationwide broadcast), *The Guardian* (28 November 1991), 6.
28. See, for example, "Rivers State SDP Gubernatorial Primaries—the Truth by Mr. A. K. Dikibo," *Vanguard* (21 November 1991).
29. Personal communication with Lucky Eleanya, University of Port Harcourt. Incidentally, Mr. Eleanya worked for MAMSER as a social mobilization officer for some years.
30. For full details see *Participation in Politics and Elections (Prohibition) Decree No. 25 of 1987* Lagos, Federal Republic of Nigeria (Official Gazette), 74, no. 57 (9 October 1987).

31. See Ibrahim Babangida, *Portrait of a New Nigeria: Selected Speeches of IBB* (Lagos, Nigeria: Precision Press, n.d.).
32. See "Bloodbath in Kano: Religious Fanatics Strike Again," *TELL* (28 October 1991); "Bauchi: Danger Looms Again," *TELL* (3 June 1991); "Jeddah Crash: Why Okojie is Fighting," *The African Guardian* (5 August 1991); and "Kaduna Burns," *Newswatch* (1 June 1992).
33. Mokwugo Okoye, "Death of a Dream," *African Concord* (13 April 1992).
34. Yakubu Mohammed, "Killing the 3rd Republic," *Newswatch* (5 August 1991), 6.
35. Ibid.
36. Sully Abu, "Politics in Retreat," *The Guardian* (14 October 1990), A9.
37. Ibid.
38. "Magic Makers," *African Concord* (25 November 1991), 40. Full details are contained in Humphrey Nwosu, "Parties Breached Rules of the Primaries."
39. Ibid.
40. "Newbreed Politicians," Editorial, *The Guardian* (18 May 1991), 6.
41. Ibid.
42. "Magic Makers," 40.
43. Ibid.
44. Ibid., 41.
45. Obinna Anyadike, "Nigeria: New Breed Old Politics?" *Africa Report* (May–June 1991), 47–48.
46. Ibrahim Babangida quoted in "Magic Makers," 39.
47. See Onome Osifo-Whiskey, "New States, New Challenges," *TELL* (9 September 1991).
48. See Adekunle Adekoya, "Mired in Crisis," *Sunday Vanguard* (28 June 1992).
49. There were a few exceptions here and there. For instance, Jonathan Zwingina, the director for Gongola State, and Jerry Gana, the former national chairman, have clear records of identification with popular ideas and ideals, at least before they joined MAMSER. With MAMSER, they did try to influence overall policy based on their political convictions. They failed because the system did not have provisions for a social conscience. The current national chairman, a retired policeman, has no record whatsoever of identification with the people or of belief in mobilization. If anything, his background and record are bound to promote demobilization rather than mobilization.
50. Cited in "Transition Programme: Third Republic Lies on Weak Foundation," *Newbreed* (1 October 1990), 29.
51. Ibid.
52. Adidi Uyo, cited in "Five Years After: What Nigerians Expect," *The African Guardian* (3 September 1990), 27.
53. Eluem Emeka Izeze, "Open Confusion," *The Guardian* (21 October 1990), A9.
54. Bosah Iwobi, "The Press and Human Rights: Bitter-Sweet Tales," *African Concord* (3 September 1990).
55. See Pita O. Agbese, "State, Media and the Imperatives of Repression: An Analysis of the Ban on *Newswatch*," *International Third World Studies Journal and Review* 1, no. 2 (1989).
56. Ibid.
57. See "Can IBB Tame the Army?" *African Concord* (16 July 1990); "Orka's Coup: The People's Verdict," *African Concord* (28 May 1990); "Coup that Failed: The Storming of Dodan Barracks," *Newswatch* (May 7 1990) and "Coups: Will They End?" *Newswatch* (21 May 1990).

58. See "Who Will Probe Babangida?" *Newbreed* (1 October 1990); "Gowon's Men Probed," *The Analyst* (Kaduna, Nigeria) (July 1986); "Corruption a Nigerian?" *African Concord* (26 March 1990); "Why Governors are Corrupt," *African Concord* (26 March 1990) and "An Era of Scandals," *African Concord* (11 February 1991).
59. See "Retired Generals: The Good Time Continues," *Thisweek* (Lagos, Nigeria) (9 May 1988).
60. "Magic Makers," 41.
61. Wole Soyinka quoted in "A Resounding No To Coup(s)," *Newbreed* (16 April 1989), 29.
62. See Claude Ake, "The Nigerian State: Antinomies of a Periphery Formation" in his collection *Political Economy of Nigeria* (London: Longman, 1985).
63. See Julius O. Ihonvbere, "The State and the Irrationality of the Bourgeoisie: An Examination of How the Nigerian Bourgeoisie Subverts its Own Future" (Paper delivered at the National Conference on "Obafemi Awolowo: The End of an Era?" organized by the Obafemi Awolowo University Press, Ile-Ife, Nigeria, 4-8 October 1987).
64. See "Nigeria: Oil Rich, Poor People," *African Concord* (2 August 1988); "Toxic Man: Sunday Nana—the Sad, Last Days," *African Concord* (2 April 1990); and "Drums of Death: Nigeria's Toxic Waste Scandal," *The African Guardian* (20 June 1988).
65. Eddie Madunagu, *Problems of Socialism: The Nigerian Challenge* (London: Zed Press, 1982), 40.
66. See "A Generation Wasted?" *Sunday Champion* (Lagos, Nigeria) (1 October 1990).
67. See "SAP Wars: A Nation on the Boil," *The African Guardian* (12 June 1989); and "Religion—Zaria: The Wounds are Healing," *Newbreed* (16 April 1989).
68. ABECOR Country Report, *Nigeria* (Prepared and distributed by Barclays Bank Economics Department, London, July 1990).
69. See "Where do We Turn," *African Concord* (8 October 1990); "The Colour of Crime," *The Nigerian Economist* (3 September 1990); "Five Years of Strangulation," *Newbreed* (1 October 1990); Mokwugo Okoye, "A Time of Sadness," *The African Guardian* (24 September 1990); "SAP: Nigerians Dismantle Family Libraries for Cash," *Newbreed* (20 August 1990); "Ola's Ogre: Ola is One of Millions of City Slickers Who Find Life With SAP a Nightmare," *Africa Event* (October 1989); "New Drug War," *Newswatch* (20 August 1990); "Nigeria: The New Rich . . . The Rising Cocaine Profile," *Thisweek* (April 2 1990); and "I Want to Die—8 Year Old Eno Ufot," *The Sunday Magazine* (3 June 1990).
70. See Julius O. Ihonvbere, "Between Reform and Disaster: The Choice Before Africa in the 1990s." Mimeo, University of Toronto, Ontario, Canada, 1991; and Adebayo Adedeji, "Economic Progress: What Africa Needs," *Transafrica Forum* 7, no. 20 (Summer 1990).
71. See "The Gulf War: U.S. Hails 'New World Order'—but Many Fear Era of Intolerance," *The Toronto Star* (3 March 1991) and "Bush Goes for Mass Murder," *Workers Vanguard* (Toronto) (18 January 1991).
72. "419 Business, Nigeria's Image and the Organized Private Sector," *The Nigerian Economist* (9 December 1991), 7.
73. Ibid.
74. See Julius O. Ihonvbere, "The Dynamics of Change in Eastern Europe and Their Implications for Africa," *Coexistence* 29 (1992), 277-86.

6

Nigeria in the 1990s: The Future of Politics and Democracy

> If you don't really put people to work, you can't produce. I think the Babangida regime has tried all the tricks that they know and they don't work. By trying to give room to a new crop of people to come to power, I think new ideas will surface and we may be able to solve the economic problems.[1]

> Politicians must now begin to set the agenda, to seek a vision that can set the agenda, to seek a vision that can truly mark a new beginning for this country. Decades of cruel abuse of the citizenry by the political class—military and civilian—have produced a thoroughly alienated populace but important segments of which are angry, very angry. What this means is that we cannot carry on much as before, as if all there is to power is its pomp perquisites.[2]

A discussion of the future of politics and democracy in Nigeria must of necessity take due cognizance of the past and the present in order to make viable prescriptions and projections for the future. Ironically, the current state of deprivation, repression, impoverishment of the middle classes, capital flight, and political instability contain the seeds for a more stable, productive, and progressive future for Nigeria. The experimentation with political and regime forms, and with economic models—import substitution, indigenization, partial nationalization, and more recently structural adjustment—have not made fundamental differences to the conditions of dependence, underdevelopment, foreign domination, and exploitation. As well, political independence and the various political and economic experiments have not altered, in any significant way, the largely corrupt, dependent, unproductive, and undisciplined character of the Nigerian bourgeoisie.

The state remains the main avenue to capital accumulation. The structures and institutions of the state still command limited credibility and legitimacy. It remains incapable of effectively managing the economy, controlling the environment, instilling discipline within the ranks of the dominant classes, and providing for the basic needs of the vast majority of the people. Thus, since achieving political independence in 1960, the vast majority of Nigerians have had to contend with poverty, deprivation, humiliation, and harassment from a desperate and non-hegemonic state and a corrupt and unproductive bourgeois class.

These conditions, contradictions, and conflicts have generated very deep-rooted problems for politics, social relations, and democracy in Nigeria. The accentuation of ethnic and religious riots, coups and countercoups, and the frequent breakdown of law and order are direct precipitates of the colonial experience and the postcolonial alignment and realignment of class forces. The creation of states and hundreds of local governments, an oil boom, a civil war, military regimes, and other institutional innovations have hardly addressed the national question: inequalities within and between classes, and the fundamental underdeveloped status of Nigeria in the international division of labor.

Nigeria is organizing a transition to democracy at a very difficult time in both its history and the world system. The Western world in increasingly diverting its attention and interest to Eastern Europe and the Middle East. Investors are also shifting their resources to these areas rather than to Africa. Western responses to the crisis in Eastern Europe and the Middle East as compared to responses to similar developments in Ethiopia, Liberia, Somalia, Sudan, and Angola demonstrate clearly their decreasing interest and concern for the African region. By the time the UN decided to send just five hundred troops to Somalia in August 1992, it already had over two thousand troops in Yugoslavia. Aid poured into Yugoslavia from all nooks and corners of the Western world. Yet, compared to the long-standing tragedy of Somalia, the Yugoslav crisis is a very recent one. As Babangida complained in his address to the forty-sixth session of the UN General Assembly in 1991, African efforts at democratization were virtually being ignored by the West and Japan in sharp contrast to the enthusiasm showed for similar efforts in Eastern Europe. Thus, Nigeria's efforts at political and economic restructuring are taking place at a very difficult period in global relations (see chapter 2).

The instability, corruption, institutional inefficiency, and mismanagement in Nigeria have not helped matters. In fact, as we showed in chapter five, the Central Bank of Nigeria and some ministers have been busy alerting the international community on the dangers of doing business with Nigeria and its people.

At the internal level, the implementation of an orthodox structural adjustment program is creating problems of unimaginable proportions. Never in the history of the country, not even during the civil war, have things been that bad. The system has virtually collapsed. Every Nigerian has practically become obsessed with either emigrating from the country or laying hands on the dollar and/or pound sterling by any possible means. With devaluation and liberalization, coupled with a floating interest rate, industries are simply collapsing as they cannot compete with foreign imports. In any case local investors cannot borrow from the banks under the floating interest rates.

As for the masses of the people, unemployment, hunger, and poverty have converted them into political opportunists and thugs, vulnerable more than ever to manipulation and exploitation. Diseases like yellow fever, cholera, and guinea worm continue to cause disaster all over the country. As the Committee for the Defence of Human Rights (CDHR) reported recently,

> Thousands of poor citizens were afflicted in at least 6 States by cerebro-spinal meningitis. "A mysterious killer disease," recently suspected to be yellow fever, has taken at least 700 lives in Ika Local Government within 6 weeks . . . cholera epidemic . . . claimed 2,161 lives in 15 states of the country's 21 states . . . between May and July (1991) in Ado Local Government Area alone, 71 people were killed. In the entire local government there is no single hospital and the people last year had been ravaged by Guinea Worm.[3]

Thus, with the privatization and neglect of public hospitals and other health delivery systems, the situation in Nigeria today "is that you either have money to pay for your treatment or die off. At the same time, government functionaries, officials and their friends are flown abroad for treatment at colossal public expense."[4] Rents have gone up by over 500 percent in most urban centers especially in the new local government headquarters and state capitals. In places like Lagos, "a room which rented for between N35–N50 per month last year (1990) now costs between N80–N250. Yet the new minimum wage is N250! . . . landlords who used to collect 6 months' rent in advance now insist on 12–18 months' rent in advance while advance payments for flats, which used to be one year, is now 2–3 years."[5] To make matters worse and as further demonstration of the social and economic war declared against the poor by the military government, in July 1990, 300,000 inhabitants of Maroko in Lagos State were given only seven days, with no alternative arrangements made, to get out their homes and seek new shelter in Lagos, which was already heavily congested. At the end of seven days they were bulldozed out of the area; their homes and over fifteen primary and postprimary schools in the area were destroyed. As Emevwo Biakolo has noted on the action, "Half a million people, some of whom have known no other habitation than Maroko, were last Saturday tossed out of this piece of land like so many useless bundles of rags. Miscarriages were recorded, pregnant women had premature births."[6] The displaced residents, many of whom had been retrenched from their jobs as a result of the adjustment program, took to begging, crime, and prostitution while the majority, who had no relatives to fall back on, simply moved under the bridges and overpasses all over Lagos. Today, Maroko, reclaimed and cleaned up by the military government, is sprouting some of the most breathtaking and expensive designer houses in the world.[7]

Since the introduction of SAP, the "cost of fuel per litre has risen by over 350 per cent; drugs by over 500 per cent; eggs by over 400 per cent; milk by over 1000 per cent; bus fare by over 500 per cent; toilet soap by over 300 per cent; baby food by over 600 per cent etc."[8] With the privatization, commercialization, and desubsidization programs of the government came massive retrenchment of able-bodied workers in the teaching and health services, the Nigerian Railways Corporation, the Federal Radio Corporation, the Nigerian Television Authority, the Nigerian Ports Authority, and other parastatals and government departments. In a country without any social insurance scheme and without any form of benefits for fired workers, the results of these retrenchments have been devastating. Many of those who were to serve the political parties as thugs were persons who had been retrenched by the state and its agencies. This is hardly the environment for building democracy, consensus, harmony, dialogue, and encouraging the spirit of creativity and national unity.

Unfortunately, the Nigerian state and its crop of opportunists, praise singers, "intellectual rationalizers," and bureaucrats continue to believe absolutely and uncritically in the prescriptions of the World Bank and the IMF. To be sure, it is virtually impossible to extricate a nation from the influence of these institutions in the context of the decline of Eastern Europe, the triumph of the market, and the increasing marginalization of

Africa in the emerging unipolar security and multipolar economic world order. Yet, it should be clear to Third World leaders that the World Bank and the IMF cannot empower them to a level where they can compete with the centers of global capitalism or to a level where they can significantly affect the global deployment of capital. These institutions were not set up for underdeveloped countries in the first instance. Policies that impoverish the people and destroy the socioeconomic fabric of society cannot be expected to lead to growth and development at the same time. What appears to be happening in the world is a gradual redeployment of capital away from Africa. As well, we are witnessing a situation in which a recolonization of African economies is taking place under the guidance of the World Bank and the IMF. At a time when the rest of the world is reconstituting itself into trade blocs, when economic protectionism dominates Western trade relations with the outside world, and when the Western governments are busy increasing subsidies to investors especially in the agricultural sectors, poor, dependent, underdeveloped, and crisis-ridden African countries are being asked to open up their economies, devalue their currencies by over 1000 percent, liberalize their economies completely, and remove all subsidies, especially from health, education, and social services. The point is that there is not one country that has benefited from such misguided policies in the world except in the books of the IMF.

The World Bank would not be bold enough to claim that its policies have succeeded worldwide because the facts are there for all to see. It even admits in its 1989 report on Africa that a large proportion of its projects in the region have been total disasters.[9] The whole notion of rolling back the state and the recent near fetishism of market forces are not only misguided, but fraudulent. African leaders now think that the only way to be in the good books of the United States and international capital is to state and restate their commitments to free market forces and free enterprise, even if their policies reflect the exact opposite. For instance, as part of several threats issued by General Babangida following nationwide riots in May 1992 was a restatement of his commitment to the free market: "Our destination, in concrete terms, is military disengagement and the return to democratic civilian rule as well as the modernization of Nigeria into a private enterprise, free market economy."[10]

In the United States, the government continues to pour money into education, road construction, and agriculture. It subsidizes a whole range of services from health, to education, to drug rehabilitation. It also subsidizes agriculture. The 1992 campaigns in the United States were about government's ability to create more jobs, provide for the needy, support local businesses, rehabilitate infrastructures, and provide initiative and leadership. It was not about dismantling the state and all the achievements of the past. The Canadian government provides free health care services, subsidizes abortions, builds low-cost housing, and subsidizes public transportation. So, what is all the noise about too much government in Africa? The real point is that Africa is in trouble not because of too much government, but because there is hardly any government at all. The ramshackle structures, desperate for stability and legitimacy, organized and presided over by armed gangs who call themselves soldiers or thieves who call themselves politicians, can hardly pass for governments. Hence, their policies are misplaced, they are so cowardly that they swallow hook, line, and sinker all instructions from the IMF and the World Bank and are totally incapable of fashioning a national agenda for growth and development.

The state was and remains a major actor in the process of accumulation and development in the capitalist countries. There was never a time when the state was not present in the accumulation process. When the U. S. automobile industry was going under, the state bailed it out. When banks are collapsing, the government steps in. During the recent savings and loans scandal, the state is providing the $500 billion bailout. In December 1991, the American president made a trip to Australia, Japan, and Asia only to negotiate for markets for American capitalists. All the talk about too much government in Africa should rather focus on the *type* of state and the *nature* of its custodians.

All the recent talks about democracy will lead nowhere. This is because people appear to be caught in the euphoria of the "American Century" and the decline of the Soviet Union both as a superpower and as a nation; Western notions and models of democracy are now seen as the only credible and appropriate models. Many African states, including Nigeria, have devoted much time and many resources to copying the U. S. model of government without copying the historical specificity of America, its traditions, history, political culture, and other factors that contribute to the strength of bourgeois democracy in the United States.

This assumes in the first place that this model is flawless. More importantly, it assumes that the American and other Western models can easily be transferred to underdeveloped, poverty-stricken, debt-ridden, neocolonial economies that are already marginalized in a highly exploitative global economy. In the capitalist countries of North America and Western Europe, the basis of development was not democratic. The slave trade, colonialism, the destruction of indigenous cultures and political institutions, the looting of resources by Western transnational corporations, and the billions of dollars that are stolen from the Third World and stored in Western banks are not part of the democratic culture. In Britain, women did not have the right to vote until the twentieth century, and in the United States, women did not enjoy the right to vote until 1920. Till this very day, in several parts of the United States, blacks are still discriminated against and issues of affirmative action are still on top of the national agenda. When capitalism was being established, child labor was permitted and workers had no rights or compensation whatsoever. It was only recently that human rights and democracy became part of the political culture of the West. To now lay down political conditionalities for African countries, after exploiting, dominating, underdeveloping, and disarticulating their economies, and after shoring up maniacal regimes all over the world for decades, is to pretend that the West was always democratic and that democracy can easily be established overnight and that there is a direct relationship between the development of capitalism and democracy.

While it is true that, once established, democracy can nurture capitalist relations, the establishment and consolidation of a capitalist system cannot follow a democratic path as the U. S. government tries to make it look. As Olusegun Obasanjo rightly warns,

> We must be aware and wary of what is called "democracy trap," that is, believing that once we have democracy, all other things will be added unto it. Democracy is easier to have than food production and increase in economic well-being. Democracy by itself does not produce these things. . . . We must not copy blindly and sheepishly. Neither must we allow democracy to become destabilising, disabling, divisive and a stumbling block. Democracy, like the market, is no panacea but it is an essential support on which the rest of the structure can hang.[11]

American capitalism was not built on the platform of democracy. The reality is that democracy cannot be decreed into existence as the Babangida regime in Nigeria seems to think, and it cannot be imposed on a society either. It has to emerge from the collective struggles and experiences of the people at the levels of politics, economy, and society.

Unfortunately for a country like Nigeria, it has never been blessed with leaders who have vision and who have not put religious, regional, and ethnic interests above the national interest. As Joy Akanwa has put it in assessing the country's experience with political independence, "What is even the essence of this independence you are talking about? Our leaders have no interest of the masses at heart. They are so interested in their own pockets. They don't want to know if you are starving. To me, Nigeria's independence is nothing but sadness. No responsible government since we started ruling ourselves in this country."[12] There has always been a huge gap between official pronouncements and policy actions. Today, the country has no leader who commands national respect and acceptability. In spite of vast natural and human resources, Nigeria remains poor, underdeveloped, marginal in the global system, and totally incapable of exploiting its resources in the interest of its citizens. To make matters worse, the Babangida regime has emerged as an arrogant, repressive, and corrupt government that has set the country back by almost a century.

Repression can drive popular forces underground or into exile while it builds a false sense of security for a regime. As well, it can generate a suffocating atmosphere of mediocrity and sycophancy. The net result is that a particular regime begins to believe its own lies and praisers. This moves it very far from the people and can push it to rely on more repression and the manipulation of the divisions in society. The Babangida regime is one such government. As the Campaign for Democracy has noted,

> Under this dispensation, the basic rights of Nigerians to life, work, decent accommodation, freedoms of speech, association, movement, assembly, etc. have been trampled upon. The trade unions are being denied the right to express their grievances, while independent non-governmental organizations are denied the right to peaceful protest. Instances abound when Nigerians are killed as a result of their open commitments and efforts to enforce their rights.[13]

The Committee for the Defence of Human Rights (CDHR), in a special edition of *Victims*, its official newsletter, expressed its concern that "life has become very intolerable, nasty and short" in Nigeria, that "cases of extra judicial murders by the police have been on the increase," and that the "periodic massacre of villagers such as those witnessed in Otta, Ogun

State; Irri, Bendel State and Umuchem in Rivers State and of course innocent citizens on the campuses, Oko Oba in Lagos State, Bauchi etc." had become too rampant.[14] The CDHR concluded that the Babangida regime "is the worst violator of Human Rights among all the regimes we have had since independence."[15] It is interesting to note that this very regime came to power promising to protect the human rights of all Nigerians.

The Nigerian military government is one regime that doctors data and lies to itself about its achievements. For instance, in Babangida's address to the nation on 27 August 1991, he correctly identified the state of the economy when his regime forced its way into power:

> Six years ago, this administration came into power at the height of deepening economic, social and political crisis. On the domestic front, there were huge fiscal imbalances and inflationary deficit financing, reckless expenditure of oil windfalls on unproductive projects and poor management of the national economy. Consequently, there was an increased role of government in the management of the national economic life as well as strangulating rules and regulations of the public bureaucracy. On the international front, the country was in deep balance of payments crisis, with diminishing foreign exchange reserves, instability in the oil market and the virtual cessation of non-oil exports. The fixing of the foreign exchange rate by administrative fiat had encouraged massive imports, discouraged exports and drastically curtailed the competitiveness of domestic producers.[16]

Babangida went on to claim that his administration had fostered a "basis for participatory democracy and protect the rights and interests of individuals, as well as social groups." Furthermore, he claimed that

> it is very gratifying to observe that so far, we have succeeded in implementing most of our programmes to the satisfaction of the generality of Nigerians. The physical and economic landscape of this country has been transformed to the extent that we now look inwards for a large measure of our requirements. We are beginning to be proud of "made in Nigeria goods" which now compete favourably with the imported ones. Indeed, with the Structural Adjustment Programme (SAP), we have undeniably achieved the objectives of developing the spirit of self-reliance . . . there is clear evidence of its gains in terms of reduction in the level of our external dependency, increased productivity, increased opportunities for rural development, and enhanced creativity and inventiveness of our people.[17]

As we have demonstrated in chapter 5,the claims by Ibrahim Babangida are very far from the truth. The regime has falsely claimed that: it has laid a basis for self-reliance in Nigeria; it has succeeded in implementing most or all of its programs; the "generality of Nigerians" are satisfied with the regime; there is a fundamental improvement in the appreciation of "made in Nigeria goods" to the extent that if imported alternatives were available, Nigerians would not prefer them; there is a reduction in the country's external dependency; there are increased opportunities in the rural areas; and Nigerians are better off today than they were under the colonial government. As we have noted above, Babangida's government is more repressive than the colonial government was. Poverty has never been so widespread. Reports in the national dailies and weeklies attest to this. The rural areas are worse than they were under colonialism. Industries have practically collapsed; the economy is still absolutely reliant on oil exports for foreign exchange earnings; the size of the state, in spite of the retrenchment of thousands of workers, is yet to be reduced as the regime has created scores of institutions, panels, and other bodies that continue to increase public expenditure.

The democratization process was subverted by the military right from the beginning. The country's foreign debt more than doubled, in spite of structural adjustment, moving from about $15 billion in 1986 to $35 billion in 1992. Corruption has become part of Nigerian life; absolutely nothing can get done in Nigeria without kickbacks. There is virtually no financial accountability in the country. The American ambassador to Nigeria noted recently that "financial discipline has broken down" in Nigeria since late 1990.[18] The *Financial Times* of London noted in 1991 that "there may be governments on the continent as corrupt as Nigeria's, and there certainly are governments that are worse managed. *But few, if any, compared with Nigeria in the scale of the problems that have to be confronted, . . . the size of export earnings open to misappropriation.*"[19] A few examples will suffice here: Vice President, Admiral Augustus Aikhomu was accused by businessman Alhaji Bashiru Bashir of taking a N.5 million bribe; Jennifer Madike accused the former assistant inspector general of police and director of the National Drug Law Enforcement Agency (NDLEA) of taking bribes from drug suspects up to the tune of N800,000;[20] the Federal Bureau of Investigation revealed in July 1991 that the Central Bank of Nigeria and some other banks perpetrated large scale frauds totaling over N1 billion in 1990; the *National Concord*, quoting *TIME* magazine, reported on 26 July 1991 that BCCI granted a facility of N11 billion to Nigeria as gratification in the bank's efforts to cover up its illegal activities; the *National Concord* reported on 16 August 1990 that Nigerians have $33 billion of stolen money in foreign reserves and this was just a "tip of the iceberg"; and in August 1991, a special military tribunal heard how three officers of the Army Corps of Artillery diverted N9 million into their own accounts.[21] The list is simply unbelievable and endless.

More Nigerians have been executed by the Babangida regime than by any other regime in the country's history. Amnesty International reported in March 1991 that the regime executed "over 120 people . . . in 1990, including 69 soldiers sentenced to death after secret, unfair trials for alleged involvement in a coup attempt."[22] There are more lunatics and prostitutes in Nigeria today than ever before. As we noted earlier, Nigeria became a major actor in the international drug business under the Babangida regime and the first case ever of murder by parcel bomb occurred under the regime. More universities have been closed and more students suspended or killed by the Nigerian police since 1986 than at any other time in the country's history. The greatest attacks against popular organizations and the labor movement occurred under the regime than at any time in the country's history. The Academic Staff Union of Universities (ASUU) was proscribed twice under the regime, a record in itself. There have been more religious riots, nationwide riots, and massacres of Christians by Moslems under Babangida's government than at any other time. There have been more attempted coups under the regime than at any other time. More Nigerians, youths, intellectuals, and social critics have fled the country and made claims for political asylum abroad under the regime than at any other time, including during the civil war.[23] More newspaper houses have been closed, journalists jailed, and social critics thrown into jail than at any other time in Nigeria's history.[24] It was under this regime that for the first time, commissioners resigned their appointments in protest against corruption by military governors. Under the Babangida regime, Nigeria was reclassified by the World Bank as a Low Income Country, was ranked number thirteen in the International Index of Human Suffering, and Nigerians became immediate suspects at international airports the world over. Today, Nigerians can no longer visit other countries abroad as all Nigerians are now seen as potential immigrants, drug carriers, and criminals. The image of Nigeria, the pride of the people, the creativity of the masses, and the ebullience of the population have taken a ruthless beating under the regime. What was once an active, creative, productive, and "quarrelsome" society is now permeated with fear, uncertainty, violence, crime, prostitution, corruption, waste, and the enthronement of mediocrity and praise singing by hangers-on and intellectual rationalizers who take delight in writing beautiful speeches with no basis in reality for the military leaders.

This is the way Sam Aluko, one of Nigeria's leading economists, assessed the economic achievements of the Babangida regime recently:

> The economy today is substantially weak in the production sector. . . . The agricultural sector is gradually collapsing in the sense that the poultry industry, for example, has virtually collapsed because of the input which is mainly imported, and is now very expensive. The real production in terms of food is itself very expensive in labour cost and input. The export products, cocoa for example; if you have a cocoa farmer today, you will find that he is groaning. It is not like before when some people wanted us to believe that the structural adjustment programme, SAP, gave boost to the export of cocoa. The cocoa farmer is worse off economically today because he is groaning under heavy cost compared with diminishing revenue. Then you find that the cost of purchase here is higher than the export price in the world market. And part of SAP is that there should be no subsidy. The US, for instance supports agriculture . . . the greatest subsidy to agriculture is given by Europe and America. And yet, it is the same people who tell our government that they must not subsidize agriculture. . . . Even the industries that are producing can't sell and when an industry cannot sell, it cannot expand . . . the investment climate which the government is trying to improve and promote is again devastated by high rates of interest and low returns . . . the economy is very poor.[25]

In another interview with *TELL* magazine, Aluko described Babangida's economic and political policies as "one of the worst." In support of this assessment, Aluko noted

> what he (Babangida) has done with our naira. There is a lot of hardship in the country, and at no time has there been greater hardship than now. In addition, have you ever heard of a country where government forms parties? Is it not party that forms government? So, how come that the Babangida government should form parties for the country? You can see from what is going on in the two parties (SDP and NRC) that there is no party. It is just an assemblage of incompatibles who are forced to come together. That's why there are troubles, actions and counter actions in the two parties. . . . Who is a soldier to tell us what is grassroots democracy?[26]

It is not only Aluko who has spoken out against the ways in which the current military administration is laying the basis for anarchy, religious fanaticism, disorder, and even civil war. Its responses to the frequent massacres of Christians in the north has been so lukewarm that Christians and southerners in general are once again anticipating attacks like those that took place before the civil war. In fact, many of them have started to move their properties back home or to relocate themselves.[27] The *Nigerian Observer* reported recently that "26 families from Asaba capital of Delta State resident in Kano arrived here over the last weekend following the religious riot last month. The families . . . said that although Kano has for sometime now remained calm, there was the belief that it is no longer a safe place for non-indigenes . . . some quarters in Kano have become a no go area . . . recent killings, lynching of people alive instilled fears in them."[28] As Lewis Obi notes, "It is hardly worth commenting on because massacres will occur again and again because those in a position to call a halt tend to profit from them. So there is no incentive to resolve the issues."[29] The increasing insecurity that Nigerians experience once they step out of their ethnic bases has been heightened since the advent of the Babangida regime. Nonindigenes are regarded and treated as "foreigners," discriminated against in employment, and charged higher fees in schools once they venture to move to other states. This has increased the stake in politics and highlighted critical issues pertaining to the national question. It was under this regime that for the first time, in the country's coup history, soldiers tried to execute a coup on behalf of the Middle Belt and the southern states in April 1990.[30] Though the coup failed, it was clear that in several ways it was a reaction to the gross inequality in the distribution of power, national resources, and the annoying arrogance with which the Babangida regime and a handful of extremely wealthy elements displayed their wealth in the faces of the poor majority even when they cannot seriously account for the sources of their wealth. This is one reason why Lewis Obi opines that there is a critical issue yet to be resolved in Nigeria: "whether Nigerians have a right to live in other parts of the country other than where they have their ethnic roots."[31] It is indeed unfortunate that such questions can be raised in contemporary Nigeria after a thirty-month civil war and numerous structural changes. What such questions show very clearly is that the war and the supposed changes have not led to progress, the nation remains dependent, dominated, and distorted. Until such critical issues are resolved, how can Ibrahim Babangida claim to have achieved anything? When citizens are afraid to invest in other parts of their own country because of religious violence and the lackadaisical attitude of government to gross violations of the rights of others, the implications cut across political and economic areas.

We have already mentioned the unprecedented increase in corruption. The Babangida regime not only rehabilitated disgraced politicians, it also restored the ranks and allowances of military governors who were probed, found guilty of corruption and gross abuse of office, and consequently dismissed under the General Murtala Muhammed regime in 1976.[32] Such an act was nothing short of a celebration of irresponsibility, mismanagement, and corruption. It was also under this regime that, for the very first time in the country's history, military officers who had voluntarily retired or who had been compulsorily retired from the armed forces were promoted to higher ranks. As well, the country witnessed its first case of nationwide riots, the "Ebony riots," protesting corrupt practices by the president, his wife, and his deputy.[33] Not one of the several ministers and governors accused of corruption has been punished by this regime. In fact, many of them were rewarded with promotions! Today, the tendency to privatize public office and loot the national purse is seen by almost all Nigerians as a patriotic duty. No nation can survive such pillage when the very custodians of the state and its treasury lead the attack on the vaults. As Lateef Jakande has rightly noted on this issue of corruption:

> It is stating the obvious to say that there was corruption in public life in the first and second republics. There was corruption in the military interregnum between the two republics. And there is corruption in the present military interregnum that will take us to the third republic. . . . In the present military era, corruption has become all pervading, unabashed, uncontrolled, unavoidable, and persistent. Few persons in public life care to deny blood-curdling allegations of corruption in both the public and private sectors of the economy and high and low places. It is fast becoming an integral part of Nigerian culture.[34]

The degree of corruption in a grossly mismanaged economy has direct implications for foreign investment and the redirection of resources to *productive* sectors of the economy.

In his 27 August 1991 address, General Babangida also claimed that "millions of our rural women have been mobilized into the national and global development process and multilateral cooperation" and this is seen as "welcome development and one of the most effective catalysts for producing a new socio-political order." This is indeed very far from the truth. The two major planks on which this claim is based, the Better Life for Rural Women Programme (sometimes called Better Life for Rural Dwellers or Better Life Programme, as demonstration of the lack of focus) and the recently established National Commission for Women, are yet to reach the rural areas. The former is the pet project of the president's wife involving elegantly dressed and heavily perfumed urban women, socialites, wives of top military officers and military governors, as well as spouses of chairmen of local governments. No one in Nigeria takes it seriously and it is incorrect to say that the program has mobilized "millions" of Nigerian women. The National Commission for Women is just what its name suggests, a commission. Its impact is yet to be felt anywhere. Though the Hunger Project in the United States humored the president's wife by awarding her the 1991 Prize for the Sustainable End of Hunger, it is clear that the Hunger Project, just like the Nigerian government, is out of touch with the Nigerian reality. More Nigerians are starving today and more are unable to meet the minimum internationally required daily caloric intake than ever before. Food prices have gone up by over 500 percent in most cases and where is Mrs. Babangida providing an answer to the problem of hunger? Assuming it were true, in any case, what is the purpose of the prize awarded by the Hunger Project? How many prizes has the Hunger Project awarded to presidents in the United States for responding to hunger in many parts of the world and for keeping down the price of food in America? Such useless awards are what makes the government believe that its policies are working even when the reality is much different. As Sam Aluko has noted on the Better Life Programme:

> The programme . . . is a ruse. That's what they do in East Africa and Southern Africa. They call it better life for rural women, women in industry, women in development and so on—just to humour women, to make them forget their sorrows. . . . It is just a ruse. They say that life has changed, even in my own village . . . I . . . go home frequently. The place is supposed to be enjoying from the rural electrification project, but most of the time in the month, there is no light. It is the same women who are now saying that some are using the programme to steal.[35]

Thus, rather than pay attention to the decay and dislocation in the rural and urban centers, the Nigerian state has busied itself wasting scarce resources in sponsoring all sorts of candidates to positions in virtually all international organizations including the United Nations. Ibrahim Babangida himself, not satisfied with being the most powerful leader ever to rule Nigeria both in terms of the number of offices under his direct command and the degree of autonomy he enjoys in relation to other power blocs, became not just chairman of the Economic Community of West African States for the third time in six years, but also the chairman of the Organization of African unity.[36]

Playing the "superpower" of Africa, the regime was spending hundreds of millions of dollars in sponsoring a peace-keeping operation in Liberia and in shoring up the embattled Momoh government in Sierra Leone until it was overthrown in a coup in 1992. While the government calls on Nigerians to be disciplined, to make sacrifices, to avoid waste and conserve resources, and to reform their life-styles and attitudes to work, it is busy squandering the nation's wealth on sports, useless international summits, the purchase of private presidential jets, paying allowances to previously dismissed and discredited soldiers, and buying expensive cars for military officers and top government functionaries. The CDHR has noted that "reckless spending such as purchasing another presidential jet worth over N160 million; donating N10 million to a musicians association to host a gala night; N10 million to the Bar Association for not being 'confrontational'; N35 million to Arewa House; N10 million to Ekpoma University and the very costly adventure of ECOMOG in Liberia and Sierra Leone" show very clearly that "the government's economic priorities do not take into account our major difficulties as a people."[37] As Nosa Igiebor has noted:

> But if the lavishness with which the Abuja Organisation of African Unity, OAU summit, was hosted is any indication, the government itself badly needs to reform its lifestyle. As if it was dramatising the fact that Mercedes Benz is the ultimate status symbol car in the country, the government purchased over 50 six-door limousine versions of the German luxury car for the summit, which was hardly reflective of an economy that is being structurally adjusted.
>
> Far more than ever before SAP was put in place, there are now Mercedes Benz and many other luxury cars plying Nigerian roads. Apart from cars, thousands of different kinds of luxury goods are brought into the country daily, and the shelves and showrooms of many supermarkets are filled with them, although the president believes Nigerians "are beginning to be proud of Nigerian goods."[38]

Sam Aluko also draws attention to this extravagant tendency in the Nigerian state that negates all the principles of adjustment and belies the poverty and impoverishment visited on the vast majority by the same government:

> The only thing we are emphasizing now is service banks, insurance, games, athletics, etc., which are evidences of a highly matured economy. When you find that four or five per cent of your population can produce the food you eat, then you can afford to allow the rest to play soccer, play tennis, swim, etc., because you are producing enough food anyway. But in a country where 60 per cent of the population cannot produce enough food for us, you are spending a lot of time on frills, all these international competitions, wasting money on sports, things that should be mere hobbies, these are the things we are concentrating so much upon. Banks are quite good because they can promote industry but the banks today are not lending money

> for direct production. They are laundering credit, foreign exchange, they are buying and selling money. But buying and selling money causes more inflation . . . inflation diminishes productive capacity. We are not doing structural adjustment. Because structural adjustment means that you are improving from primitive agriculture to mechanized agriculture. Then you are improving from substantially depending on agriculture to increased industrialization. In fact, *most of the industries in Nigeria are collapsing.*[39]

Yet, the Nigerian government claims that its structural adjustment program is achieving all its set goals and that it has laid a foundation for self-reliance and development!

We cannot but agree with Aaron Gana that in spite of the heavy participation of some intellectuals in the government, it is clear that its conceptualization of reality, its understanding of the realignment of forces in the global system, its understanding of the patterns of alignment and realignment of class forces in Nigeria are essentially "informed by the same superficial comprehension of the dynamics of our crisis. It explains the administration's rejection of the profound analysis of the Nigerian political economy contained in the Political Bureau Report and the central recommendations of the Panel."[40] Gana concluded his convocation lecture at the University of Jos by noting that the legacies the Babangida military regime will bequeath to Nigerians include: (1) a repressive atmosphere; (2) subversion of the people's will; (3) corruption and abuse of office; (4) "the decoration of prominent members of the ruling class, (whose track records as public servants are known to border on criminality) with the highest honours of the land"; (5) "the perversion of justice by men and women entrusted with the sacred duty of managing public affairs"; (6) "conspiracy of pessimism," "apathy," and "uncertainty" about the future political order; (7) "politicisation of religion," which has "provided a launching pad for the intensification of religious bigotry and the manipulation of religious sensibilities for political ends"; and (8) "the consolidation of the neo-colonial economy through the Structural Adjustment Programme inspired by the IMF and the World Bank," which is bound to "deepen the crisis of accumulation with dire consequences for the Third Republic."[41]

There is, therefore, enough reason to be skeptical about the future of politics and democracy in Nigeria.[42] The economic basis for the sustenance of rational and consensual politics is just not there. There is no reason whatsoever not to expect more military coups; for not only does the military control and monopolize the means of coercion, but it also believes it has the right to determine and decide how, when, and by whom the country should be ruled. To make its job easier, the politicians have not demonstrated any appreciable level of discipline, responsibility, or willingness to reduce the tensions, violence, thuggery, manipulation, and the accentuation of primordial loyalties. Politics is still essentially a business.

The domination of the transition program by corrupt individuals, young and old, poses a major threat to the nation's quest for democracy. In spite of the efforts of the military to husband the transition program to reflect its narrow interests, the old politicians, even before the government lifted the ban on them out of frustration, were fully in charge of the transition program. For instance, John Ebimah Ogbeide, who had contested for the gubernatorial nomination in the National Republican Convention (NRC), the more conservative of the two parties, resigned from the party claiming that "few individuals with selfish personal interests and who would want to reap where they did not sow" had joined and taken over the party. Ogbeide also alleged in a press conference that "in Edo State, . . . the National Republican Convention has been sold completely to the highest bidder by some members of the National Executive Committee of the party, such that unless you are a member of this notorious clique of auctioneers, speculators and buyers encapsulated [sic], you cannot aspire for anything in the party" and that "bribery, thuggery, greed and avarice have been institutionalized in the party . . . the NRC in Edo State is now synonymous with an overbearing money bag" who had, on 16 October 1991, "invited the chairmen and secretaries of the party at the ward, local government and state levels who he installed anyway to his wonderland . . . for one night where thousands of naira were brazenly dished out to buy their conscience."[43] In late November 1991, *The Observer* reported that Jerry Gana, then national chairman of MAMSER, "alerted Nigerians on the threat posed to democracy by the political elite, whom he said, are hell bent on violating electoral rules and regulations for purely selfish reasons. These political elite, the MAMSER boss contended, have learned practically nothing from the historical experiences of the past and are therefore now pre-occupied with bastardizing democratic institutions."[44] The paper also reported that in his first reaction to the conduct of the primaries by the two government-created political parties, Ibrahim Babangida "expressed serious reservations, and *noted with fright the large scale frauds* and blatant irregularities that attended the exercise."[45] The Nigerian Bar Association (NBA) in the face of pronouncements by the leaders of the NEC and CDS about their intentions to disregard the orders of the courts had cause to caution "the parties and NEC on the grave dangers posed to the survival of democracy by the disobedience, disregard and violation of court orders."[46] Similarly, at a one-day conference on "Peace and Security as a Pre-condition for a Successful Third Republic" held in November 1991, Gana described as "a dangerous development," "the growing influence of money in determining victors in political contests" that "might sound the death knell for the national quest for a stable democracy." His Edo State representative at the conference, P. E. B. Uku, lamented the fact that "political aspirants still believe strongly in the use of money to secure votes at the expense of their opponents."[47] These statements from the leaders of the MAMSER show that the institution has failed woefully in its mission and wasted the hundreds of million of naira sunk into its activities since it was created as a major instrument of the transition program in 1987. Yet, Gana, in a press conference at the end of 1991, claimed that in the areas of political education, mass mobilization for self-reliance and economic recovery, social justice, and mass literacy promotion, the MAMSER "had justified its existence."[48] Such claims, which have no relationships to reality, are part of the contradictions of governance, responsibility, and accountability in Nigeria. The excessive reliance on self-glorification to justify huge expenditures tend to encourage public officers to continue in their old ways since they are usually accountable to themselves anyway. The truth is that one cannot expect much from the politicians currently campaigning to run the Third Republic.

The masses of the people are so poor and desperate that they are easily vulnerable to manipulation, exploitation, and recruitment as thugs. The debt profile is high, the state is unstable, the economic base is fragile, and the general culture of politics and society is permeated with greed, avarice, ostentatiousness, glorification of wealth, the abuse of power by the rich and powerful, and the fetishism of foreign exchange. Civil society is highly fragmented and opposition forces are weak, poorly organized, lack resources, and are vulnerable to domestication and incorporation. It will be tantamount to an exercise in academic fraud to speak glowingly of the prospects of the Nigerian economy or of democracy in Nigeria. The truth about the country today is that it is on the path to disaster:

> There is too much leakage in the economy. We spend too much abroad. . . . Our president and ministers, they roam around the world like locusts. . . . Nigeria is a debtor nation and yet we are behaving extravagantly. . . . Today, we have about 10.6 naira equal to one dollar. It is by government fiat. It is not by free market because if you allow people to determine, nobody will pay such high rate. Government has been manipulating the rate of exchange. . . . An economy that is not yet fully industrialized cannot afford to keep the value of the naira like this. We can't buy vehicles today. No young man can build a house today. . . . Why are all the banks concentrated in Victoria Island? And none of them is lending money for direct production. They are trading in foreign exchange; they are buying and selling currency, . . . we are owing about $35 billion. Part of the problem is the interest rate. The other part is that we have been borrowing money for various useless things. We borrow money to buy books. We borrow money for water; we borrow money for environmental sanitation; we borrow money for hospitals. That is what we call unproductive ventures . . . there have been a lot of foreign flights of capital. Foreign investment has not been coming in because the environment is not conducive. . . . People are lifting oil, selling it and keeping the money abroad. They are not bringing such money back home for investment. When you get to Lagos these days, the traffic hold-up there is more than that of New York. People bring in all sorts of junk in the name of cars. . . . It is a cardinal mistake to devalue the naira to the tune of 90 per cent. No government can do it and survive. . .
>
> This is the only country in the world where people publish black-market rate in the newspaper.[49]

The Future

From our analyses thus far, the future does not seem too bright. Yet, there is hope for the future. The failure of the Nigerian state to meet the basic needs of the people as well as the repressive atmosphere engendered by the military has forced a coalescence of interests and social forces. As well, the perpetuation of gross inequalities in power and opportunities, the proletarianization of the upper-middle and lower-middle classes, the repression of labor, students and other popular groups, and the decay in the rural areas have encouraged the breakdown of old orthodoxies, the strengthening of cross-class and cross-ethnic group interests, and the forging of stronger political relations. The unbridled corruption of the Nigerian state and the arrogance of power exhibited by the ruling elite have served to convince the working classes and other nonprivileged groups that it cannot be relied upon to move the country toward self-reliance and popular mobilization. The impoverishment of nonbourgeois forces through the implementation of the structural adjustment program and the grossly unequal distribution of the pains of adjustment have served to expose the class bias of the state and its custodians, and demonstrate to the victims of the adjustment program that the unequal alliance between the Nigerian bourgeoisie and foreign capital cannot be in the interest of the people or the country.

The sudden creation of nine new states and 136 new local government areas, the abrupt dismissal of elected local government officials, as was the case in the Enugu local government, the indiscriminate banning of politicians in the name of the transition program,[50] the frequent changes made to the transition program as many as forty times, and inconsistency on the specific date of hand over of power to civilians have tended to give the Nigerian public the impression that the regime: (1) is trying to provoke Nigerians in order to find an excuse to hang on to power; (2) has a hidden agenda unknown to the public; (3) hopes to sufficiently discredit the politicians to justify the extension of military rule as the civilianization of Babangida's junta; and (4) is attempting to manipulate the transition program to enable its favored party or individuals to succeed it.[51] Thus, in the past six years or so, several popular and civil liberty organizations have emerged in Nigeria. These include the Committee for the Defence of Human Rights (CDHR), the Civil Liberties Organisation (CLO), the Constitutional Rights Project (CRP), the Campaign for Democracy, National Association of Democratic Lawyers (NADL), Gani Fawehinmi Solidarity Association (GFSA), National Consultative Forum (NCF), Women in Nigeria (WIN), and of course the National Association of Nigerian Students (NANS). Support for these associations come from some trade unions, critical scholars, and even militant religious leaders. Religious organizations, especially the Christian Council of Nigeria (CAN), have become very militant, concerning themselves with economic and political issues and confronting the state openly on issues of human rights, social justice, and freedom of religion.

The agenda of these organizations transcend the campaigns for transition to the Third Republic under the guidance of the military. For instance, the objectives of the Campaign for Democracy, an association of eight popular groups, include:

1. restoration of the sovereignty of the Nigerian people, allowing them to choose how to be governed, who to govern them, and the procedure or process through which they will be governed;
2. the right of the people to form their own political parties without interference;
3. termination of military rule for all time;

4. the replacement of imposed transitional agencies by independent and impartial transitional agencies including the immediate establishment of impartial electoral bodies;
5. respect of fundamental human rights, the rule of law, and the abrogation of all decrees;
6. termination of economic policies that have caused the people hardship, poverty, disease, hunger, unemployment, retrenchment, and illiteracy;
7. the abrogation of military rule in Nigeria no later than 1 October 1992 and the immediate restoration of democracy.[52]

It is clear from the above that there is a major emphasis on the *political* aspects of restructuring, recovery, democratization, and development in Nigeria. Just as the World Bank is beginning to recognize and acknowledge the salience of the political dimensions of the African crisis and has specifically in its 1989 report addressed the issues of repression, mismanagement, corruption, the suffocation of civil society, the nonempowerment of the people and their organizations, the existence of disabling environments, and the reproduction of underdevelopment and inequalities through unequal power relations in African countries, the civil liberty organizations believe that Nigeria's problems are more political than economic.

Economic underdevelopment, foreign domination and exploitation, rural decay, urban dislocation, unemployment, inflation, poverty, inequality, institutional fragility, and other manifestations of backwardness in oil-rich Nigeria are precipitates of political contradictions and inequalities in the control and distribution of political power in the country. With repression, closure of political spaces, the harassment of popular forces, the ruthless exploitation of women, the virtual abrogation of all fundamental human rights, and the inability of the people to attain the highest points of the creative and innovative abilities, the economic crisis takes on new and higher dimensions. Economic development cannot take place in the absence of an enabling environment. Foreign investment cannot flow in when the economy is not competitive and political instability, violence, and human right abuses as well as coups and countercoups permeate the system. Growth and accumulation cannot occur when people cannot invest, cannot save, and cannot produce. Finally, development will remain a mirage when corruption has become a way of life, the state is weak and unstable, and the dominant elites have no commitment whatsoever to the future of the nation. We share Lateef Jakande's view that

> if the Third Republic is to survive longer than any of its civilian or military predecessors, there must be a new social order. It should be the overriding policy of the new social order to make use of all available talents regardless of their political leaning. . . . The next prerequisite of the new social order must be to review those aspects of current national economic policies which have brought unnecessary pain and agony to our people. . . . The new social order must review the structural adjustment programme. . . . The new social order must move with the greatest possible speed to terminate the present sufferings of our people of all categories. I refer specifically to the high rate of inflation, the lack of jobs for millions of Nigerians able and willing to work, the inadequacy of places in higher educational institutions resulting in the exclusion of about 200,000 qualified students from higher education every year, the confused state of our primary and secondary education, the inadequacy of health care facilities, the inadequacy of support and subsidy for agriculture, the deplorable housing conditions, and the scarcity of potable water in most parts of Nigeria. . . . The new social order must, of course, tackle the problem of corruption.[53]

To achieve these and other objectives, there is need for greater political unity among democratic and progressive forces in the country. What is actually going on in Eastern Europe, rather than the pedestrian and misguided interpretations and deductions made about the situation by bourgeois scholars and political opportunists, should strengthen progressive, democratic, and popular forces on the need for clarity, specificity, relevance, democracy, accountability, and flexibility in the constitution and composition of political and ideological models and the relationship of theory to praxis. Developments in Eastern Europe are lessons on the implications of excessive bureaucratization, and the massive concentration of resources on security and military development. As well, the East European experience demonstrates the fundamental obstacles to socialism in a world economy dominated by capitalist relations. There are more countries in the world where capitalism as an economic model has been a disaster. There is not one country in Africa where it has worked. Yet, people do not see this as a demonstration of the uselessness or failure of capitalism. In the absence of colonies and slaves and in the absence of neocolonies, African countries are caught in a major contradiction that militates against the ability to promote primitive accumulation by looting other societies. This means that the contemporary order calls for a careful and clever ability to exploit the productive and progressive aspects of both the capitalist and socialist ideologies anchored on the principles of democracy, accountability, social justice, and the dominance of the will of the people. The struggle for such a society is already on in Nigeria but there is no reason to expect a quick consummation of the struggle.

Notes

1. Sam Aluko, "We Are Behaving Like Father Christmas," *TELL* (7 October 1991), 50.
2. Sully Abu, "Politics in Retreat," *The Guardian* (14 October 1990), A9.
3. Committee for the Defense of Human Rights (CSHR), "Nigeria in Danger—the Way Out," *Victims* 2, no. 4 (4 August 1991), 4.
4. Ibid.
5. Ibid., 5.
6. Emevwo Biakolo, "Maroko and Other Indignities," *The Guardian* (21 July 1990).
7. Ibid. Also see, Sully Abu, "Ode to Maroko—Reflections on a Sick, Sad Country," *The Guardian* (22 July 1990); Emevwo Biakolo, "Maroko and Other Indignities"; and "Maroko: The Final Solution," Editorial, *The Guardian* (24 July 1990). For the rationalization of the demolition exercise by the military governor of Lagos State, Colonel Raji Rasaki, see "Why Maroko Residents were Evacuated, by Rasaki," *The Guardian* (24 July 1990).
8. Committee for the Defense of Human Rights (CSHR), "Nigeria in Danger—the Way Out," 2.
9. See World Bank, *Sub-Saharan Africa: From Crisis to Sustainable Growth—a Long-Term Perspective Study* (Washington, DC: The World Bank, 1989).
10. Ibrahim Babangida, "Our Salvation Is in Our Hands," *New Nigerian* (26 May 1992).
11. Olusegun Obasanjo, "The Nigerian Society and the Third Republic," *The Guardian* (14 March 1992), 9.
12. Joy Akanwa, "All These 'Suffer, Suffer'," *TELL* (7 October 1991), 17.
13. "Campaign for Democracy" (Text of Address at the Inauguration of the Campaign for Democracy, Lagos, 11 November 1991).
14. "Nigeria in Danger—the Way Out," 1.
15. Ibid.
16. Ibrahim Babangida, "Consolidating the Gains of Development." (Nationwide address on the sixth anniversary of the regime, 27 August 1991.) Text reproduced in *Newbreed* (16 September 1991).
17. Ibid.
18. "Between Dream and Reality," *The African Guardian* (2 December 1991), 28.
19. *Financial Times* quoted in *Victims-CDHR Newsletter* 2, No. 4 (August 1991), 3.
20. See "Why Oyakhilome was Removed," *Newbreed* (1 April 1991); "The 'Sacking' of Oyakhilome," *Newswatch* (25 March 1991); and "Jennifer Madike: The Road to Prison," *Newswatch* (4 March 1991).
21. "Army Officers on Trial," *Newswatch* (12 August 1991); *Victims*; and Pita Agbese and Julius O. Ihonvbere, *The State and The Politics of Structural Adjustment in Nigeria* (Forthcoming).
22. "Nigeria: A Summary of Human Rights Concerns in 1990," Amnesty International, AI Index: AFR 44/04/91 (March 1991), 1.
23. See for instance "764 Nigerians Seek Asylum in Germany," *New Nigerian* (27 November 1991), 8.
24. See the newsletters of the CLO and the CDHR for comprehensive details.
25. Sam Aluko, "We are Behaving like Father Christmas," 50–51.
26. Sam Aluko, "We are All Liars," *TELL* (15 April 1991), 52.
27. See "Religious Fanatics are Back: Death, Destruction in Bauchi," *TELL* (6 May 1991) and *African Concord* (25 November 1991).

28. *The Nigerian Observer* (22 November 1991), 8.
29. See Lewis Obi, "The Kano Massacres," *African Concord* (25 November 1991).
30. See Julius O. Ihonvbere, "Structural Adjustment, the April 1990 Coup and Democratization in Nigeria," *Africa Quarterly* 29, nos. 3-4 (1990), 17-39 and "Coup that Failed: The Storming of Dodan Barracks," *Newswatch* (7 May 1990).
31. Ibid.
32. See Ndukwe Eke, "Aikhomu Clears Air on Assets of Dismissed Military Governors," *The Statesman* (13 April 1991).
33. See "SAP Wars: A Nation on the Boil," *The African Guardian* (12 June 1989).
34. L. K. Jakande, "Building a New Nigeria," *Newswatch* (5 November 1990), 7.
35. Sam Aluko, "We are All Liars," 54.
36. See "Ruling the World—Amid Serious Domestic Problems, President Babangida Makes a Personal Impression on Global Politics by Hunting for Key Posts in World Bodies," *African Concord* (17 June 1991).
37. Committee for the Defense of Human Rights (CDHR), "Nigeria in Danger—The Way Out," 2.
38. Nosa Igiebor, "Splash and Dash," *TELL* (9 September 1991), 16.
39. Sam Aluko, "We are Behaving like Father Christmas," 50 (emphasis added).
40. Aaron Gana, *The Limits of Political Engineering: A Critique of the Transition Programme* (12th Convocation Lecture, University of Jos, Nigeria, 2 February 1990), 15.
41. Ibid.
42. See "A Foreigner's Impression," *African Concord* (27 January 1992); Andy Ike Ezeani, "The Ultimate Circus," *Daily Champion* (9 March 1992); "Assassins Again," Editorial, *Daily Champion* (9 March 1992); and Labaran Maku, "Presidency: 35 Vying for SDP Ticket," *Daily Champion* (9 March 1992).
43. "The Hour of Truth" (Press statement delivered by Dr. John Ebimah Ogbeide, MBBS, MBA, NRC gubernatorial aspirant, Benin City, Edo State), *The Observer* (22 November 1991), 12.
44. "Threats to Democracy," Editorial, *The Observer* (22 November 1991), 4.
45. Ibid.
46. Ibid.
47. "Bribe Nobody to Vote for Candidates," *The Observer* (22 November 1991).
48. "Gana Lauds MAMSER," *The Observer* (22 November 1991), 2.
49. Sam Aluko, "We are Behaving like Father Christmas", 51-53.
50. See "Agbalajobi, Sarumi, Others Banned," *Vanguard* (26 November 1991).
51. See "Campaign for Democracy in Nigeria" (Text of Press Conference Announcing the Inauguration of the Campaign for Democracy in Nigeria, Lagos, 11 November 1991).
52. Ibid.
53. L. K. Jakande, "Building a New Nigeria," 7.

Select Bibliography

Achebe, Chinua. *The Trouble with Nigeria*. Enugu, Nigeria: Fourth Dimension, 1982.

Adam, Mohammed. "Nigeria: The Busted Boom." *International Perspectives* (January-February 1987).

Adamolekun, Lapido. *The Fall of the Second Republic*. Ibadan, Nigeria: Spectrum, 1985.

Adedeji, Adebayo, and Timothy M. Shaw, eds. *Economic Crisis in Africa: African Perspectives on Development Problems and Potentials*. Boulder: Lynne Reinner, 1985.

Adekanye, Bayo J., ed. "The Military, Social Classes and Revolution." *Studies in Politics and Society* 5 (special issue, 1989).

Adeotun, Phillips, and E. C. Ndekwu, eds. *Structural Adjustment Programme in a Developing Economy: The Case of Nigeria*. Ibadan, Nigeria: NISER, 1987.

______. *Economic Impact of Nigeria's Structural Adjustment Programme*. Ibadan, Nigeria: NISER, 1990.

Agbese, Pita. "State, Media and the Imperatives of Repression: An Analysis of the Ban on *Newswatch*." *International Third World Studies Journal and Review* 1, 2 (1989).

______. "The Impending Demise of Nigeria's Third Republic." *Africa Today* 37, no. 3 (1990).

Ake, Claude. *Revolutionary Pressures in Africa*. London: Zed, 1978.

______. *A Political Economy of Africa*. London: Longman, 1981.

______, ed. *Political Economy of Nigeria*. London: Longman, 1985.

Akeredolu-Ale, E. O. *The Underdevelopment of Indigenous Entrepreneurship in Nigeria*. Ibadan, Nigeria: Ibadan University Press. 1975.

Aluko, Olajide. "Necessity and Freedom in Nigerian Foreign Policy." Inaugural Lecture, University of Ife, Ile-Ife, Nigeria, 17 March 1981a.

______. *Essays in Nigerian Foreign Policy*. London: George Allen & Unwin, 1981b.

______. "The Study of International Relations in Nigeria." *Millenium* 16, no. 2 (Summer 1987).

Aluko, Sam. *The Burden of Economic Structural Adjustment: The Nigerian Scenario*. Ile-Ife, Nigeria: Convocation Ceremony Lecture, 1987.

Amadiume, Ifi. *Male Daughters, Female Husbands*. London: Zed, 1987.

Andrae, Gunilla, and Bjorn Beckman. *The Wheat Trap: Bread and Underdevelopment in Nigeria*. London: Zed, 1985.

———. *Industry Goes Farming: The Nigerian Raw Material Crisis and the Case of Textiles and Cotton*. Uppsala, Sweden: Scandinavian Institute of African Studies, Research Report no. 80.

Ate, Bassey. *Decolonization and Dependence: The Development of Nigerian-U. S. Relations, 1960–1984*. Boulder: Westview, 1987.

Ayu, Iyorchia D. *Essays in Popular Struggle: Fela, Students' Patriotism and the Nicaraguan Revolution*. Oguta, Nigeria: Zim Pan-African, 1986.

Bach, Daniel. *Le Nigerian Contemporain*. Paris: Editions du CNRS, 1986.

Baker, Pauline H. "A Giant Staggers: Nigeria as an Emerging Regional Power." In *African Security Issues: Sovereignty, Stability and Solidarity*, edited by Bruce E. Arglinghaus, 76–97. Boulder: Westview, 1984.

Bangura, Yusuf. "Structural Adjustment and the Political Question." *Review of African Political Economy* 37 (1986).

———. "IMF/World Bank Conditionality and Nigeria's Structural Adjustment Programme." In *The IMF and the World Bank in Africa*, edited by Kjell J. Havenik, 95–116. Uppsala, Sweden: Scandinavian Institute of African Studies, 1987.

———. "The Crisis of Underdevelopment and the Transition to Civil Rule: Conceptualizing the Question of Democracy in Nigeria." *Africa Development* 13, no. 1 (1988).

———. "Authoritarian Rule and Democracy in Africa: A Theoretical Discourse," in *Authoritarianism, Democracy and Adjustment: The Politics of Economic Reform in Africa*, edited by Peter Gibbon, Yusuf Bangura, and Arve Ofsted. Uppsala, Sweden: Scandinavian Institute of African Studies, 1992.

Barber, Karin. "Popular Reactions to the Petro-Naira." *Journal of Modern African Studies* 20, no. 3 (September 1982).

Beckman, Bjorn. "Imperialism and the 'National Bourgeoisie.'" *Review of African Political Economy* 22 (October–December 1981).

———. "Whose State: State and Capitalist Development in Nigeria." *Review of African Political Economy* 23 (January–April 1982).

______. "Neo-Colonialism, Capitalism, and the State of Nigeria." In *Contradictions of Accumulation in Africa: Studies in Economy and State*, edited by Henry Bernstein and Bonnie K. Campbell, 71–113. Beverly Hills: Sage, 1985.

______. "Whose Democracy? Bourgeois versus Popular Democracy in Africa." *Review of African Political Economy* 45/46 (1989).

Bello, M. "Economics of Garri or Garrinomics." *Business Concord* (20 January 1989).

Berry, Sara S. "Oil and the Disappearing Peasantry: Accumulation, Differentiation and Underdevelopment in Western Nigeria." *African Economic History* 13 (1984).

______. *Fathers Work for Their Sons: Accumulation, Mobility and Class Formation in an Extended Yoruba Community*. Berkeley: University of California Press, 1985.

Bienen, Henry, and V. P. Diejomaoh, eds. *The Political Economy of Income Distribution in Nigeria*. New York: Holmes & Meier, 1981.

Biersteker, Thomas J. *Distortion or Development? Contending Perspectives on the Multinational Corporation*. Cambridge: MIT Press, 1978.

______. *Multinationals, the State, and Control of the Nigerian Economy*. Princeton, NJ: Princeton University Press, 1987.

Caccia, Goffredo. "Nigeria: Oil Plot or Oil Glut?" *Journal of African Marxists* 3 (1983).

Campbell, B., and J. Loxley, eds. *Structural Adjustment in Africa*. London: Macmillan, 1989.

Carlsson, Jerker, and Timothy M. Shaw, eds. *Newly Industrializing Countries and the Political Economy of South-South Relations*. London: Macmillan, 1988.

Clarke, Peter. "Islamic Reform in Contemporary Nigeria: Methods and Aims." *Third World Quarterly* 10, no. 2 (April 1988).

Cohen, Robin. *Labour and Politics in Nigeria*. London: Heinemann, 1984.

Coleman, James S. *Nigeria: Background to Nationalism* (Berkeley: University of California Press, 1958).

Crowther, Michael. *The Story of Nigeria*. London: Farber, 1978.

______. *West Africa Under Colonial Rule*. London: Hutchinson, 1981.

Daddieh, Cyril Kofie, and Timothy M. Shaw. "The Political Economy of Decision-Making in Africa: The Cases of Recognition of Biafra and MPLA." *International Political Science Review* 5, no. 2 (January 1984).

Diamond, Larry. "Nigeria in Search of Democracy." *Foreign Affairs* 62, no. 4 (Spring 1984).

______. "Issues in the Constitutional Design of a Third Nigerian Republic." *African Affairs* (April 1987a).

______. "Nigeria: Between Deictatorship and Democracy." *Current History* (May 1987b).

______. *Class, Ethnicity and Democracy in Nigeria: The Failure of the First Republic*. London: Macmillian, 1988.

______. "Nigeria's Search for a New Political Order." *Journal of Democracy* 2, no. 2 (Spring 1991a).

______. "Nigeria's Third Quest for Democracy." *Current History* (May 1991b).

Dudley, Billy J. *Parties and Politics in Northern Nigeria*. London: Frank Cass, 1968.

______. *Instability and Political Order: Politics and Crisis in Nigeria*. Ibadan, Nigeria: Ibadan University Press, 1973.

______. *An Introduction to Nigerian Government and Politics*. London: Macmillan, 1982.

Economist. *The Political Economy of Nigeria*. London: The Economist, 1984.

Economist Intelligence Unit. *Nigeria: Economic Prospects to 1985. After the Oil Glut*. London: EIU Special Report Number 123, 1982.

Ekekwe, Eme. *Class and State in Nigeria*. London: Longman, 1986.

Ekoko, A. E., and M. A. Vogt, eds. *Nigerian Defence Policy: Issues and Problems*. Lagos, Nigeria: Malthouse, 1990.

Ekundare, R. O. *Economic History of Nigeria 1860–1960*. London: Methuen, 1973.

Ekwe-Ekwe, Herbert. "The Nigerian Plight: Shagari to Buhari." *Third World Quarterly* 7, no. 3 (July 1985).

Evans, Peter. *Dependent Development: The Alliance of Multinational, State and Local Captial in Brazil*. Princeton, NJ: Princeton University Press, 1979.

Fadahunsi, Akin. "A Review of the Political Economy of the Industrialisation Strategy of the Nigerian State, 1960–1980." *African Development* 4, nos. 2/3 (April–September, 1979).

Fadahunsi, Akin, and B. U. N. Igwe, eds. *Capital Goods and Technological Change and Accumulation in Nigeria*. Dakar, Senegal: CODESRIA, 1989.

Falola, Toyin, ed. *Britain and Nigeria: Exploitation or Development?* London: Zed, 1986.

Falola, Toyin, and Julius O. Ihonvbere. *The Rise and Fall of Nigeria's Second Republic, 1979–1983*. London: Zed, 1985.

______, eds. *Nigeria and the International Capitalist System*. Boulder: Lynne Reinner, 1988.

Fashoyin, Tayo. *Industrial Relations in Nigeria*. London: Longman, 1981.

Fasipe, Akintayo, ed. *Nigeria's External Debt*. Ile-Ife, Nigeria: Obafemi Awolowo University Press, 1990.

Feinstein, Alan. *African Revolutionary: The Life and Times of Nigeria's Aminu Kano*. 2d ed. Boulder: Lynne Reinner, 1987.

Forrest, Tom. "Recent Developments in Nigerian Industrialisation." In *Industry and Accumulation in Africa*, edited by Martin Fransman. London: Heinemann, 1982.

______. "The Political Economy of Civil Rule and the Economic Crisis in Nigeria, 1979-84." *Review of African Political Economy* 35 (May 1986).

Freund, Bill. "Oil Boom and Crisis in Contemporary Nigeria." *Review of African Political Economy* 13 (May-August 1978).

______. *Capital and Labour in the Nigerian Tin Mines*. London: Longman, 1981.

Gambari, Ibrahim. *Party Politics and Foreign Policy: Nigeria Under the First Republic*. Zaria, Nigeria: Ahmadu Bello University Press, 1980.

Garba, Joe. *Diplomatic Soldiering: Nigerian Foreign Policy, 1975–1979*. Ibadan, Nigeria: Spectrum, 1980.

Graf, William. *The Nigerian State*. London: James Currey, 1989.

Hatch, John. *Africa Emergent: Africa's Problems Since Independence*. Chicago: Henry Regenery, 1974.

Helleiner, Gerald K. *Peasant Agriculture, Government and Economic Growth in Nigeria*. Homewood, IL: Irwin, 1974.

Ihonvbere, Julius O. "Resource Availability and Foreign Policy Change: The Impact of Oil on Nigerian Foreign Policy since Independence." *Afrika Spectrum* 2 (1982a).

______. "Oil Revenues, Underdevelopment and Class Struggles in Nigeria." *Scandinavian Journal of Development Alternatives* 2, no. 2 (June 1982b).

______. "Social Aspects of Economic Integration: The Case of the Economic Community of West African States." *Korean Journal of International Studies* 14, no. 1 (winter 1982/83).

______. *The Oil Industry in Nigeria: An Annotated Bibliography*. Montreal, Canada: Centre for Developing-Area Studies, McGill University, 1983a.

______. "Internal Dimensions of Nigeria's Foreign Policy towards the West African Sub-Region." *ODU- A Journal of West African Studies* 24 (July 1983b).

______. "Foreign Policy of Dependent States: The Impact of Oil on Nigeria's Foreign Policy, 1960–1982." *Indian Journal of Political Science* 13, no. 1 (January 1984).

______. *The 1983 Elections and the Buhari Coup in Nigeria: Contradictions in a (Semi) Peripheral Political Economy*. Halifax, Nova Scotia, Canada: Center for African Studies, 1985.

______. "Contradictions of Multi-Party Democracy in Peripheral Formations: The Rise and Demise of Nigeria's Second Republic, 1979–1983." In *Democracy and the One Party State in Africa*, edited by Peter Meyns and Dani Wadada Nabudere. Hamburg: Institute for African Studies, 1988.

______. ed. *The Political Economy of Crisis and Underdevelopment in Africa: Selected Works of Claude Ake*. Lagos, Nigeria: JAD, 1990a.

______. "The African Debt Crisis: Responses and Options." In *The African Debt Crisis*, edited by G. O. Olusanya and A. Olukoshi. Lagos, Nigeria: NIIA, 1990b.

______. "The Changes in Eastern Europe and Their Implications for Africa's International Economic Relations." *The Nigerian Journal of International Affairs* 16, no. 2 (1990c).

______. "Nigeria as Africa's Great Power: Constraints and Possibilities in the 1990s." *International Journal* 46, no. 3 (1991b).

______. "Structural Adjustment, the April 1990 Coup and Democratization in Nigeria." *Africa Quarterly* 29, nos. 3/4 (1991d).

______. "A Critical Evaluation of the Failed 1990 Coup in Nigeria." *Journal of Modern African Studies* 29, no. 4 (December 1991e).

______. "Africa and the New World Order: Prospects for the 1990s." *Iranian Journal of International Affairs* 4, nos. 3–4, (Fall–Winter 1992).

______. "Structural Adjustment and Nigeria's Democratic Transition." *Trans-Africa Forum* 8, no. 3 (Fall 1991).

______. "The Economic Crisis in Sub-Saharan Africa: Depth, Dimensions and Prospects for Recovery." *The Journal of International Studies* 27 (July 1991).

______. "The Dynamics of Change in Eastern Europe and Their Implications for Africa." *Coexistence* 29 (1992).

Ihonvbere, Julius, and Eme N. Ekekwe. "Dependent Capitalism, Structural Adjustment and Democratic Possibilities in Nigeria's Third Republic." *Afrika Spectrum* 3 (1988).

Ihonvbere, Julius, and Toyin Falola, eds. *Oil and Nigeria's Political Economy.* Lagos, Nigeria: Longman, 1991a.

Ihonvbere, Julius, and Kola Olufemi. "Towards a Radical Study of Foreign Policies of Peripheral Societies." In *Issues in the Administration of Nigeria's Public Sector*, edited by A. O. Sanda and Olusola Ojo. Ile-Ife, Nigeria: Ife University Press, 1986.

Ihonvbere, Julius, and Timothy M. Shaw. "Nigerian Oil Workers in Contextual and Comparative Perspective." In *Labour and Unions in Asia and Africa: Contemporary Issues*, edited by Roger Southall. London: Macmillan, 1988a.

______. *Towards a Political Economy of Nigeria: Petroleum and Politics at the (Semi-) Periphery.* Aldershot, England: Gower, 1988b.

Ikoku, S. G. *Nigeria's Fourth Coup d'Etat: Options for Modern Statehood.* Enugu, Nigeria: Fourth Dimension, 1985.

International Labour Office. *First Things First: Meeting the Basic Needs of the People of Nigeria.* Addis Ababa, Ethiopia: Jobs and Skill Programme for Africa, 1981.

Iyayi, Festus. "The Primitive Accumulation of Capital in Neo-Colony: the Nigerian Case." *Review of African Political Economy* 35 (May 1986).

Joseph, Richard. "Affluence and Underdevelopment: the Nigerian Experience." *Journal of Modern African Studies* 16, no. 2 (1978).

______. "Class, State and Prebendal Politics in Nigeria." *Journal of Commonwealth & Comparative Politics* 21, no. 3, (November 1983).

______. "The Overthrow of Nigeria's Second Republic." *Current History* 83 (March 1984).

______. *Democracy and Prebendal Politics in Nigeria: The Rise and Fall of the Second Republic.* Cambridge: Cambridge University Press, 1988.

Kraus, Jon. "Nigeria under Shagari." *Current History* 81, no. 473 (1982).

Lubeck, Paul M. "Labour in Kano since the Petroleum Boom." *Review of African Political Economy* 13 (September-December 1980).

______. ed. *The African Bourgeoisie: Capitalist Development in Nigeria, Kenya and the Ivory Coast.* Boulder: Lynne Rienner, 1986.

______. *Islam and Urban Labour in Northern Nigeria: The Making of a Muslim Working Class.* Cambridge: Cambridge University Press, 1987.

Madunagu, Edwin. *Problems of Socialism: The Nigerian Challenge*. London: Zed, 1982.

______. *Nigeria: The Economy and the People*. London: New Beacon, 1984.

Mazrui, Ali A. "Nigeria and the United States: The Need for Civility, the Dangers of Intimacy." *Orbis* 25 (Winter 1982).

Miles, William F. S. *Elections in Nigeria: A Grass Roots Perspective*. Boulder: Lynne Rienner, 1988.

Mohammed, Siddique, and Tony Edoh, eds. *Nigeria: A Republic in Ruins*. Zaria, Nigeria: Gaskiya Publishers, 1985.

Nnoli, Okwudiba. *Ethnic Politics in Nigeria*. Enugu, Nigeria: Fourth Dimension, 1978.

______, ed. *Path to Nigerian Development*. Dakar, Senagal: Codesria, 1981.

Nwankwo, Arthur. *Can Nigeria Survive?* Enugu, Nigeria: Fourth Dimension, 1981.

Nwosu, E. J., ed. *Achieving Even Development in Nigeria: Problems and Prospects*. Enugu, Nigeria: Fourth Dimension for EDI, University of Nigeria, 1985.

Odama, J. S. "SFEM in the Context of a Developing Economy." In *The Nigerian Economy Under (S) FEM*, edited by J. Attah. Zaria, Nigeria, Ahmadu Bello University: Department of Economics, 1985.

Oculli, Okelo. "Dependent Food Policy in Nigeria, 1975–1979." *Review of African Political Economy* 15/16 (May–December 1979).

Odetola, T. O. "Economic Development and the Structure and Process of Economic Decision-Making." *Nigerian Journal of Economics and Social Studies* 17, no. 1 (March 1975).

Ofeimun, Odia. *The Poet Lied*. Lagos, Nigeria: Update Communications, 1989.

Ogunbadejo, Oye. "Nigeria's Foreign Policy under Military Rule, 1966–79." *International Journal* 35, no. 4 (Autumn 1980).

Ogunbambi, R. O. "The Dilemmas of Nigeria's African Policy." *Journal of African Studies* 12, no. 1 (Spring 1985).

Ogunsanwo, Alaba. *Our Friends; Their Friends: Nigeria's External Relations, 1960–1985*. Yaba, Nigeria: Alfa Communications, 1986.

______. *Japanese Companies, Labour & Society: Lessons for Nigeria*. Lagos, Nigeria: NIIA, 1989.

Ogwu, U. Joy. *Nigerian Foreign Policy: Alternative Futures*. Lagos, Nigeria: NIIA with Macmillan, 1986.

Ogwu, U. Joy, and R. Omotayo Olaniyan, eds. *Nigeria's International Economic Relations: Dimensions of Dependence and Change*. Lagos, Nigeria: NIIA, 1990.

Ohiorhenuan, John F. E. "The Political Economy of Military Rule in Nigeria." *Review of Radical Political Economics* 16, no. 2/3 (Summer and Fall 1984).

"Oil, Debts and Democracy: Nigeria." *Review of African Political Economy*. 37 (December 1986).

Okolo, Amechi. *Foreign Capital in Nigeria: Roots of Underdevelopment*. Lagos, Nigeria: Heartland, 1987.

Olaniyan, Omotayo, and Chibuzo Nwoke, eds. *Structural Adjustment in Nigeria: The Impact of SFEM on the Economy*. Lagos, Nigeria: Nigerian Institute of International Affairs (NIIA), 1990.

Olatunbosun, Dupe. *Nigeria's Neglected Rural Majority*. Ibadan, Nigeria: OUP for NIIA, 1975.

Olojede, Dele, and Onukaba Adinoyi-Ojo. *Born to Run: The Story of Dele Giwa*. Ibadan, Nigeria: Spectrum, 1987.

Olusanya, G. O., and R. A. Akindele, eds. "Nigeria's External Relations: Agenda for the Future." *Nigerian Journal of International Affairs* 12, nos. 1 and 2 (1986).

Olusanya, G. O., R. A. Akindele, and Adebayo Olukoshi, eds. *The African Debt Crisis*. Lagos, Nigeria: NIIA, 1989.

Oni, Ola, and Bade Onimode. *Economic Development in Nigeria: A Marxist Alternative*. Ibadan, Nigeria: Nigerian Academy of Arts, Sciences and Technology, 1975.

Onimode, Bade. "A Critique of Planning Concepts and Methodology in Nigeria." *Review of Black Political Economy* 7, no. 3 (Spring 1977).

______. *Imperialism and Underdevelopment in Nigeria*. London: Zed, 1982.

Osoba, Segun. "Ideology and Planning for National Economic Development, 1946-72." In *Nigeria: In Search of a Viable Polity*, edited by Mahmud Tukur and Tunji Olangunju. Zaria, Nigeria: ABU Press, 1972.

______. "The Nigerian Power Elite, 1952-1965." In *African Social Studies-A Radical Reader*, edited by Peter C. W. Gutkind and Peter Waterman. New York: Monthly Review, 1977.

______. "The Deepening Crisis of the Nigerian National Bourgeoisie." *Review of African Political Economy* 13 (May-August 1978).

______. "The Economic Foundations of Nigeria's Foreign Policy During the First Republic, 1960-1965." In *Topics on Nigerian Economic and Social*

History, edited by I. A. Akinjogbin and S. O. Osoba. Ife, Nigeria: University of Ife Press, 1980.

Osundare, Niyi. *Songs of the Market Place*. Ibadan, Nigeria: New Horn Press, 1987.

Othman, Shehu. "Reflections on Nigeria Super Power Relations." *Nigerian Journal of International Affairs* 12, nos. 1 and 2 (1986).

______. "Classes, Crises and Coups: The Demise of Shagari's Regime." *African Affairs* 83, no. 333 (October 1984).

Panter-Brick S. K., ed. *Nigerian Politics and Military Rule*. London: Athlone, 1970.

______. *Soldiers and Oil: The Political Transformation of Nigeria*. London: Frank Cass, 1978.

Parfitt, Trevor, and Stephen Riley. *The African Debt Crisis*. London: Routledge, 1989.

Rimmer, Douglas. "The Overvalued Currency and Over-Administered Economy of Nigeria." *African Affairs* 84, no. 336 (July 1986).

Sano, Hans-Otto. *The Political Economy of Food in Nigeria, 1960–1982*. Uppsala, Sweden: Scandinavian Institute of African Studies, Research Report Number 65, 1983.

Schatz, Sayre P. *Nigerian Captialism*. Berkeley: University of California Press, 1977.

______. "Nigeria's Petro-Political Fluctuation." *Issue* 11 (Spring and Summer 1981).

______. "The Nigerian Economy Since the Great Oil-Price Increases of 1973–74." *Africa Today* 29, (Third Quarter 1982).

______. "Nigerian Coups and Foreign Policy." *International Perspectives* (November/December 1985).

______. "Nigeria Restrained: Foreign Policy under Changing Political and Petroleum Regimes." *The Annals* 489 (January 1987).

Shaw, Timothy M., and Julius Ihonvbere. "Nigeria." In *Corporatism in Africa*, edited by Julius Nyang'oro and Timothy M. Shaw. Boulder: Westview, 1989.

Shaw, Timothy M., and Olajide Aluko, eds. *Nigerian Foreign Policy: Alternative Perceptions and Projections*. London: Macmillan, 1983.

Shaw, Timothy M., and Orobola Fasehun. "Nigeria in the World System: Alternatives Approaches, Explanations and Projections." *Journal of Modern African Studies* 18, no. 4 (December 1980).

Shaw, Timothy M. "Nigeria in the International System." In *The Political Economy of Nigeria*, edited by I. Williams Zartman. New York: Praeger, 1983.

Shenton, Robert W. *The Development of Capitalism in Northern Nigeria*. London: James Currey, 1986.

Sklar, Richard S. *Nigerian Political Parties*. Princeton, NJ: Princeton University Press, 1963.

Smock, D. *Conflict and Control in an African Trade Union: A Study of the Nigerian Coal Miners Union*. Stanford, CA: Stanford University Press, 1969.

Takaya, Bala J., and Sonnie Gwanle Tyoden, eds. *The Kaduna Mafia: A Study of the Rise, Development and Consolidation of a Nigerian Power Elite*. Jos, Nigeria: Jos University Press, 1987.

Toyo, Eskor. *The Working Class and the Nigerian Crisis*. Ibadan, Nigeria: Sketch Publishing Company, 1967.

Turner, Terisa. "Multinational Corporations and the Instability of the Nigerian State." *Review of African Political Economy* 5 (January-April 1976a).

______. "The Transfer of Technology and the Nigerian State." *Development and Change* 7 (1976b).

Usman, Yusufu Bala. *For the Liberation of Nigeria*. London: New Beacon, 1979.

______. *Nigeria Against the IMF: The Home Market Strategy*. Kaduna, Nigeria: Vanguard, 1986.

______. *The Manipulation of Religion in Nigeria, 1977–1987*. Kaduna, Nigeria: Vanguard, 1987.

Waterman, Christopher Alan. *Juju—A Social History and Ethnography of an African Popular Music*. Chicago: University of Chicago Press, 1990.

Waterman, Peter. *Aristocrats and Plebeians in African Unions? Lagos Port and Dock Workers Organisation and Struggle*. The Hague: Institute for Social Studies, 1983.

Watts, Michael J., ed. *State, Oil and Agriculture in Nigeria*. Berkeley: University of California, Institute of International Studies, 1987.

Williams, Gavin. "Taking the Part of Peasants: Rural Development in Nigeria and Tanzania." In *The Political Economy of Contemporary Africa*, edited by P. C. W. Gutkin and I. Wallerstein, 131–54. Beverly Hills: Sage, 1976a.

______, ed. *Nigeria: Economy and Society*. London: Rex Collings, 1976b.

______. *State and Society in Nigeria*. Idandre, Nigeria: Afrografika, 1980.

Women in Nigeria. *WIN Document: Conditions of Women in Nigeria and Policy Recommendations to 2000 AD*. Zaria, Nigeria: WIN, 1985.

______. *Women in Nigeria*. London: Zed, 1986.

Wright, Stephen. "Limits of Nigeria's Power Overseas." *West Africa* 3339 (27 July 1981).

______. *Nigeria: The Dilemmas Ahead. A Political Risk Analysis*. London: EIU, Special Report # 1072, November 1986a.

Young, Andrew. "The United States and Africa: Victory for Diplomacy." *Foreign Affairs* 59, no. 3 (1981).

Zartman, I. William, ed. *The Political Economy of Nigeria*. New York: Praeger, 1983.

Index